JURGEN O. SCHULZ

What Story Have We Fallen Into?
Copyright © 2021 by Jurgen O. Schulz

All rights reserved. No part of this publication may be reproduced, distributed, or transmitted in any form or by any means, including photocopying, recording, or other electronic or mechanical methods, without the prior written permission of the author, except in the case of brief quotations embodied in critical reviews and certain other non-commercial uses permitted by copyright law.

All Scripture quotations, unless otherwise indicated,
are taken from the *Holy Bible, New International Version.*
Copyright © 1973, 1978, 1984, by International Bible Society.
Used by permission of Zondervan Publishing House.
All rights reserved.

Cover and interior design: Jurgen Schulz
Cover artwork: *Garden of Eden* by Nolan Nasser

ISBN
978-1-7778496-0-3 (Paperback)
978-1-7778496-1-0 (eBook)

DEDICATION

~

This book is dedicated to a woman
whose goodness is beyond human.
She is beautiful in her spirit
and strong in her faith.
She is a joy-bringer, a God-lover,
a woman of prayer,
and a spreader of blessing.
She is a treasure.
I am blessed beyond words
to have her as my wife.

CONTENTS

Acknowledgements
Introduction
1. The Over-Arching Story • 15
2. The Story Begins • 25
3. The Original Word • 35
4. The Matrix of the Story • 45
5. Love Was Here First • 57
6. Expansive Goodness • 69
7. Amusing Grace • 79
8. God's Self-Portrait • 91
9. The Giver of Life • 101
10. Dispelling the Darkness • 113
11. The Twist in the Story • 125
12. The Big Blunder • 137
13. The God Who Stoops • 149
14. The God Who Is Abba • 161
15. The Human Face of God • 173
16. The Story of His Glory • 185
17. Grace and Truth • 195
18. Outrageous Grace • 207

19. Step Aside, Moses • 219
20. The Unveiling of God • 231
21. The Way to the Father • 243
22. The Giver of the Spirit • 253
23. A New Place to Live • 263
24. A Ladder to Heaven • 273
25. A Deep Connection • 283
26. Living in His Love • 293
27. Learning to Fly • 303
28. The Sacred Romance • 313
29. The Ultimate Makeover • 323
30. A Fabulous Finale • 335

Endnotes

ACKNOWLEDGMENTS

~

Writing a book is not unlike building a house—materials from many sources are brought together, people with different skills assist in the process, and one never knows all of those who will step inside and benefit from the final result. I am indebted to all who assisted in the "construction" of this book.

I am specially grateful to several friends who read the manuscript and made helpful recommendations—Alan Yoshioka, Sarah Clarke, Paula Boshoff and Shirley Vargas. Carolyn Wilker and Mike Allen provided valuable help with the editing. My mother-in-law, Margaret Horton, deserves special mention; no one has shown more enthusiasm, or given away more copies of my books than she has. My wife Wendy was wonderfully supportive, in spite of being awakened on a regular basis by her husband who writes best in the early hours of the morning.

Above all, I am thankful to God. As I reflected on the extreme goodness of the Good News presented in John's Gospel, I felt like Moses who peered through a chink in the rock on Mount Sinai. The staggering beauty and wonder of the Gospel sent me to my knees. It made my heart beat faster. Thank you, Lord, for the privilege of sharing with others something of the richness and glory of Your Story.

Finally, I am indebted to readers like you, who open this book and venture into the rooms of this "house." I trust it will be a memorable visit. I cannot promise a wardrobe leading to a "Narnia" adventure. However, it is highly possible that you will catch sight of the overwhelming beauty and wonder of the Divine Drama into which we have fallen.

*We must certainly be in a novel;
What I like about this novelist is that
he takes such trouble about
his minor characters.*

—G. K. Chesterton

INTRODUCTION

~

IN TOLKIEN'S great fantasy epic, *Lord of the Rings,* Sam turns to Frodo as they journey toward Mordor and asks: "I wonder what kind of a tale we have fallen into?"

He suspects there is something bigger going on. Something larger than the moment they are living. Some kind of a story—and they appear to be in the thick of it.

Have you ever asked yourself that question?

What kind of a story do we find ourselves in?

We have every reason to believe it's an extraordinary one.

Take a look around. We are bolting through space on a blue-colored sphere at about 67,000 miles per hour. That's almost three times faster than the speed of most rockets, so hang on to your hat. For some unknown reason, our planet has not yet been stopped for speeding. While blazing through the sky, this globe also *spins*—so tack on an extra 1,000 miles per hour. And try to keep your balance!

This space trekker called Earth is also a complex ecosystem where remarkable things take place. Caterpillars turn into butterflies, sandpipers swoop in unison, bees convert nectar into honey, orcas leap out of the ocean, and coal is crushed into diamonds. A vast array of living creatures navigate the Milky Way together: dolphins, warblers, buffalo, parrots, giraffes, peacocks, penguins, gazelles, dragonflies and a million others.

Humans are on a planet where we experience sunsets, ice cream, romance, strawberries, hummingbirds, waterfalls, coffee, kittens, roses and rainbows. And even chocolate.

It is more astonishing than we could possibly imagine.

Einstein was right: "There are only two ways to live your life. One is as though nothing is a miracle. The other is as though everything is."

When did we lose our sense of wonder? This is not an ordinary, run-of-the-mill world; *it is incredible.* If we could open our eyes and see it for the first time, it would leave us speechless and breathless with wonder. It is more astonishing than any fairy tale.

Searching For Answers

So, what kind of a story are we in?

Science has attempted to provide an answer. Much has been discovered about neurons, enzymes, quasars and quarks, but very little about the mystery of our existence. Some in the scientific community, after examining the vastness, the complexity, the precision and marvels of creation, have given their verdict—*there is no story.*

These men in white coats have managed to flatten the mysteries of life down to formulas, equations and categories. They inform us that everything can be explained by natural mechanisms, and that humans are no more than a fortuitous combination of molecules. Love and joy and loyalty and beauty are accidental by-products of a huge explosion. To consider anything as "sacred" or "miraculous" is silliness and superstition. We are left with no plot, no meaning, no explanation, no climax, no resolution and no happy ending.

Just one random cosmic accident.

Not a very comforting thought.

Science leaves us, as someone said in the language of Lewis's novels, with "all wardrobe and no Narnia." It is a bleak restricted vision of reality that is less than satisfying. An ancient poet described it well: *"a dry and parched land where there is no water"* (Psa. 63:1).

Scientist John Polkinghorne writes:

INTRODUCTION

> Science, by itself, would be a hopelessly limited and impoverished view of things. Music would be vibrations in the air. A beautiful painting would just be a collection of specks of paint of known chemical composition… Nearly all that makes life worth living slips through the wide meshes of the scientific net.[1]

"Not everything that counts can be counted," pointed out William Bruce Cameron.

French scholar Étienne Gilson observed: "To minds tormented by the divine thirst, it is useless to offer the most certain knowledge of the laws of numbers and the arrangement of the universe."

Human hearts yearn for something more.

"Embedded in each is the insatiable longing to know we are part of a story greater than our own," writes Karen Angela Ellis.

A Better Story

Most of us sense that life is more than a random, meaningless sequence of accidental events. "The sacred exists and is stronger than all our rebellions," insists acclaimed author Czeslaw Milosz. We find it difficult to believe our existence is simply "a tale told by an idiot, full of sound and fury, signifying nothing." We suspect there is a story; something larger is going on.

Is this not what the poets, mystics and writers have told us? They insist that to truly see something one must look beyond it and see something more. To delight in the splendor of a rose or a majestic sunset is to contemplate something greater than a flower or a night sky. It is to connect with the infinite. It is to transcend the physical realm and peer into another world.

"In our world . . . a star is a huge ball of flaming gas," says Eustace in one of C. S. Lewis's novels. Eustace is given this answer: "Even in your world, my son, that is not what a star is, but only what it is made of."[2]

Science tells us what stars are made of. Scripture tells us that stars carry messages about the Star-Maker—*the heavens proclaim the glory of God.* There's more to stars than flaming gas.

WHAT STORY HAVE WE FALLEN INTO?

There is a bigger story. It is recorded in Holy Scripture. It is an overarching narrative that is unspeakably beautiful, wonderful and good. It's the Father's Story. It's the only story large enough to account for the beauty and brokenness of our world, and to make sense of the longings and dreams of our hearts.

"The whole point of Christianity is that it offers a story which is the story of the whole world," declares Professor N. T. Wright.[3]

I am persuaded that there is nothing as amazing, as extraordinary, as staggering as the story God is telling in our world. The more you discover about it, the more remarkable it turns out to be. It is a divine conspiracy of goodness—*extreme goodness*. The jaw-dropping, heart-stopping kind.

Many people find this hard to believe.

What they have been told about God and the Bible has been less than exciting. Often it has been life-quenching, joy-killing and uninteresting. They heard the doctrines, the duties, the principles, the fundamentals of the faith.

But they didn't hear the Story.

The Story had been deconstructed, codified, truncated, diminished. It was turned into lessons about sin avoidance, correct behavior, and right belief. People learned doctrinal facts. But they missed the shocking, heart-grabbing, counterintuitive wonder of the Gospel. *They missed the glory of the Story.*

What if the Gospel story is truer, richer, and more beautiful than we ever imagined?

What if it is the most astonishing story of all?

Missing the Magnificence

A friend dropped in one day on the English writer, Gilbert K. Chesterton, and found him packing his bags for a trip. He asked Chesterton where he was going.

"To Chamberwell," responded the writer.

"Aren't you getting absentminded like the proverbial professor?" questioned his friend. "You are in Chamberwell. This is where you live."

INTRODUCTION

"Yes," said Chesterton, "and that is why I am going away. I'm too close to Chamberwell to see it properly. Things have become too familiar for me to notice them."

Has this happened to readers of the Bible? Have we become too familiar with it to notice the magnificence of this Story?

Novelist Dorothy Sayers described God's Story as "the most exciting drama that ever staggered the imagination of man... this terrifying drama in which God is the victim and the hero. If this is dull, then what, in Heaven's name, is worthy to be called exciting?"[4]

Through the Eyes of John

This book explores God's unfolding drama from the standpoint of John's Gospel and particularly his prologue. The first eighteen verses of John's book are a microcosm of the biblical narrative. Probably no other portion of the Bible is so densely packed with great theological themes. Alexander Whyte asserts that it contains "far more philosophy; far more grace, and truth, and beauty, and love; than all the rest that has ever been written by pen of man, or spoken by tongue of man or angel."[5] We are struck with the feeling that, as one writer put it, "we are in the realm of the wonderful and the profound." John's prologue will be our launching pad to delve into the mystery of God's "grand narrative" that is unfolding in this world.

The apostle shares with us a vision of God—a God more gracious, giving and awe-inspiring than we imagined. A Divine Lord whose conspiracy of goodness is more astonishing than a fairy tale.

The Gospel writer unveils the Real Story.

He dares us to believe that truth is more wonderful than fiction.

To live in the world without becoming aware of the meaning of the world is like wandering about in a great library without touching the books.

—MANLY P. HALL

CHAPTER ONE

THE OVER-ARCHING STORY

In the beginning...
JOHN 1:1

LET ME TELL YOU A STORY... There is hardly a better way of grabbing a person's attention than that.

Propositions and facts are fine—but what really fascinates us is *stories*. They inspire us, they move us, they touch us deeply. They bring out the childlike in us. It is no surprise that more novels are read than books on science, self-help, or anything else. Fiction tops the list. People love stories.

Stories are food for the soul. They speak not just to our minds, but also our hearts. "We are narrative creatures, and we need narrative nourishment—narrative catechisms," contends N. D. Wilson.[1]

G. K. Chesterton dared to state: "Literature is a luxury; fiction is a necessity."

Good stories have the potential of shifting our perception of life. They allow us to taste, feel and be stirred by a new glimpse of reality. Stories are transformative.

Stories have a strange power. They slip past our rationalistic filters. They have an uncanny way of sneaking under the radar we normally use to filter out unwelcome ideas, and rudely awakening us. "If you want to change the world, don't bring in the politicians who make the laws," advised one scholar. "Bring in the poets who tell the stories."

Discovering a New World

I have a vivid memory from my childhood of borrowing a large volume of fairy tales from the classroom library. As a new reader, this was my first time to take out a book from the library. Settling down on our living room couch, I plunged into an enchanting realm of dwarfs and beanstalks, perils and princes, dungeons and wizards, wonder and beauty. I read ancient tales full of mystery, marvels and magic. It was my first taste of literary ecstasy. *I had discovered a new world!*

I became so captivated that, scarcely stopping for supper, I didn't put the book down until it was time to go to bed. When I returned the book the following day, my teacher refused to believe that I had read the entire tome. She insisted on interrogating me on the stories in the book, until she finally conceded, with some amazement, that somehow I had managed to devour the whole collection in one day.

What is it about stories? Why do they have such an appeal?

Could it be that stories intrigue us because we find ourselves in a large narrative played out on Planet Earth? Is it how we attempt to make sense of our personal stories? Do we love tales with happy endings because they satisfy our longing for the ultimate overthrow of evil and the triumph of good?

We all want our lives to find their place in some greater story. We yearn for a happy resolution to the turbulent human drama when everything will be made right, when *"the crooked roads shall become straight, the rough ways smooth"* (Lk. 3:5). We long to hear our hero announce: *"Take heart! I have overcome the world"* (Jn. 16:33). It is the story we most want to be true. Stories inspire hope for redemption.

The Quest for Meaning

A story, of course, implies the existence of a Story Writer.

"I had always felt life first as a story," confided G. K. Chesterton, "and if there is a story, there is a storyteller."

If a transcendent Author does *not* in fact exist, as some suggest, then the whole drama turns out to be a huge nonstory.

Neil Postman, a professor at New York University, insisted that people require a story to give meaning to their existence. "Without air, our cells die," he said. "Without a story, our selves die." It defies logic that an indispensable ingredient for human happiness should *not* actually exist. A world without meaning is a world unfit for human habitation.

The Greek thinker Plato believed that man is a being in search of meaning. The great philosopher insisted that we cannot simply eat, sleep, work and reproduce—there is a deep longing in us to figure out why we are here. Not surprisingly, "What is the meaning of life?" is one of the 100 most asked questions on the Google search engine.

> *The deepest need is the need for meaning, purpose, and hope.*
> —Peter Kreeft

The Scientific Approach

The discoveries of science are remarkable, valuable and greatly beneficial. Science answers the question, How does it work? The questions it does *not* answer are: Why is it here? Why are *we* here? Who's in charge? Why is there such beauty and order in our world? What is this all about?

This is what we all long to know.

Science is adept at analyzing anatomy, algorithms and atoms, but clumsy at explaining faith and love and dreams and beauty and goodness. Science sheds much light on the question of "what," but comes up short when it attempts to unravel the question of "why?" It can tell us the distance to the nearest galaxy, but has no answers regarding the meaning of life.

"The Great God Science. It has failed us, because it was never meant to be a god, but only a few true scientists understand that," comments author Madeleine L'Engle.[2]

Scientists are well equipped to study natural phenomena, but the instruments in their toolbox are incapable of prying open the mystery of life. Their tools were never designed for the task. Would it not be absurd to expect a plumber to perform brain surgery, or to call on a truck driver to check our cholesterol level? We should not expect good results when people operate outside their field of expertise. Nor should we hope for reliable answers when science operates beyond its prescribed domain.

> *Creation is too large to be contained in the tight fist of reason.*
> —MARILYNNE ROBINSON

The Basic Formula

For many years brilliant men of science like Albert Einstein, Stephen Hawking and others were engaged in the search for the "theory of everything," a cohesive explanation for how the universe works. This master theory would provide an all-encompassing framework to answer the big questions, eliminate the mysteries, and explain everything in a unified and coherent manner.

For the scientist, to find the "theory of everything" is to uncover the secret to the universe; it is to discover the mystical formula at the heart of reality. It would account for everything from aardvarks to zygotes, from snowflakes to supernovas. It would allow us to penetrate the mind of the Maker.

However, this foundational equation proves to be rather elusive, and continues to be one of the major unsolved problems in physics. Great minds are still baffled about what makes things tick.

A Need For Revelation

Madeleine L'Engle wrote: "But I did feel, and passionately, that it wasn't fair of God to give us brains enough to ask the ultimate questions if he didn't intend to teach us the answers."[3]

Has the Script Writer left no clues regarding the great questions of life? Has our Maker left us completely in the dark?

Fortunately, He hasn't. He has let us in on the secret. We are not limited to speculation—thankfully a revelation has taken place. The One who authored our existence also authored a book we call the Bible. Inspired Scripture came to us through *"holy men of God [who] spoke as they were moved by the Holy Spirit"* (2 Pet. 1:21 NKJV). While many questions remain unanswered, important features of our story surface in the biblical record.

> *For lo, the one who forms the mountains, creates the wind, reveals his thoughts to mortals...* (Amos 4:13 NRSV).
>
> *There is a God in heaven who reveals secrets* (Dan. 2:28 NASB).
>
> *In the past, God did not tell his plan to people. But now the Holy Spirit has shown it to his holy apostles and prophets* (Eph. 3:5 WE).
>
> *This secret was hidden throughout the ages and generations but has now been revealed to his saints* (Col. 1:26 ISV).

Heaven has shed light on our story.

The Big Picture

A computer program called Google Earth allows us not only to zoom in and view the exact spot in the world where we live, but also to zoom out and get a bird's eye picture of our whole city, region and country. If we continue to zoom out we can survey Planet Earth from space—a round blue ball hanging in the sky. If we keep going, we get a panoramic view of our location in the Milky Way solar system. It's remarkable!

Imagine if we could do a zoom-out on the mini-story of our lives and see the big picture. What is the mega drama we are a part of? What is the Grand Central Story being played out on the stage of our world?

A purely secular interpretation of the universe reduces all reality to molecules and matter. Living in this kind of a world, suggests Professor Nancy Pearcey, is like living in a bunker with no windows. The biblical narrative, on the other hand, invites people to "open the door and come out . . . of a small, cramped world into one that is expansive and liberating."[4]

Scripture contends that there is rich meaning to our story, and provides a wide-angle Google Earth view of what's going on. It tells an epic saga of a paradise lost, a tangled plot, a crucified king and a glorious resolution.

> *The solution to the riddle of life in space and time, must come from beyond space and time.*
> —Ludwig Vidkinstein

The world's a stage where a wild, startling, delightful and fearful drama of majestic beauty unfolds, and we appear to be in the thick of it. It has all the makings of a fairy tale, and is not without a prince, a villain, romance, seduction, danger—and even a dragon.

Far-fetched? Perhaps. But skim through the last book of the Bible, and you will find that "dragon" shows up at least twelve times. In the inspired narrative, a fearsome evil power is on the loose. And that shouldn't surprise us. We have all had nasty dragons to contend with in our lives. "Always remember," declares one writer, "it's simply not an adventure worth telling if there aren't any dragons."[5]

The Divine Script Writer

If the infinite Lord were to write a story, it would be the ultimate masterpiece—a breathtaking, mind-boggling, heart-warming, spine-tingling epic of majestic beauty.

Nothing like our flimsy fables.

That's only to be expected. He is the inventor of creativity, artistry and imagination. William Shakespeare, Charles Dickens and J. K. Rowling are still learning their ABC's. The Divine Scriptwright is in a league of His own.

Human authors write things like fiction, legends, poetry and essays. The Almighty writes a universe. People put words on paper. The Lord God sends galaxies spiraling into space. Creative writers make up stories. God actually *creates* them. He speaks His word and reality happens—in real time.

You and I find ourselves in His Story, written into the narrative by the Author Himself. We did nothing to make it happen. Our existence was entirely His idea. The Divine Author believed the Story would not be complete without us, and He wrote us into the script.

An immense privilege, indeed.

The Real Story

The cosmos is filled with purpose because there is a God above.
—Dan DeWitt

In the opening moments of the movie *The Matrix* (1999), we are introduced to Neo, a man who sees himself as an ordinary guy living an ordinary life. As time goes by, Neo realizes there's something much bigger going on. He can't figure out what it is until he takes a red pill and discovers what he thought was the real world was only a simulated reality. His eyes are opened to a totally different narrative for his existence.

Like Neo, there's a deep longing in all of us to see the reality of things and to connect our lives to the Real Story. Life is too precious and too short to live a fictional one.

Inspired Scripture invites us to stop living on the outskirts of reality and to open our eyes to the Grand Story, the God-given drama in which we find ourselves.

Admittedly, there are areas of mystery in the human story that lie beyond our reach. No one can claim to have full and final answers to the deep problems of life in this world. "*Even if the wise claim they know, they cannot really comprehend it,*" confessed a man of great wisdom (Eccl. 8:17). Having said that, there are exciting hints found in Scripture that highlight the broad contours of our story. We do not have all the answers, but the inspired record provides breathtaking insight into the divine plot.

What is the Almighty up to? What is this story all about? The biblical record brings to light a narrative of compelling beauty, depth and richness we never could have come up with on our own.

> *It was a secret hidden from the beginning of the world. But now it is for us to know. The early preachers wrote about it. God says it is to be preached to all the people of the world so men can put their trust in God and obey Him* (Rom. 16:25-26 NLV).

C. S. Lewis adduces: "In science we have been reading only the notes to a poem; in Christianity we find the poem itself."[6]

The apostle Paul stated:

> *But it is just as the Scriptures say, What God has planned for people who love him is more than eyes have seen or ears have heard. It has never even entered our minds!* (1 Cor. 2:9 CEV).

The Bible provides fascinating information about this story-shaped world. "The Gospel is not just a series of facts to which we yield our assent but a dramatic narrative that replots our identity," writes Michael Horton.[7] It gives us a compelling "big picture" of reality and our place in it.

When the Author of the universe says: "Let me tell you a story...," we must pay close attention. This is not fiction. This is not fanciful conjecture. This is inside information on the secret that lies behind everything.

This is truth about the fantastic tale we have fallen into.

PRAYER

LORD GOD, You rule on high and we are here below, confused and longing to make sense of our brief existence. We feel there is something in life we have missed. We are here only for a fleeting moment—far too short to spend stumbling in the dark. Shine Your light upon us. It is only in Your light we see light. Rouse us from our sluggishness. Open our understanding to perceive the glory, the wonder, the beauty of Your purposes of grace. Help us to discern the splendor of the Story in which we find ourselves. And lead our feet on the path where Your light shines ever brighter till the fullness of day. Amen.

*The heart of the world's life
is its literature.
The heart of all literature
is this sacred Book of God.
The heart of this Book is the Gospels.
The heart of these four Gospels
is John's.*

—S. D. Gordon

CHAPTER TWO

THE STORY BEGINS

In the beginning...
JOHN 1:1

IN HIS NOVEL, *THE HOBBIT,* one of Tolkien's characters declares, "Truly songs and tales fall utterly short of the reality."

Could Tolkien be right?

Could the Real Story be bigger than we thought? This world has produced a wide array of awe-inspiring songs, stories and poems. Could reality be more wonderful still? Chesterton thought so: "Truth, of course, must of necessity be stranger than fiction, for we have made fiction to suit ourselves."[1]

Have we perceived too feebly and faintly the unfathomable splendor of the drama we find ourselves in?

There is no better place to turn to explore the mystery of our story than the Gospel of John. It has been said that John's book is like a pool a child can wade in, and yet deep enough for an elephant to swim in. With simplicity and profundity, John expands our view of God, and compels us to see that the Good News is extraordinarily rich and beautiful and astonishing.

The Gospel of John is perhaps the most profound book ever written. One scholar states: "The thought of this Gospel reaches dizzying heights, its majestic language spirals and soars..."[2] The story seems straightforward, but there are multiple levels of meaning, hidden truths awaiting discovery. John is a master of metaphor. Every narrative is thick with symbolic meaning. We can read the book time and again, yet we sense there is mystery, richness and wonder we have not yet grasped.

A Gospel Like No Other

John, the only one of the twelve apostles not martyred, lived until the final years of the first century. As he grew older, his teaching grew simpler and more focused. It is reported that he spoke always and only of one thing—*the love of God*. According to an old tradition, one of his disciples complained: "Why don't you talk about anything else?" John's response was, "Is there anything else?"

John, the son of Zebedee, was fond of referring to himself as "the disciple that Jesus loved." It was not that he was loved more than the others, but he was the one who best understood the fact—and reveled in it. He had gained rich insight into the love of God.

And he was intoxicated by it.

The apostle John had comprehended something so stupendous that it filled his whole horizon. He caught a vision of something so magnificent he could not cease talking about it.

Mark Buchanan mused:

> How did he know with such lucid, fervid certainty that God's essential nature is love—extravagant, sacrificial, heartbreaking, breathtaking love? How did he know with such cartwheeling joy that he was God's child, awash in love?[3]

Thankfully, before dying, the beloved disciple wrote a book on the subject.

The Gospel of John, as best we know, was the last book of the New Testament to be written. After spending years in exile on the Isle of Patmos, the apostle John, possibly in his nineties, resided in Ephesus. The vision contained in the book of Revelations had been given to him while on Patmos. But, there was one final message God was going to reveal through him.

The best wine comes last.

Matthew, Mark and Luke had written their biographies of Jesus over thirty years earlier. The Good News, while spreading throughout the Roman empire, was now under siege by numerous false teachings. A variety of conflicts had emerged in the Christian church, and there was a need for followers of the Messiah to strengthen their grasp of the Gospel message. The other evangelists had recorded the outward facts of the Gospel story. The time had come for someone to expound their deeper meaning.

No one was more suited for the task than the son of Zebedee.

The Apostolic Author

Of the twelve disciples who walked the dusty roads of Israel with the Rabbi from Nazareth, three formed an inner circle. John was part of that select group. Of the three, there was one who enjoyed special intimacy with Christ—John. At the Last Supper, he reclined beside the Lord and even leaned his head on His chest. Did he hear the heartbeat of God? Perhaps. What is clear is that the disciple "whom Jesus loved" captured better than anyone the deeper truths the Son of God came to reveal.

The beloved apostle had spent three years traveling with the Master. He then pondered that momentous experience for six decades. When he finally sat down to write as an old man, it was "from the snowy summit of ninety winters," as Dean Farrar put it. Years of reflection and prayer had deepened and enriched his understanding of the mystery of the incarnate Christ.

Before dying, Jesus committed to John the care of Mary, His mother (Jn. 19:26,27). Did He not have several siblings to whom this responsibility could have been given? Yes, He did. However, one suspects what our Savior had in mind was not simply that the son of Zebedee would care for His mother, but that he would *learn* from her. She was the woman who had brought Jesus into the world. She had spent more time with Him than any other human being.

WHAT STORY HAVE WE FALLEN INTO?

What fascinating conversations John and Mary must have had! The insights gained by the apostle no doubt played a vital role in preparing him to be the instrument God would use to write a Gospel that was unique, profound and insightful.

Over and above all of this, was the illumination of the Holy Spirit. He was sent to bring to remembrance the words of Christ and guide His followers into all truth (Jn. 14:26; 16:13). The Apostle John was led to an extraordinary apprehension of the richness of the divine drama. He declared:

> *And we know that the Son of God has come and has given us understanding, so that we may know him who is true…* (1 Jn. 5:20 ESV).

It is worthy of note that, of the twelve apostles, John was the only one referred to by the Church fathers as "The Theologian." His book was described by Clement of Alexandria as the "spiritual Gospel." It is likely that no other living person obtained sharper insight into the mystery of Christ than John himself.

> *The Gospel according to John is the most original, the most important, the most influential book in all literature.*
> —PHILIP SCHAFF

The Final Record

Tradition tells us that in his latter years John was approached by a group of his disciples who urged him to put into writing what he had taught them. John proposed three days of prayer and fasting to seek guidance on the matter. That same night, in a place of solitude in the hills, divine confirmation came.[4]

The aged apostle set to work, and when the manuscript was finished, he had left on parchment the most profound exposition we have of the message and mind of Christ. It does more than retell the life of Jesus of Nazareth. It unveils the deep spiritual meaning of His coming. It opens up unparalleled vistas into the unsearchable riches of Christ.

It is no exaggeration to say it is a window into the inner life of God, a revelation of His heart.

The writer of the Fourth Gospel didn't simply open a window; he opened a floodgate from which pours forth refreshing streams of living water.

The Story Begins

A good opening line is essential. John has a great one, borrowed from the first verse of the Bible.

"In the beginning" was a radical idea. It pointed to a moment in time when everything began. (Scientists now agree that this appears to be the case.) We are not trapped in endless cycles. There is a beginning and an end. Time moves forward. There is a plot, there is a plan… *this is a story.*

John does not launch his Gospel account, as Mark does, with the testimony of John the Baptist. Nor does he go back, as Luke does, to the story of Jesus' birth. He does not even return, as Matthew does, to the genealogy of Messiah starting with Abraham. John takes us even further back to the very beginning, when there was no one else but God.

The Bible does not commence with a thesis statement, or like the Quran, with a command. It starts with a *story*. It begins not with ideas, but with a narrative, with events. This is significant. We are not simply told what to do. There is something *we should know*. The Spirit of God is shedding light on what is really going on. He is explaining *The Story* to us.

Inspired Scripture contains a wide array of literary genres and styles, but above and beyond all else—*it is a story*. Running through this tapestry of history, precept, parables, visions, letters and songs is a fabulous Story which moves relentlessly forward. Before it was codified, systematized or institutionalized, the Christian faith was understood as a narrative.

WHAT STORY HAVE WE FALLEN INTO?

Many see the Bible as . . .

- A treasure chest of promises
- A theological text of God-facts
- A self-help manual for living well
- A legal code of divine edicts
- A compass for navigating life

But first and foremost, the Bible tells a *Story*. We should cherish the promises, learn the facts, observe the laws, live the lessons—*but we should not miss The Story.*

The Christian faith fulfilled two deep longings of the human soul, states Chesterton: "It met the mythological search for romance by being a story, and the philosophical search for truth by being a true story."[5]

It is a huge, wild, wonderful, perplexing and awe-inspiring Story that seeks not just to inform and advise, but to *enthrall*. It is an unfolding drama of peril, tragedy, suspense, mystery and surprise that winds up with an unsurpassable celebration of jubilant gladness. It concludes with the greatest "they lived happily ever after" ending of all.

Getting Back Into the Story

When my children were small, they loved to watch *Winnie the Pooh* videos. In one of them, Tigger, the bouncing tiger, gets himself into some trouble. He bounces right out of the story, and into the branches of a large tree. In the storybook shown on the screen, the tree is located right beside the printed words the narrator is reading. A frightened Tigger cries, "For goodness sakes, narrate me down from here!" The narrator laughs, and tilts the book to one side. Tigger drops from the tree, and lands on the print on the page. The narrator then rights the book, and Tigger bounces down the words onto the ground. He's back in the story. A delightful interlude.

In another video, Pooh, a honey-loving bear, turns and questions the narrator of the story. Tigger reacts, "That's the narrator! You don't argue with the narrator!"[6]

It's true—characters in stories shouldn't be talking to the narrator or the audience. They are locked in their storyworld. This amusing twist, occasionally used in fictional media, is called "breaking the fourth wall." The phrase comes from the fact that a theater stage is made up of three walls, the fourth wall is invisible, separating the world of the actors from the audience. When a character speaks directly to the spectators, he demonstrates his awareness of his fictional nature. He is "breaking the fourth wall."

In Genesis 3, human beings "bounced" themselves out of the Story and into a tree. It was the tree of the knowledge of good and evil—the one we were warned about. We ended up in a tragic nonstory. What do we do now? Could we expect any help from the Narrator? Could we "break the fourth wall" and get in touch with Him? Would He be there for us after we blundered so badly? Is there any way back into His Story?

This is what John's book is all about.

The Word who spoke the universe into being comes to speak again. He enters the human drama with *"words of eternal life"* (Jn. 6:68). He comes to bring us into a God-story that surpasses anything we imagined. The one who wrote the story of creation has come to write a story of redemption.

The Center of Everything

Journey to the Center of the Earth is one of the great classics in the genre of science-fiction, written by nineteenth century French author Jules Verne. The book tells the story of an intrepid professor, his quaking nephew and their trusty guide who go on an expedition down an extinct Icelandic volcano to the Earth's very core. Verne tells an entertaining and adventure-filled tale of this group's quest to uncover the planet's primordial secrets.

John's Gospel takes us on a journey even more spectacular—not to the center of the Earth, but to the very center of the *universe,* to the matrix of everything.

Scholars point out that the words *in the beginning* mean more than "before all else." The phrase in Greek combines two meanings: "in the beginning of history," and "at the root of the universe."7 John frequently uses expressions with multiple levels of meaning, and it is likely he does so here. "In the beginning" can refer to the fundamental reason why all things exist, the underlying logic behind everything.

S. D. Gordon states: "The whole of the God-story in the larger picture of the whole Book is given in few simple clear lines in this exquisite little thing commonly called John's Gospel."8

The apostle uncovers the hidden enigma behind God's creation. Unlike Verne's novel, this is *not* a work of fiction, but a book containing divinely revealed truth. If we are to awaken to the true secret of the human story, this part of Scripture is essential reading.

> *The good news is bigger, better, fuller than you ever imagined.*
> – N. T. Wright

This God-story, if the truth be fully known, is "unimprovable." Theologian J. Gresham Machen ventured to say, "In the gospel there is included all the heart of man can wish."9

Poet and theologian Evelyn Underhill once suggested that many Christians are like deaf people at a concert. They study the program, they believe what it says, they comment on the quality of the music, but only manage to hear faint snatches of it. They have no notion of the "mighty symphony" of God, the overwhelming beauty, and the astonishing goodness of His eternal purposes of love.10

It's time for this symphony, this Mega-Story, to burst out of its religious encasement, take the stage, and subvert the false scripts of our culture and our world. We need to let the Grand Story transform our mind, fire our imagination, and captivate our hearts.

As we track the divine drama in Scripture, we will discover it to be exceedingly more beautiful than we imagined.

PRAYER

LORD OF HEAVEN AND EARTH, You are the one who at the beginning of time said, "let there be light." You are the one who floods our world with light at the dawn of each new day. Dispel all darkness from our hearts. Awaken us to the wonder of Your Story. Enlighten our minds to the mystery of our existence. Open our eyes to the splendor and richness of the divine drama in which we find ourselves. Free us from the lies that so easily entangle us, and flood our minds with the truth that sets us free. Teach us to live with gratitude and joyful surrender in the wonder of Your unfolding Story. Amen.

*John has the immortal honour
of having conceived and meditated
and indited the most magnificent passage
that has ever been written
with pen and ink.*

—Alexander Whyte

CHAPTER THREE

THE ORIGINAL WORD

In the beginning was the Word...
JOHN 1:1

IN THE NOVEL *The Man Who Was Thursday*, G. K. Chesterton's character, Syme, exclaims, "Shall I tell you the secret of the whole world? It is that we have only known the back of the world. We see everything from behind... If we could only get round in front."[1]

To "get round in front" is the task that has long occupied the minds of philosophers and theologians. Somehow we sense there is *more* going on than meets the eye. It seems that our existence is connected to a greater reality, and we long to know what it is.

Looking Through the Cracks

If the Bible is, as it claims to be, a book inspired by the One who crafted the cosmos, we should expect it to provide insight into the true story of our world. Holy Scripture, like a crack between time and eternity, should allow us to peer through and catch sight of the meta-narrative of our existence.

No section of this ancient book is better suited to help us than John's Gospel. "John excels in the depths of divine mysteries," affirmed early Christian scholar Jerome. The ancient Church

Fathers referred to the Gospel of John as the "spiritual" Gospel. Its chapters are steeped in transcendence, riddled with spectacular vistas of divine truth.

One scholar called the first verse of the Fourth Gospel the "most compact and pulsating theological statement in all of Scripture." Here the beloved apostle pulls back the curtain to let us see what was going on *before* everything else began. The text conveys an ocean of truth teeming with mystery.

In the beginning was the Word (Logos) (Jn. 1:1).

Before the story began there was Someone. A secular interpretation of the universe traces everything back to a "what." The biblical narrative starts with a "who." We must pay close attention. John is presenting to us the Script Writer, the Divine Author of the whole narrative. Someone called "the Word" holds the key to the mystery of our existence.

Verse one reveals remarkable facts about the Word:

- His eternity - *"in the beginning"*
- His singularity - *"was the Word"*
- His personality - *"was with God"*
- His deity - *"was God"*

John doesn't immediately reveal the surprising identity of the Logos. He doesn't mention the name Jesus Christ until verse 17. But, it soon becomes clear that this is who the apostle is talking about.

When God Speaks

Why is Jesus given the codename: Word?

This name alerts us to the fact that God has a message for us, and this message is—Jesus. "John intends that the whole of his Gospel shall be read in the light of this verse (Jn. 1:1)," wrote biblical scholar C. K. Barrett. "The deeds and words of Jesus are the deeds and words of God."[2] The prologue tips off the reader to see the whole Gospel story as God's word to the world.

Jesus is God revealing His heart to us.

> *God, after He spoke long ago to the fathers in the prophets in many portions and in many ways, in these last days has spoken to us in His Son...* (Heb. 1:1-2 NASB).

Almost one hundred times in the Bible, we run into the phrase: "*The Word of the Lord came unto...*" Prophets of old received messages from heaven, and made them known to the people. Their job was to pass on God's words.

But something new took place.

> *The Word became flesh and made his dwelling among us...* (Jn. 1:14).

The Word of the Lord did not come as before—verbally, audibly, occasionally. The Word became *flesh*. The Word of the Lord took human form. God was now speaking "*in His Son*" (Heb. 1:2)—an unusual phrase that implies that the Son not only brought the message, but *was* the message. *Messenger and message merge.* Jesus of Nazareth is God's utterance, heaven's pronouncement.

Jesus is what God has to say.
–Brian Zahnd

Never before had the Lord of heaven and earth spoken like this.

Previously, God had spoken through patriarchs, sages and prophets. They gave us *words* about God. Their messages were the Word made a precept, an ethic, a commandment, a sermon. They were attempts to communicate the transcendent with the feeble medium of human vocabulary. Mere words were not up to the task. They could never carry the weight of the message! A superior communication took place—*Jesus was the Word made flesh.* A Word you could touch, you could see, you could hear. The Living Word.

The Divine Word had become human.

C. S. Lewis states: "If the thing happened, it was the central event in the history of the Earth—the very thing that the whole story has been about."[3]

God Has a "Word" for Us

A person may have magnificent ideas in their mind, but they remain hidden and unknown until words are used to express them. Words are the primary way we use to share our thoughts; words transmit ideas. We use words to make ourselves understood and known.

The Logos is the Word that breaks the silence and makes known the mystery of God.

The true plot to God's Story would forever remain hidden unless He revealed it to us. We needed light from heaven; we needed a word from God—*and that is exactly what we have!* Not a multitude of words but *the* Word. Not a verbal word but a living Word. A life-giving, beauty-making, truth-revealing, evil-destroying, goodness-spreading, joy-bringing Word.

Glen Scrivener writes, "Jesus is the Word of God. He is not the best Word. He is not the ultimate Word. He is not the seal of series of improving words. He is *the* Word."

Jesus Christ is the alpha and omega of what God has to say. He is the first word, and also the last. And when this Word finishes saying what He is going to say, there will be nothing left to say. When the truth about the Real Story is finally and fully revealed, the entire cosmos will bow and worship in wordless wonder. When He brings the Story to its grand finale, every tear will be wiped away, and every tongue will sing as all creation dances in the *"glorious liberty of the children of God"* (Rom. 8:21 NKJV).

You will not want to miss it!

Making Sense of Our Story

The One who authored creation's script is appropriately referred to as the Word—the *Logos* (from which our word logic comes). Logos is a loaded term. It was used in ancient Greek philosophy to refer to the mind or intelligence behind the order and structure of the universe. It resembles the Hebrew concept of wisdom, God's companion and co-worker in the task of creation.

Sixteen centuries ago, the great theologian Athanasius stated: "The Logos is the logic of the universe." He meant that in Christ we find the explanation, the reason, the rationale behind everything. "Christ is the clue to all that is," asserted Lesslie Newbigin.

History is not merely a confusing assortment of chaotic incidents or an unending cycle of pointless events. Rather, there is a *Logos*—a logic to it all. History is not meaningless. It has a beginning, a middle and an end. It is going somewhere.

John is saying, "I have something important to say, so listen closely: The secret of the universe? This may sound audacious—but I know what it is. Or, more accurately, I know *who* it is."

The apostle has inside information. If we are to make sense of our story, we must listen to what He says. The truth about our world is found in the *Logos*. Our unfolding drama originates in Him. The key to reality, the secret to the universe, is not found in some abstract principle, but in the divine person made known to us through the incarnation of Jesus of Nazareth. Christ declared,

> *The reason I was born and came into the world is to testify to the truth* (Jn. 18:37).

Paul asserted,

> *For it is in him, and in him alone, that men will find all the treasures of wisdom and knowledge"* (Col. 2:3 Phlp).

Scripture affirms that the Logos is...

- The reality behind the cosmos
- The explanation of the world
- The logic of the universe
- The secret to everything

Our Starting Point

The Logos is the starting point of all things. If we are to understand God's Story, it is here we must begin—*Christ*. If you start in the wrong place, you end up in the wrong place. In the beginning was the Word. Not the Bible, not a doctrine, not a theological system but the *Word*. If we start anywhere else, we will get things wrong. We must begin with Jesus. He precedes Genesis. He precedes *everything*. He is the Alpha and Omega. Christ needs to be our interpretive key.

The apostle Paul dares to say all things *"hold together"* in Christ (Col. 1:17). Outside of Him, everything—even our best theories—fall apart.

In the fourth century, theologian Athanasius asserted, "The only system of thought into which Jesus Christ will fit is the one in which He is the starting point." Failure to understand this is like inserting a button into the wrong buttonhole when putting on a shirt. When you begin in the wrong place, things simply don't "fit" properly.

E. Stanley Jones writes:

> The Gospel begins with Jesus, the Incarnate. If you don't begin with Jesus, you don't begin—you don't begin with anything except roads with dead ends. We know little or nothing about God, and what we know is wrong, unless we begin with Jesus. If you do not see God in the face of Jesus, you see something other than God—and different.[4]

Theologian Michael Horton cautions, "Don't start with the question of the existence of some vague deity, start with the particular God who showed up in our world, the one we have access to in history."[5]

We don't simply believe in God. We believe in *this* God.

Our starting point is the Lord Jesus Christ—the Incarnate Word.

He Is Not Silent

Many people visualize Almighty God reigning on a distant throne, inaccessible, aloof and indifferent to the concerns of mere mortals. We should not expect to hear from Him.

Such a view is false.

God is neither remote or wordless.

> *For God does speak—now one way, now another—though no one perceives it* (Job 33:14).

> *In the past God spoke to our ancestors through the prophets at many times and in various ways"* (Heb. 1:1).

He is never speechless, never at a loss for words. He takes the initiative to disclose Himself. His very name is "The Word."

Words are wonderful things. They do much more than communicate—they create fellowship. Sharing intimate thoughts and feelings transports us beyond a mere exchange of information; it creates connection. It builds relationship. It takes us into the mystery of communion.

The biblical term *logos* literally means "that which enables you to be in relationship with another."[6] It is wonderful that God would seek to inform or to enlighten us—but that's just the beginning! The phrase "*in the beginning was the Logos*" implies that the Author of the universe chooses to relate to and be in conversation with human beings. He seeks to bring us into something that staggers the imagination—*He desires fellowship.*

This could turn into an exciting story!

> *At the very heart of God is the passionate disposition to be in loving fellowship with you.*
>
> —Richard Foster

God Speaks Again

When the Word spoke at the beginning of history, creation sprang into existence. Heaven and earth, oceans and rivers, trees and flowers, fowl and fish, animals and humans. Everything that was made came to be through God's spoken Word.

But somewhere along the way things went off the rails. Our world came to ruin, and stood in desperate need of repair. This "repairing" required God to speak once more—and no one but the Logos was up to the task.

So the Word speaks again. This time the Word becomes flesh and He "immigrates" into His creation in the person of Jesus. And when He speaks, redemptive things happen—healing and forgiveness, light and life, goodness and grace, hope and mercy. At His word salvation comes.

The Creator becomes the Redeemer. At His life-giving word, what is crooked is made straight, what is fallen is raised up, what is damaged is made whole. His stated purpose in coming to a world under the reign of death was to bring life—life in abundance (Jn. 10:10).

The Creator Who Looks Like A Carpenter

Almost no one in Israel suspected that the God of glory and Jesus of Nazareth were the same person. The man from Galilee worked with wood, attended weddings, befriended outcasts, hugged children, told parables and dined with sinners. He looked like a normal Galilean.

But there is more than meets the eye.

- Eternity has intruded into time.
- The Creator has entered His creation.
- Infinity has been squeezed into humanity.
- The Lord of heaven has come to earth.
- The Light shines in the darkness.

According to John's record, the Script Writer of the cosmic drama came among us incognito. Nothing more staggering has ever happened. He came to our planet to salvage the story, and when he finishes writing the last chapter, everything will be made new. The earth will be flooded with the glory of God as the waters cover the sea.

PRAYER

HIGH GOD OF HEAVEN, we are grateful that we do not find ourselves lost and alone in the vastness of the cosmos. You are there and You are not silent. It is comforting to know that the Lord of the universe is not a cold cosmic force or a deity who dwells in distant aloofness. You are a God who speaks, who makes Himself known—Your name is the Word. Thank You for writing us into your script and for giving us a role to play in your unfolding drama. Amidst the din and the noise of this busy world, help us to be attentive to your "still small voice." Teach us to live in the light of Your presence, and to find our joy in knowing You. Amen.

*Every once in a while . . . someone
asks how I can believe in the Trinity.
My answer is always the same.
I would still be an agnostic
if there was no Trinity, because
there would be no answers.
Without the high order of personal unity
and diversity as given in the Trinity,
there are no answers.*

—Francis A. Schaeffer

CHAPTER FOUR

THE MATRIX OF THE STORY

*And the Word was with God,
and the Word was God.*

JOHN 1:1

THE BRILLIANT PHYSICIST and inventor Nikola Tesla once said: "If you want to find the secrets of the universe, think in terms of energy, frequency and vibration."

Really? That's what life is all about?

Not exactly a heart-warming thought!

Humans long for meaning and romance and adventure and relationship and joy and love. It would be enormously disappointing to discover that the core issue of the cosmos comes down to some impersonal quantifiable force. If that's the heartbeat of reality—*we must be in the wrong universe!*

The worldview that emerges from Holy Scripture is radically different. The apostle John brings to light the secrets of the universe—and they are astonishingly wonderful!

John launches his Gospel with the most revolutionary statement in the history of human thought about God. He reveals there is more going on within the Almighty than anyone had imagined. He boldly overturns all previous notions of deity. The apostle leads us to an understanding of the infinite Lord that is astounding, extravagant and unique.

Let's fasten our seatbelts and delve into this mystery.

And the Word was with God... (Jn. 1:1).

In eternity, God was *not* alone—somebody else was there. He had company.

The Greek term translated "with" literally means "turned toward God." There was face to face *interaction* going on. There was intimacy; there was connectedness. One scholar translates the verse, *"the Word was very close to God."* The relationship was both dynamic and intimate.

Don't miss this detail.

"The Word was with God" involves something huge. The unpretentious term "with" doesn't usually get much attention. But look closely. Behind these four letters lies a world of mystery, beauty and ecstasy. There is a symphony of life and goodness here. Mind-blowing things take place inside this "with-ness," and for centuries theologians have tried to wrap their minds around it. The apostle is going to help us explore this mystery—and he's going to take us deeper than we imagined.

Divine Togetherness

The Word is not "with" God in the way a hammer is together with a chisel in a toolbox. The "with-ness" John talks about is much deeper. It is more like a musical note that teams up with two others and blends with them to make a three-voice chord. The notes get inside one another, they interact, harmonize, and enhance each other generating a pleasant fuller sound called a triad or a chord. Each note retains its identity while becoming part of something greater and richer.

God is also the blending of three. He is not a solitary note; He is the harmony of multiple notes.

He is polyphonic.

God is the perfect harmony of the original melody that is so indescribably rich, so unsurpassably beautiful, so wildly expansive it ran the risk of spilling over into the creation of a universe.

Which, as you might suspect—is *exactly* what happened.

One and More Than One

The writer adds a fascinating detail:

> *And the Word was God* (Jn. 1:1).

This is where our brains get bent out of shape.
Three facts stand out:

- There is a person called the *Word*.
- This person is *with* God.
- This person *is* God.

In the same breath, the apostle *distinguishes* Him from God and *identifies* Him as God.

How do you put that together?

If I were to state: "I am *with* the boss, and I *am* the boss." You would probably exclaim: "That's ridiculous! Which one of the two is it?"

John is saying something equally puzzling about God.

It took the early Christians a few centuries to process this mystifying connection between the Logos and God.

How can the Word "be" God, and at the same time be "with" God?

Welcome to the glorious enigma of the Trinity!

It is here we come to the very heart of reality, the matrix of everything. This is the marvelous mystery at "the very center of the very center." It is of huge importance and has fabulous ramifications on the narrative that enfolds. Let's take a closer look.

In the Beginning

The very first phrase in the Bible, *"in the beginning God,"* underscores the rock bottom truth that there is ONE and only one God. Singular. He has no rivals. He alone is God.

> *The Lord is God in heaven above and on the earth below. There is no other* (Dt. 4:39).

The first verse in the Gospel of John takes it a step further. It lets us in on the secret that something dynamic and beautiful takes place *within* God. In God, there is both oneness ("was God") and community ("with God"). The oneness of God includes *otherness*.

There's more going on inside of God than we realized!

We are not talking about an *absolute* oneness (like one apple or one book), but a *composite* oneness (like one team or one audience). *God is both one and more than one.*

Don't write this off as some bizarre oddity. Stay with me. There is something indescribably wonderful here.

There are religions which claim belief in "one God," and still others that worship many gods. But only Christianity brings "one" and "more than one" together. It embraces a belief in *the Tri-unity of God*—a remarkable concept![1]

Trinity establishes relationship and community as fundamental truths about God. Trinity is not one of the many attributes like holiness, mercy, patience, wisdom, power, etc., that describe how God acts. *Trinity is the primary fact about God.* This is who He is. We cannot speak accurately about God apart from His triune existence, because God isn't God apart from His triune existence.

Trinity is about relationships

God does not live in aloneness; He lives in togetherness—in the loving interaction of Father, Son and Holy Spirit. The foundational reality of God's being is not the individual persons of the Godhead but their deep *relatedness*. Everything else we can say about Him springs out of this. Every one of His attributes flows out of this loving union of Three Divine Persons.

This is the central issue.

Relationships did not start up with Adam and Eve—they existed eternally within God. The Creator who said in Genesis: *"It is not good for man to be alone,"* has never been alone. The triune life of God has always been one of community and togetherness.

"There is no such thing as the silence of eternity," writes Robert W. Jenson. "What is eternal is not silence, but discourse."

The Most High inhabits the Eternal Conversation.

He is a relational God.

God on Display

John's Gospel forces us to scrap the notion of a distant deity who is a shapeless, passionless, colorless being living somewhere in outer space in eternal boredom.

John blows this idea off the map, and declares: "You've got it all wrong! In the beginning there was life and joy and overflowing goodness. There was a Dance—and it was indescribably wonderful."

All through his book, the beloved apostle gives us glimpses of the inner life of this Three-In-One God. Jesus' connectedness with His Heavenly Father was the central factor of His life. The way He related to *Abba* during His earthly life reveals fascinating aspects of what goes on within the Trinity. A number of features stand out:

- Intimacy (Jn. 1:18)
- Companionship (Jn. 5:19; 16:32)
- Love (Jn. 3:35; 14:31; 15:9)
- Unity (Jn. 10:30)
- Transparency (Jn. 5:20)
- Harmony (Jn. 5:19)
- Honor (Jn. 8:29,54)
- Joy (Jn. 15:11; 17:13)

WHAT STORY HAVE WE FALLEN INTO?

This is the inner life of God! There is interaction, there is dialogue, there is closeness, there is gladness, there is fellowship. A divine dance is how early Christian theologians pictured the triune life of God.
And it has been going on forever.
Listen to C. S. Lewis:

> The most important difference between Christianity and all other religions [is] that in Christianity God is not a static thing—not even a person—but a dynamic, pulsating activity, a life, almost a kind of drama. Almost, if you will not think me irreverent, a kind of dance...[2]

Unlike the remote, solitary, aloof, faceless deity that exists in the minds of many, the stunningly beautiful truth about the true God is this: *He is a Holy Trinity.* The blending of Three Persons. A joyous interchange of love, honor, creativity and goodness.
And this universe has never seen anything like it.

More Than a Mystery

Trinity is possibly the most delightful truth we know about the Lord of glory. It has been sadly neglected and frequently reduced to a philosophical debate that entirely misses the sheer beauty and main point of it all.

The truth of God's tri-unity is not meant to mystify; it is cause to *marvel.* It is not a philosophical puzzle we are meant to unravel, it is reason for wonder.

"The triunity of God is the secret of his beauty," argues Swiss theologian Karl Barth. "If we deny this, we at once have a God without radiance and without joy."[3]

God's beauty is not found in eternal motionless serenity but in free-flowing togetherness. In the full, rich and passionate concert of life shared by Father, Son and Holy Spirit.

This Three-In-One God dwells in the fullness of loving, holy, joyful togetherness. He has never been bored or lonely or listless!

He has no needs, no unfulfilled desires. Nothing diminishes His joy. He lives in a circle of endless goodness, blessedness and glory. He knows only fullness, only thriving, only limitless flourishing, joy and delight.

> *God's oneness and threeness is God's beauty.*
> — A. J. Swoboda

No one else had *ever* thought of the Almighty this way. No other religion spoke of a vibrant fellowship of life and love within the Divine Community. It is Abba's Son who reveals to us this remarkable truth.

A Trinitarian Story

Our Story begins with *this* God, for there is no other. It begins with this Trinitarian togetherness of other-focused love, indescribable goodness and unbounded joy. Trinity is the deepest truth about God—not holiness, not sovereignty, not power—*but Trinity*. The essential bedrock truth about God is that He is the eternal loving union of Father, Son and Holy Spirit. *This relationship is the heartbeat of reality.* This is the explanation for everything else.

Michael Reeves writes:

> The Trinity is not some inessential add-on to God, some optional software that can be plugged into him. At bottom, this God is different, for at bottom, He is not creator, ruler, or even "God" in some abstract sense: He is the Father, loving and giving life and love to his Son in the joy of the Spirit. A God who is in himself love, who before all things could "never be anything but love." Having such a God happily changes everything.[4]

Trinity is a game changer. It is bedrock truth that alters the whole logic of the universe, and the logic of our existence. At the centre of reality is the stunning beauty of the Triune Community of love—and this transforms the entire Story.

Far from being theological baggage, Trinity is what makes our Story indescribably beautiful. It takes a black-and-white picture and fills it with living color. It provides a breathtaking backdrop to our drama.

This is the matrix of reality. To get our story right, we must begin here.

The Heart of Reality

Trinity is the good news that rich exuberant togetherness lies at the epicenter of reality. It tells us that at the heart of all things rules a relational God. Trinity is the biblical answer to the lurking fear that we may be lost in an impersonal and loveless universe. Trinity dispels that false narrative. It informs us that love, personality, and communication have always existed, and have eternal value.

A Creator whose very essence centers in relatedness explains a lot of things! One of the deepest longings in human beings is to relate to others. We want to connect and belong. Our greatest joys are associated with family, friends and falling in love. Nothing in life contributes more to our well-being than the experience and quality of our interpersonal relationships, and nothing can cause greater pain.

Our true humanity is expressed, not as individuals but as persons in community. Our connection with others gives our lives dignity, richness and meaning. It is the source of our identity. The words we use to describe who we are—father, mother, husband, wife, son, daughter, brother, sister, etc.—are all *relational* words. No one exists as an unattached "individual," without social ties. "To be," declares one philosopher, "is to be in relations."

"Adam wasn't lonely because he was imperfect," states Timothy Keller, "but because he was perfect. The ache for friends is not the result of sin." The "ache for friends" is the result of being human. It wasn't enough to live in paradise. Human life requires friendship, conversation, community.

"I am convinced that human beings instinctively seek two things," writes Philip Yancey. "We long for meaning, a sense that our life somehow matters to the world around us. And we long for community, a sense of being loved."[5]

When we come to the final days of our life, what will matter most to us? The car parked in the garage? The university degree framed on the wall? The state of our finances? Of course not. What will matter most will be *people*.

We are relational to the core... and now we know *where* that came from.

> *If you cut existence it bleeds Trinity.*
> — JEFF TURNER

Togetherness is at the hub of the universe. We long for intimacy because we were made in the image of a Father-Son-and-Spirit God—a community of Three Persons inseparably united in love. The Christian understanding of God as a 3-in-1 Divine togetherness makes sense of our deepest longings.

Thomas Merton points out, "To say that I am made in the image of God is to say that Love is the reason for my existence, for God is love."

In his book, *Experiencing the Trinity*, Darrell Johnson writes: "At the center of the universe there is a relationship… It is out of that relationship that we were created and redeemed, and it is for that relationship we were created and redeemed."[6]

The Secret of the Universe

Before the universe came to be, before the heavens and the earth were called into existence, before there was anything else, there was the great fountain of life of the triune God. The center and the matrix of the universe is not an equation—it is a dance, a symphony, a circle of passion and glory, an interaction of love between Father, Son and Holy Spirit.

This is the deepest mystery at the heart of all of reality.

- God is not a bachelor
- God is not a solitary divinity

- God is not an impersonal force
- God is not a despotic ruler

God is a holy circle of love, light and life. A Tri-unity of abounding goodness and splendor.

To borrow Tesla's phrase: If you want to find the secrets of the universe . . . think in terms of the loving unity of Father, Son and Holy Spirit.

This alters the whole logic of the universe.

Timothy Keller states, "This astonishing, dynamic conception of the triune God is bristling with profound, wonderful, life-shaping, world-changing implications."[7]

If an incomparable celebration of eternal joy upholds and undergirds reality, if this is the matrix of our existence—this is the best news we have ever heard.

This transforms the whole story.

PRAYER

GLORIOUS TRIUNE GOD, *for many of us, the idea of Trinity was an awkward, difficult, perplexing concept, best left in the creed. Little did we realize there was such rich beauty and inexhaustible goodness to be discovered. Thank You for helping us to perceive a little more of the wonder of who You are. We praise You, Father, Son and Holy Spirit, for the perfection of your oneness, and the splendor of your threeness. We rejoice in the fact that it is a joy-filled, love-driven togetherness of glory that lies at the center of all things. How wonderful You are, oh Lord God. Continue to open our eyes to the blessed magnificence of your holy Three-in-Oneness. Amen.*

*God loved us before he made us;
and his love has never diminished
and never shall.*

—J‍ULIAN OF N‍ORWICH

CHAPTER FIVE

LOVE WAS HERE FIRST

He was with God in the beginning.
JOHN 1:2

WHAT WAS THERE before anything else existed? Silence? Boredom? Energy? Emptiness?

No, none of the above.

The biblical answer may come as a surprise.

In the beginning there was... love.

Before there were planets or protoplasm or people, God was not lonely. God was not bored or brooding. The Almighty was not wondering what to do.

Nothing of the kind.

Something beautiful was going on inside of God—love flowed like a cascading river between a Father and His Son in the unfettered joy of the Holy Spirit. God is love, and love is what God does. Before anything else, there was a magnificent interchange of other-focused affection and mutual delight.

Love was here first.

Ultimate reality has to do with love.

Does that surprise you?

Scripture reveals that at the center of the cosmos we do not find an absolute and all-determining Ego. We do not find a Celestial

Caesar. We find a rich fellowship of love and intimacy—a Holy Trinity. The shining radiance of love is at the very core of existence. It is here, at the headwaters of all life and goodness, that we find the secret to our story.

Glen Scrivener writes:

> So, to find the pulse of the universe (if you want to tap into the heartbeat of reality) what do you find? You find fierce, passionate, determined, life-giving love that flows between the Generous Father, His Beloved Son and the Life-Giving Spirit.[1]

This delightful fact challenges the somber narrative so many people have believed. If love is what truly lies beneath and behind everything else, then the story "we have fallen into" could turn out to be a most fascinating one indeed!

Uncovering the Story

In his Gospel, John takes us on an expedition into the heart of God. On this journey, the son of Zebedee intertwines theology with poetry and packs multiple meanings into a word or phrase. He cracks open the door of eternity.

Few other lines have so intrigued theologians and inspired musicians and artists as John's opening statement:

> *In the beginning was the Word,*
> *and the Word was WITH God,*
> *and the Word was God.*

Not only does the apostle state in verse one that the Word was "with" God, he then repeats it for good measure in verse two. At the end of his prologue, he mentions it again (Jn. 1:18). What's more, he alludes to this close-knit "with-ness" all throughout his book. It appears the author is saying: "Do not miss this truth. You must get a hold of this." It is perhaps the most important concept the author is going to unpack.

Before Time Began

"Before the foundation of the world" is an intriguing phrase that shows up four times in Scripture. Notice how the Lord Himself used this phrase. He prayed: *"Father . . . You loved Me before the foundation of the world"* (Jn. 17:24 NKJV). Christ is pulling back the curtain and giving us insight into the pre-creation past.

What is He telling us?

Before everything else existed, there was love.

A Father and His Son delighted in each other with an "omnipotently fervent love," as one writer put it. Past eternity was not bland, boring or uneventful. There was an exuberant exchange of self-giving love going on that was over-flowing and relentless.

This is who God is.

Could we even begin to imagine what a nonstop interchange of infinite love, absolute goodness, unlimited power, boundless creativity and overflowing joy would actually look like?

We are trying to capture the ocean in a teacup.

Theologian Michael Reeves points out, "It is only when you grasp what it means for God to be a Trinity that you really sense the beauty, the overflowing kindness, the heart-grabbing loveliness of God."[2]

A Community of Joy

So what was God doing in eternity past?

I am not being flippant, or irreverent when I say this, but I think *He was having a blast.*

And that is putting it mildly.

If you look at the Bible references that speak about God in eternity, you keep running into words like: rejoicing, delight, glory, love, joy. Look at Proverbs 8:30: "*I was filled with delight day after day, rejoicing always in his presence.*" The psalmist said: "*In His presence is fullness of joy* (there is an awful lot of it) *and at right hand are pleasures forevermore*" (there's no end to it) (Psa. 16:11 NKJV).

C. S. Lewis stated it well, "Joy is the serious business of heaven."

Scholars of the early church reflected deeply on the inner life of the triune God, and used the word *perichoresis* to describe the "dance of mutual indwelling." They had come to understand that the being of God is involved in a dynamic choreography of free-flowing togetherness and joy.

In 1 Timothy 1:11, Paul described Him as *"the blessed God."* One translation reads *"the blissful God."* Not bored, disgruntled or grouchy. Not depressed. He is enjoying Himself fabulously.

What is God so happy about?

He is enjoying *togetherness*. He's not misery seeking company. He's Three-in-One bursting with life. Joy spilling over. God is Father, Son and Spirit inextricably *intertwined* in an exuberant connectedness of love and goodness. Their devotion to each other is so rich, so strong, so deep that they actually become *one*. This intense, eternal overflow of love generates a rhapsody of mutual delight.

> **The trinity is not a maths problem. The trinity is the good news that God is love.**
> – GLEN SCRIVENER

The attribute of God most celebrated in the Old Testament is His *"chesed"*—His faithful love. The New Testament takes it a step further—it declares that *"God is love"* (1 Jn. 4:8,16). This is a profound statement. *Love isn't just something God does, it's who God is.* Think about that. Love has to do with the *essence* of the divine being. Love is what goes on "inside" of God.

Holiness, Righteousness and Wrath

There are those who are quick to say, "Yes, God is love, BUT He is also..." They then speak of the holiness, righteousness or wrath of God. There is no question that all the attributes of God are to be taken seriously, but to think that there is an "unloving" or darker side to God is a mistaken view.

John's bold, paradigm-altering statement "God is love," is not followed by a word of caution. There's no need to qualify it. There's no need to balance it. Nothing needs to be added.

C. H. Dodd writes:

> To say "God is love" implies that all His activity is loving activity. If He creates, He creates in love; if He rules, He rules in love; if He judges, He judges in love. All that he does is the expression of his nature, which is—to love.[3]

Divine attributes are not at odds with each other. Holiness is not something that keeps God from going overboard in loving people. Divine wrath is not when God ceases to show love. Justice and love are not God's yin and yang. Holiness, wrath and justice are not opposed to love. *Rather, they are manifestations of the love of God.* When God demonstrates His wrath or justice, He is not being unloving. He is doing what love *should* do when faced with evil and corruption. Everything God does is inspired by love.

All divine attributes are attributes of love. Love is not one of the many attributes of God—*love is the essence of God*. It is the center from which everything else flows:

- Omnipotence is the power of love.
- Omnipresence is the sphere of love.
- Holiness is the beauty of love.
- Faithfulness is the steadfastness of love.
- Justice is the rightness of love.
- Wrath is the fire of love.
- Goodness is the benevolence of love.

D. Martyn Lloyd-Jones writes, "You cannot think of God and must not think of Him except in terms of love. Everything that God is and does is coloured by this."[4]

Rather than viewing the love of God as one spoke in a wheel —one among many—it may be better to think of it as the hub to which all the spokes are connected. Love is not simply one of the many divine qualities; it is the central reality of the Triune God. What lies at the heart of God is not power, righteousness or wisdom—*it is love.*

Love Is Not Squishy

It should be understood that authentic love is more than a warm bubble of joy. Not only does love show tenderness, kindness and compassion, it also expresses itself in indignation against injustice and firm opposition to evil. Love should not be confused with sentimentality.

"Love," as Lewis points out, "is something more stern and splendid than mere kindness." It is ardent, fierce, relentless. It is sin-scorching, evil-destroying, goodness-spreading. God's love comforts and confronts. It is both tender and turbulent. It blazes with fiery intensity.

"It is because God loves the world he has made, and especially his human creatures, that he hates everything that spoils, wrecks, or defaces it," writes N. T. Wright.[4] The wrath of God is the vigorous opposition of Father, Son and Spirit to our destruction. It is divine love declaring: "No, I didn't create you for that!" God's wrath is not the nasty side of God. *God's wrath happens because God loves.*

Love Was Here First

If we wind back the clock into the far reaches of eternity, we will never come to a time when God was not love. The Father eternally loved the Son in the joy of the Spirit. The overflowing love of the Blessed Trinity has been going on forever. However, we cannot say this about other aspects of the Divine Being. There was a time when God was *not* Creator. There was a time when God was *not* Lawgiver, Judge or Sustainer of the cosmos. God took on these roles later on in life. They are not fundamental to who He is. The Holy Trinity was not always involved in managing a universe, *but He was always involved in love.* This is His very nature. This is who He is.

> **God is love. It isn't just that God loves. He is love. That goes to the core of his being.**
> —Dallas Willard

The Oneness of Threeness

To say that Father, Son and Spirit are one, is to say *they are bound together in love.* One of the best analogies is the oneness of the marriage relationship where two become "one flesh." Marriage is the unity of a man and a woman bound together in love. God is the unity of Father and Son, bound together in the love of the Spirit. Marriage is a picture of the ultimate mystery of love at the core of the universe.

Tragically, because of human weakness, selfishness and sinfulness, marriages often flounder. It is not uncommon for couples to argue, fight, and even divorce. For all have sinned and come short of marital perfection.

However, in the triune God, *none* of these problems exist—not even remotely! The torrential love of God flows undiminished and unhindered, generating a oneness that is perfect, spectacular and everlasting.

In the eighth century, John of Damascus wrote: "By virtue of their eternal love they live in one another to such an extent, and dwell in one another to such an extent that they are one."

There is nothing so beautiful in the entire universe!

Loves Gives

Paul affirms in 1 Cor. 13:5 that love *"is not self-seeking."* One translation states, *"love is never turned upon itself."* Love is always outwardly inclined, it is other-focused. That is what love does.

And that is what *God* does.

Timothy Keller describes the Trinity thus:

> Each of the divine persons centers upon the others. None demands the others revolve around Him. Each voluntarily circles the other two, pouring love, delight and adoration into them. Each person of the Trinity loves, adores, defers to and rejoices in the others. That creates a dynamic, pulsating dance of joy and love.[6]

This was going on before the beginning of time.

This is the heartbeat of the universe—the unquenchable, uninhibited, passionate, omnipotent overflow of love between Father, Son and Holy Spirit. This is the center of everything. At the heart of reality . . . *there is love.*

Cornelius Plantinga writes:

> At the center of the universe, self-giving love is the dynamic currency of the Trinitarian life of God. The persons within God exalt, commune with, and defer to one another. . . . When early Greek Christians spoke of perichoresis in God they meant that each divine person harbors the other at the center of his being. In constant movement of overture and acceptance each person envelops and encircles the others.[7]

Mutual Othering

Canadian singer and musician Steve Bell tells of an unforgettable moment that took place on stage in the middle of a concert. At one point, his pianist Mike began to play in a wonderfully creative, dynamic and unrehearsed way. Steve locked eyes with the pianist and began to play his guitar in response to and in support of what Mike was doing on the keyboard.

A fascinating rhythmical dialogue ensued as both musicians sought to enhance the music played by the other. Both were following and no-one was leading as they engaged together in "mutual othering." It was an ecstatic moment. Time seemed to stop, and at that instant Steve sensed God saying, "Pay attention to what is happening here. This is who I am; a free mutuality, an insoluble communion born of loving self-donation for the other." It was a ravishing taste of pure beauty and unity unlike anything Steve had ever experienced.

Neither musician was trying to outplay his fellow artist or "steal the show." Each was striving to enrich and elevate the other. They were "honoring" each other. It all blended to create an awe-inspiring moment of beauty, harmony and ecstasy.[8]

And it captures something of the inner life of the Trinity.

Father, Son and Spirit engage in a concert of "mutual othering." The Three-In-One God is an other-focused ensemble, each one pouring life and love into the other. Each one honoring and lifting up the other. And this generates an extravagant symphony of unsurpassed beauty, goodness and joy we call the Holy Trinity.

Baxter Kruger writes,

> Far from being frozen in some lifeless pose, the Father, Son and Spirit live in a circle of eager and lavish hospitality. It is a circle of passionate embracing, of mutual acceptance, delight and love, which issues forth not in sadness or depression or misery but in unchained life—joyous, overflowing fellowship. The early theologians of the church were quite right when they spoke of the triune life of God as a divine dance. It is not dead, but alive, good, right, unstifled, overflowing, creative.[9]

The Mighty Symphony

Early one morning, my wife and I headed out for a walk, something we enjoy doing. We turned onto a trail that wound through a pine forest to the waterfront where we sat to rest on a bench. We conversed and prayed and enjoyed the freshness of the dawn.

Suddenly Wendy rose to her feet and stood at attention. I was puzzled. When she broke out singing the National Anthem, I was really taken aback. I knew my wife loved her country, but this was ridiculous!

"What are you doing?" I asked.

"Don't you hear it?" she responded.

"Hear what?" I inquired.

"The music," she said, pointing across the bay to the military base.

I listened, and I could barely make out the sound of a band playing the national anthem.

My hearing was not what it used to be—and I had totally missed the melody.

We are surrounded by the mighty symphony of God's self-expression in creation. Sadly, many fail to hear the music.

Michael Reeves writes,

> Indeed, in the triune God is the love behind all love, the life behind all life, the music behind all music, the beauty behind all beauty and the joy behind all joy. In other words, in the triune God is a God we can heartily enjoy—and enjoy in and through his creation.[10]

Every enjoyment is a token of His love, a cause for gratitude. The aroma of coffee, the magic of Mozart, the taste of blackberries, the gift of hearing, sight and smell.

> *Every good and perfect gift is from above, coming down from the Father of the heavenly lights, who does not change like shifting shadows* (Jas. 1:17).

Philosopher Peter Kreeft comments on the music of creation:

> Everything in nature was designed and created to manifest the God of love… Every blade of grass is a blade of grace, a grace note in God's single Song. Nature is not blind and dumb. Nature is eloquent. Human science is blind and dumb if it does not hear this eloquence.[10]

The beloved disciple wrote his book to help us tune our ear to the heavenly melody. He calls our attention to the great symphony of life and glory shared by the Father, Son and Spirit. He helps us hear the harmony of the Father's Eternal Song.

This trinitarian song of love is the deepest truth about God.

It is what lies behind all the beauty and goodness and joy in creation.

And it is the song we were created to sing.

PRAYER

SOVEREIGN LORD, we are prone to think that You are all about power and authority and letting everyone know You are in charge. It fills us with awe to think that the Supreme Lord of heaven and earth is all about love. Blessed God, we are thankful that love sits on the throne of the universe. Not the flimsy, giddy, wobbly thing we sometimes call love, but a boundless, bottomless, unwavering, unshakeable reality of self-giving goodness. How wonderful to know that love is at the center of all things. That love has the final word. This speaks peace to our hearts. It constrains us to come before You with thanksgiving and praise. Blessed be Your Name, oh Lord, our God. Amen.

God, who needs nothing,
loves into existence
wholly superfluous creatures
in order that he may love
and perfect them.

—C. S. Lewis

God does not will to exist without us.
In all the fullness of his divinity, in which
he might well have been satisfied with himself,
he wills to exist together with us.
He wills to be in fellowship with us.

—Karl Barth

CHAPTER SIX

EXPANSIVE GOODNESS

Through him all things were made.
JOHN 1:3

GIVEN THE OVERWHELMING GOODNESS and glory of this Three-in-One God, spillover was inevitable. The Divine Dance of life was too vibrant to be confined, too exuberant to be contained. It required expression. And it comes as no surprise that in the beginning . . . there was an outburst of creativity.

And God said, let there be . . . (Gn. 1:3).

The Bible does not begin with a theory about origins, but with a Creator at work, fashioning a universe like an artist brushing beauty onto a canvas.

The Divine Artist gives shape, color, and texture to His work of art, occasionally standing back to admire His masterpiece. He speaks things into existence—and a beautiful world bursts forth full of waterfalls, butterflies, dolphins, eagles, orchids, beaches, sunsets, and Columbian coffee. The Maker's creativity is endless.

On the sixth day, the World-Maker fashions His crowning work, His *opus magnum*. Instead of words, He now uses His "hands" and makes a statue out of dust. He draws near, imparts

His own breath to the statue, and transforms it into a living being. From the breath of heaven and the dust of the earth a *"fearfully and wonderfully made"* creature comes to life in the Maker's likeness. The Creator's self-portrait.

Human beings were given a favored position on this pristine planet—male and female were stamped with the image of God. Ancient kings often set up images of themselves as visible symbols of their sovereignty over a certain territory. But in the Genesis record, the divine image is not placed on a monument, but on *humans* (Gn. 1:26,27). These representatives of God on Planet Earth are granted extraordinary dignity and value.

Our first parents were privileged actors in the divine drama, regal residents in an idyllic paradise called Eden. Great glory was bestowed upon us. We were endowed with remarkable beauty and strength, and called to exercise dominion over a new world. We were "statues of God" placed as kings over a kingdom (Psa. 8:4-8).

> *God saw all that he had made, and it was very good* (Gn. 1:31).

A creation filled with extravagant goodness—*this* is where our story begins. Not with original sin, but original *glory*. What was "original" about this world is not evil, but goodness and beauty.

What Motivated the Maker

What prompted the Divine Lord to do this? Why did Father, Son and Holy Spirit give existence to people, and romance, and forests, and beaches, and music, and laughter?

This is an important question.

A Sunday School teacher once asked his class: "Why did God decide to create the world and everything in it?" One boy gave his opinion, "Because he was bored."

Is *that* why we are here?

Nothing could be further from the truth.

> *God is not served by human hands as if he needed anything* (Acts 17:25).

God has never known one moment of boredom. From all eternity, the God who is Father, Son and Holy Spirit has lived in an eternal interchange of life, light and love. Within this holy circle of glory there is no emptiness, fear, anxiety, or unfulfilled desires. The triune God exists in the fullness of eternal bliss—totally satisfied, infinitely joyful. He does not create in order to meet some unfulfilled needs—*He has none.*

He is not lonely or in lack.

He is fullness seeking expression.

Benevolence Brimming Over

Why would a God of overflowing abundance, goodness and joy create a universe? The only motive that makes any sense is this:

He wants others to enjoy His goodness and love.

Michael Reeves writes: "Other gods need worship and service and sustenance. But this God needs nothing. He has life in Himself—and so much so that he is brimming over. His glory is inestimably good, overflowing, self-giving."[1]

C. S. Lewis said it well: "In God there is no hunger that needs to be filled, only plenteousness that desires to give."[2]

In his famous work, *A Dissertation Concerning the End for Which God Created the World,* Jonathan Edwards argues that the driving force behind God's acts of creation is His benevolent love. That the Creator was moved by a desire to share the abundance He enjoys and extend it to others. He created in order to bring more guests to the banquet of His other-focused love. He invites us to His table, to enjoy the feast with Him, and drink from His *"river of delights"* (Psa. 36:8).

Overflowing love is the reason everything exists.

Second century theologian, Irenaeus declared: "In the beginning, God formed Adam, not as if He stood in need of humanity, but so that He would have someone to confer His benefits upon."[3]

Islam's answer to the "why" of our existence comes out of its understanding of the divine Lord as sovereign power. Muslims believe God created everything to give expression to His supremacy and dominion; all creation should bow to the rule of Allah in humble submission. The frequently heard slogan, "*Allah akbar*" (Allah is great) is a reminder of His supreme authority, and of people's place of subservience. Hence the name: Islam, which in Arabic means submission.[4]

The Christian perspective is profoundly different.

The Matrix of Everything

The biblical account of our world does *not* begin with...

- A rule-maker requiring obedience
- A task-master wanting laborers
- A power-hungry king demanding submission
- A bored God looking for entertainment
- A lonely divinity seeking company
- An insecure deity needing worshippers

Nothing of the kind.

The God revealed in Scripture is a beautiful, relational, exuberant and dynamic community of love. The Maker of all things forever delighted in His Father's embrace in the joy-filled fellowship of the Spirit. This is the true backdrop to our Story—the Great Dance of Life shared by the Father, Son and Spirit.

In the beginning there was boundless love. There was a triune God of inexhaustible, irrepressible, over-flowing benevolence.

His goodness is a steady tsunami. There is an unstoppable expansiveness about it. Here, life and light and love flow with such intensity that they burst forth and bring a universe into being. Creation was an explosion of generosity, an overflow of divine love. The World-Maker was not seeking to fulfill some personal need. *He created so that others would enjoy His goodness.*

Five centuries ago, Puritan scholar Richard Sibbes wrote of the diffusive nature of God's benevolence:

EXPANSIVE GOODNESS

God's goodness is a . . . spreading goodness . . . If God did not have a . . . spreading goodness, he would never have created the world. The Father, Son and Holy Spirit were happy in themselves and enjoyed one another before the world was. But God delights to communicate and spread his goodness.⁵

The creation of the world was an explosion of joy—not a filling up, but a spilling out.

—Matt Smethurst

"Spreading goodness"—a fascinating way to portray creation! It is heaven exporting joy. The spilling over of love.

"How good is God," wrote Jonathan Edwards, "that he has created man for this very end, to make him happy in the enjoyment of himself, the Almighty, who was happy from the days of eternity in himself."

Bible expositor Alexander MacLaren states, "He created a universe because He delights in His works, and in having creatures on whom He can lavish Himself."

Staggering Generosity

One scholar writes: "What is clear in this magnificent movement or flow of the prologue [of John] is that in God there is communion, unity, love and light, and from this communion, all creation flows."⁶

Here we find the explanation for our existence.

The Logos creates, not to overcome boredom, not to obtain service, nor to placard His power. His reason for creating is spectacularly different. Pause and take this in...

*He wants to share His glory with us.*⁷

He wants to include us in the Eternal Dance of the love of God. Could anything be more astonishing than that?

> In staggering and lavish love, this God determined to open the circle and share the Trinitarian life with others. As an act of mind-boggling and astounding philanthropy, the Father, Son and Spirit chose to create human beings and share the great dance with them.⁸

WHAT STORY HAVE WE FALLEN INTO?

> *His love is, as it were, bottomlessly selfless by definition; it has everything to give.*
>
> —C. S. Lewis

The reason why we exist is because God is a Trinity—a Trinity who loves and shares. Other-centered love is the very essence of His being. Sharing is what goes on in the depths of this Three-In-One God. The Trinity is all about generosity and self-giving love—*and that's why creation happened.* When you start with a Tri-unity of love and glory, it changes the *whole* story. When we get the *who* question right, everything else falls into place.

Jeremy Berg writes:

> Please scrap your images of a lonely God hovering over a dark silent abyss, bored and looking for something to do. The universe ... was created to give further expression to the rich, vibrant, society of love and creativity that already existed within the trinitarian community of the Godhead.[9]

We can only surmise that the Three-In-One God mused, "This celebration of love and joy is far too good to keep to ourselves. Why not create billions of people in our image who could join in and be a part of this?"

There was enough goodness to fill an entire universe. It was only a matter of time before the celebration of glory would overflow its banks. The great dance of life and love would be expanded and shared with others. "Creation is about the spreading, the diffusion, the outward explosion of that love," writes Michael Reeves.[10]

Theologian Thomas Torrance writes:

> The whole raison d'être of the universe lies in the fact that God will not be alone, that He will not be without us, but has freely and purposely created the universe and bound it to Himself as the sphere where he may ungrudgingly pour out His love, and where we may enjoy communion with Him.[11]

Extravagant love is why we are here.

The Meaning of the Story

Pagans of ancient times believed the world to be at the mercy of capricious, self-serving gods who must be placated in order to obtain their favor and to ward off their indignation. Entire civilizations operated on the basis of this core narrative.

When Christianity proclaimed, *"God so loved the world,"* it challenged the very heart of the pagan worldview. No one imagined the All-powerful One to be the personification of love. The story Christians told seemed absurd and unbelievable.

"God is love" is either ridiculous fiction, or it is the best news this world has ever heard.

Christians dare to believe the latter.

They dare to give credence to the testimony of Scripture that we are part of the greatest love story ever told. They believe that we inhabit a universe drenched with magnificent meaning, and the answer to our existence is found in the love of God. He purposed to pour out His love upon us in such a way as to turn us into amazed lovers and worshippers of God.

"We were made, not primarily that we may love God (though we were made for that too), but that God may love us," asserted C. S. Lewis.[12]

This Story is better than we imagined!

The Trinitarian Dream

The biblical drama is driven by the love of the triune God. We need to stop and take a long hard look at the exuberant love of the Father, Son and Spirit. It's the central *reality* of the cosmos. It is the matrix of everything. The existence of every single human being finds its purpose and meaning in this other-centered love of the Holy Trinity.

Love is why we are here.

> Love is the foundation, the focus; the how, the why; the reason, the promise, the call, the catalyst, the flame, the

It is not hard for God to love... it is impossible, given his nature, for him not to love.

—Dallas Willard

goal, the mandate, the mantle, the method, the message, the heartbeat, the demonstration, the answer, the everything because Love is WHO HE IS.[13]

Do you know who you are? Have you come to realize you are the object of divine love, the one the Father created to be His own? Has it crossed your mind that you were made to be caught up in the overflow of God's loving exuberance?
We find ourselves in a love story.
A story that is unspeakably beautiful.

Is God Really That Good?

Some readers will have trouble with this. They're not *sure* the Lord of creation could be this good. The God inside their head looks nothing like the one described in this chapter. Their idea of God is more like Zeus with lightning bolts.
Where did that Divine Ogre come from?
He showed up when our minds were blinded by sin in the Garden of Eden. He came when we lost sight of the Trinity—the self-giving eternal fellowship of love and glory. This god with an anger problem showed up when we failed to let Jesus be our definition of God.
It messed up our whole theology.
God is calling us back to know who He really is. We don't believe in an *ogre*. We believe in the God who is Father, Son and Holy Spirit. We believe in a Divine Trinity, a rich fellowship of beauty and joy and passion and glory, whose unending goodness is overflowing and outgoing. A God whose eternal nature is self-giving. This is who God is, and this is the *only* God there is, and *ever* has been.
And this is the triune God who before the foundation of the world said, "We're going to share all we have with you."
Can you wrap your mind around that?
It is the Original Plan, the Trinitarian Dream for mankind—and it goes beyond our wildest dreams.

PRAYER

LORD OF LIFE AND GLORY, we recognize that our highest thoughts about You are ridiculously undersized. We see You so faintly, but what we are starting to see causes our hearts to beat faster. We know You are a God of goodness, but we did not suspect that your goodness was so wildly extravagant. We know You are a God of glory, but we never dreamed that You planned to share your glory with us. We thought that "Trinity" was an uninteresting theological debate. We now perceive that it is an outrageously beautiful dance. We thought that your goal was to extract something from us. We now see that You are all about giving. Forgive our false, foolish, distorted thoughts about You. Open our eyes to the unending splendor and richness of who You are, oh God, and teach our hearts to respond in wonder and worship. Amen.

*Angels can fly because
they take themselves lightly.*

—G. K Chesterton

*Whence comes this idea that if what
we are doing is fun, it can't be God's will?
The God who made giraffes, a baby's fingernails,
a puppy's tail, a crooknecked squash,
the bobwhite's call, and a young girl's giggle,
has a sense of humor.
Make no mistake about that.*

—Catherine Marshall

CHAPTER SEVEN

AMUSING GRACE

Through him all things were made.
JOHN 1:3

JOHN'S GOSPEL LEAVES NO DOUBT as to who the World-Maker and Story-Writer is. After stating that the Logos was God, and has always been with God, he identifies Him as the agent of creation.

> *Through him all things were made* (Jn. 1:3).

Then, John says it a second time:

> *Without him nothing was made that has been made* (Jn. 1:3).

And for good measure, a few verses later, he mentions it again:

> *The world was made through him* (Jn. 1:10).

The inspired author is making an emphatic statement: Not a single thing that exists or has ever existed came into being apart from the Logos. *He is the reason for everything.* All the beautifully ordered randomness of the cosmos was orchestrated by Him.

If we trace the origin of all things, if we follow every good gift to its source, we end up at the feet of the Eternal Son of God, who lives face-to-face with the Father. He is The Cause, The Meaning, The Reason, The Plot, The Point of everything. Our story starts here.

The Lord Jesus Christ is not just the founder of Christianity; He is the founder of the universe. Galaxies and cherry blossoms and waterfalls and sunsets are not random accidents. They are His invention. This startling realm of daily wonder was His idea.

He made it from scratch.

Without using pre-existing matter (there was none), He unleashed the power of His word, and pulled the universe into existence out of nowhere. First there wasn't, then there was. No raw material was required. The Logos gave the command and all things came to be from nothing. Scholars call it, "Ex nihilo." We would call it the ultimate mindblower.

His Word made worlds.

As well as... walruses, bumblebees, crunchy apples, trumpeting elephants, autumn colors, snow-clad mountains, screeching seagulls, tropical beaches, black cherries, humming-birds, alpine wildflowers, tuxedoed penguins, cascading waterfalls, chirping crickets and designer made snowflakes.

Philosopher Thomas Carlyle confessed, "This world, after all our science and sciences, is still a miracle: wonderful, inscrutable, magical and more."

"The whole order of things is as outrageous as any miracle which could presume to violate it," insisted Chesterton.

Amusing Grace

During our first years in the tropics of Bolivia, I was puzzled by a loud buzzing noise often heard in early evening. I had no idea what it was, and even wondered if something was wrong with the power lines. Then I discovered the source—swarms of cicadas, large insects that produce a strident deafening buzz. When swarms of them "chorus" together, the sound is amplified into an overpowering bedlam.

We had a small brown dog named Cocoa, and she found cicadas to be tasty morsels. Large numbers of these noise-makers would often descend upon a big tree in our yard, and screech up a storm. Sometimes I threw a stick up into the branches, and numerous cicadas would drop to the ground. Our little dog was on top of them in an instant, filling her mouth, and crunching on the noisy critters (could we call that sound bites?). It was hilarious to hear loud buzzing noises from the mouth of Cocoa as she dashed about, feasting on these noisy delicacies that had dropped from the sky.

> *The universe is not God at work but God at play.*
> —Leonard Sweet

Who is the Author of all this playfulness? What kind of God would invent creatures that are frisky, comical, playful, silly, dopey, vivacious, chirpy, cheeky, frolicsome, bouncy and prankish? He is undeniably a lover of fun. "I cannot find it in me to believe that God enjoys long faces and scowls at merriment," concludes Madeleine L'Engle.

> A thing may be too sad to be believed or too wicked to be believed or too good to be believed; but it cannot be too absurd to be believed in this planet of frogs and elephants, of crocodiles and cuttle-fish.[1]

"All nature wears one universal grin," observed novelist Henry Fielding.

The Divine Creator is often seen as a deity of unbending seriousness; He never cracks a smile. How did we ever come up with such an idea? The lighthearted charm of creation tells an entirely different story—our Maker has a playful streak. The Inventor of such amusement is not without a keen sense of humor. "No somber God could ever have made a bullfrog or a giraffe," contends George Buttrick. The Lord God is not like those who, in Shakespeare's words, have "a plentiful lack of wit."

He is a God of amusing grace.

A Mirthful Maker

The One who crafted this whimsical world must have greatly enjoyed the undertaking.

- He dressed up raccoons like bandits.
- He invented the playful silliness of kittens.
- He made monkeys with their mischievous antics.
- He trained mountain goats to do crazy climbing feats.
- He designed penguins who stroll in their Sunday best.

He created dogs that chase their tails, otters that play with pebbles, roosters that crow their hearts out, lizards that catch insects with their tongues, camels who spit at strangers, parrots who mock their owners, and excitable golden retrievers with floppy ears and tongues hanging out of their mouths.

What kind of a God would create all that?

Helen Salsbury writes:

> *Dear God, we make you so solemn,*
> *So stiff and old and staid.*
> *How can we be so stupid*
> *When we look at the things you've made?*2

Have you seen the silly arrogance of a llama?
Have you watched squirrels playing tag?
Have you heard the ridiculous bray of a donkey?

Pointless Playfulness

Creation is a mirror of God's glory, says Scripture (Psa. 19:1). It reflects His character, the magnificent splendor of who He is. The works of His hands force us to conclude that His "glory" is not just about His power—*it's also about His playfulness.*

The biblical view of reality suggests that behind this material world lies (in the words of Tolkien) "a great joy: a fountain of mirth enough to set a kingdom laughing, were it to gush forth."

For all belongs to you . . . the world, life, death, the present and the future and you belong to Christ (1 Cor. 3:21-23 MOF).

There is a "world" dominated by evil which does not belong to me, but the world made by God, full of sunrises and meadows, snowflakes and apple cider, cherry blossoms and children's laughter—that world *does* belong to me, for I belong to Christ.

All delightfulness, winsomeness, funniness, charm, amusement, enjoyment, pleasure, bliss and beauty originate from this one Source. He is the Giver of every good gift. Did humor and wit come into the world as the result of the Fall? Clearly not. Our sense of humor reflects the character of our Maker. We were made in the image of one who evidently enjoys laughter.

Surprised by Joy

A life changing event took place when a boy named Clive Staples Lewis stood beside a flowering currant bush outside his home in Ireland. Lewis was destined to become one of the most important Christian writers of the 20th century, and this childhood moment in the garden launched a lifetime quest. "It is difficult to find words strong enough for the sensation which came over me," writes C. S. Lewis. "Milton's 'enormous bliss' of Eden... comes somewhere near it." Something extraordinary took place. A feeling of the profoundest kind swept through Lewis' heart. He felt he had encountered something deeper and more beautiful than anything he had ever known. He had no idea what it was, or where it came from, but it left him breathless and longing for more.

Lewis experienced similar moments throughout his life; he called them "stabs of joy." They vanished all too quickly. He was catching glimpses of something of deep beauty from another realm. They haunted him and stirred within him an overpowering desire to find out where it came from. It became an "inconsolable longing" that led him to a long determined search to find the source of this joy.

When Lewis finally surrendered his life to God, it was shocking for him to discover that God and joy were connected. It had never crossed his mind that the two might be linked. He was astonished to realize that God was the answer to his quest.

Lewis found the answer to the riddle of life in God; he discovered the true source of joy. He was keenly aware that fullness of joy will only be reached in heaven, but he got a taste of it, and he pursued it. We are struck by the freedom, the simple, contagious joy of this man of learning. He caught a glimpse of something vast and deep and beautiful, it captivated him, and he wrote about it. His autobiography is appropriately titled, *Surprised by Joy*.

Cars and Craziness

One day, I went to the park across from our apartment and met a man who had asked to see me. He claimed to be a Christian, and seemed to know a number of my colleagues. He had arrived from another part of the country to resolve an issue with a pickup truck he had stored in a rented garage. He wanted to donate the truck to someone who was serving God, and he wondered if I knew anyone who could make good use of it. I immediately thought of Mario, a dear friend who preaches the Gospel in rural Quechua communities. For some time, he had been praying for a vehicle.

The owner of the truck was pleased with the idea, and indicated he would come back the next day to work out the details. That evening I called Mario to let him know about the offer. My friend wept with joy. He was thrilled that God was answering his prayer for a vehicle.

The following day we met again. Everything was ready to go, except for one item—money was owed to the owner of the garage. The man asked if I could give him a hand with that. I did, and he agreed to come back the next day with the truck.

That was the last I ever saw of him.

It was a scam. There was no truck to be had.

I said to my wife, "What are we going to say to Mario?" We looked at each other, wondering what to do. Our dear friend was happily waiting for a truck that didn't exist.

I came up with a wacky idea. "Wendy, what would you think if we gave Mario *our* car? We could manage without a vehicle, and it would probably serve him well." Wendy thought for a moment and replied, "If you want to do that, it's fine with me."

I called Mario and said, "Unfortunately that offer of a truck didn't work out, but we've got a Toyota SUV here that you could have instead. Would that interest you?"

It did, and our friend took an all-night bus trip to come and talk to us about it. He had money saved up that covered a quarter of the value of the car. We refused, but he insisted that we take it. It had been given to him for the purchase of a vehicle.

I was expecting to travel to speak at a conference in the area where Mario lived. We made arrangements to meet there, and I would leave the vehicle with him, and return home on a bus. Things went as planned. Mario became the proud owner of a Toyota. We had the joy of spreading some goodness and blessing a friend in need.

A few weeks later, we were notified that a gift had been deposited in our account. A sizable gift. It matched exactly what our vehicle was worth.

I turned to my wife and said, "Honey, you're not going to believe this. You know that car we gave to Mario? As it turns out, God has just paid us for it. He sent enough money to cover the entire value of the vehicle!"

We looked at each other, and broke into laughter.

Prodded by a scam, we had engaged in a reluctant act of generosity. We donated our car to a friend, and then, to top it off, God paid us for it!

The Lord does some crazy things!

Winemaking at its Best

On the last page of his book Orthodoxy, Chesterton speaks of joy, the "gigantic secret of the Christian." And he refers to something Christ mostly keep hidden:

> He concealed something ... He restrained something ...
> There was something that he hid from all men ... some one thing that was too great for God to show us when he walked upon our earth; and I have sometimes fancied that it was his mirth.⁴

Once, when Jesus attended a wedding in a small village called Cana, the unthinkable happened.

They ran out of wine.

The bridegroom had under-estimated the capacity of his guests to consume that delightful beverage—and the supply ran dry. The miscalculation threatened to put a damper on the whole celebration. A most embarrassing situation for the hosts.

It would bring major social disgrace.

The carpenter from Nazareth stepped in and saved the day. About 180 gallons of water were quietly transformed into wine. "He spoke to the water and it blushed into wine," said one.

And no ordinary wine. It was exquisite—head and shoulders above the previous batch that ran out. The celebration regained its momentum. The Master's hidden alchemy brought life back to a party that was about to wind down.

The Master of Ceremonies had not tasted anything like it. Never had he come across anything of this caliber at the local market. He's impressed, and he calls the groom over and says,

> *Everybody I know begins with their finest wines and after the guests have had their fill brings in the cheap stuff. But you've saved the best till now* (Jn. 2:10 MSG).

Where did you get this stuff?

Imagine the situation...

As the M.C. raves about the wine, there's Jesus sitting at the table with the guests. The anonymous winemaker doesn't let on. He is totally nonchalant. Perhaps others around Him comment on the quality of the wine, and He heartily agrees. "Excellent wine, indeed!" Did He smile and give a knowing nod to the waiter? Did He manage to keep a straight face as He continued to enjoy His meal? Isn't that hilarious?

The delightful playfulness of Christ! So unpretentious. So unassuming. So unreligious. A fascinating and beautiful blend of greatness, humility… and humor.

The winsome man from Nazareth pulls off a stunning miracle, and keeps it under wraps. He does it with style. He rescues a wedding that was about to fizzle. He salvages the bridegroom's honor. He leaves the host of the event flabbergasted. And almost no one found out what He was up to. It's classic!

> *It is pleasing to God whenever you rejoice or laugh from the bottom of your heart.*
> —Martin Luther

Jesus Christ is the definitive revelation of the character of God (Jn. 1:18). He said, *"Anyone who has seen me has seen the Father"* (Jn. 14:9). You read that right—the Living God is just like Jesus. And He reveals not only His love, but His joyful humor. His lightheartedness. God is not just high and holy. He is winsome.

Making wine was the first miracle Jesus performed—a sign, according to John, that *"revealed His glory"* (Jn. 2:11). It put His spectacular goodness on display. He's not a life-squelcher—He's the life-giver. He puts songs in the heart and sets feet to dancing. He is the joy-bringer.

When Wine Flows Freely

The Old Testament prophets frequently used wine as a metaphor of the coming messianic age of blessing.

Isaiah spoke of the coming age as a sumptuous Eastern banquet, *"a feast of well-aged wine"* (Isa. 25:6 ESV).

Jeremiah wrote:

> *They will come and shout for joy on the heights of Zion; they will rejoice in the bounty of the Lord—the grain, the new wine and the olive oil* (Jer. 31:12).

WHAT STORY HAVE WE FALLEN INTO?

Joel declared:

The vats will overflow with new wine and oil" (Joel 2:24).

Amos predicted:

New wine will drip from the mountains and flow from all the hills" (Amos 9:13).

Wine will flow like a river!

Obviously, this has nothing to do with drunkenness and insobriety. It has everything to do with fullness of joy, abundance and blessing under God's favor.

An Ancient Shortage

The fact is, wine ran out in this world long before the wedding in Cana. It ran out in the garden of Eden when sin invaded the world. Joy and blessing have been in short supply ever since.

When Christ shows up and mass-produces wine at a wedding, what is he saying? There's important symbolism here. He was picking up a well-known prophetic theme, and was essentially announcing, "The long-awaited messianic age has arrived. The time of God's joy, blessing and favor has come, the time for an outpouring of divine grace. Come and feast at the banquet of the Kingdom. The celebration has begun."

"Joy is the rarest and most infrequent thing in the world. We already have enough fanatical seriousness, enthusiasm, and humorless zeal in the world..." writes Karl Barth. "When we have found God our Saviour – or when he has found us – we will rejoice in him."

When this Messiah finishes writing the final chapter of our planet, it will be heart-stopping. The supreme cause for wonder. God's epic Story culminates in the greatest banquet of all.

You can count on it—the best wine will be left to the last.

PRAYER

BLESSED LORD, we read in Scripture that in Your presence is "fullness of joy." We are prone to view You as a no-nonsense God of solemn scariness. We recognize Your strong opposition to all that is twisted, destructive and wrong, but it seems that we may have overlooked Your winsomeness, Your joyfulness, Your blissfulness. Thank You for the gift of humor, and for a creation crowded with indicators of divine light-heartedness. You gave us the gift of laughter, and You provide many occasions for using it. Teach us to see these things as gifts from above, and to be more obedient to Your command that says, "Rejoice always." Amen.

*We are rags of lordship;
blurred images of
a distant King.*

—J. R. R. Tolkien

CHAPTER EIGHT

SELF-PORTRAITS OF GOD

The very life of God is what ignited the existence of man.
JOHN 1:4 (Paraphrased)

A HOMELESS MAN SLEEPING on a park bench was rudely awakened by a policeman. "Who are you? Where do you come from? And what are you doing here?" demanded the officer. After a moment's thought, the vagrant replied, "You know, those are the questions I have been trying to answer all of my life."

We are *all* trying to answer those questions.

It is normal for children to ask, "Where did I come from?" and "Where will I go after I die?" They want to understand the story of their existence.

If we are to make sense of our story, we need to discover our true origin. The Gospel of John traces our life back to its original source.

The Fountain of Life

"In him was life," writes John. This is the fountainhead, the original matrix of all life. Here is life that is eternal, uncreated, overflowing, and self-sufficient. All life and light that ever existed is derived from this inexhaustible Life-source. He is the giver and sustainer of all life.

It is here that our story begins—not with a nebulous life force, not with a cosmic explosion, not with a fortuitous combination of molecules, *but with a divine Person*. He was there before all else. We do not come from chaos, we come from a Creator. He is the reason, the plot and the meaning of our existence.

This is the true index to reality.

Our origin is in God. Humankind traces the genesis of its existence to the Logos of God who speaks and makes *"everything beautiful in its time"* (Eccl. 3:11). We are His workmanship, His idea, His inspiration. *"We are his offspring"* (Acts 17:28), declares the apostle Paul, quoting an ancient poet.

Holy Scripture is telling us who we really are.

There is something *far* more significant about our identity than the circumstances of our natural conception, whether we were wanted or unwanted, conceived by married or unmarried parents. Towering above all other considerations is a much greater fact— *our God begotteness*. We are not the invention of our parents, we are the creation of God. We are His dream come true.

Designer-Made People

> *So God created mankind in his own image, in the image of God he created them; male and female he created them* (Gn. 1:27).

It is no accident we are here. The Creator had a glorious plan and decided to make us a part of it.

> *You created all things, and by Your will they exist and were created"* (Rev. 4:11 NKJV).

God masterminded the exact combination of our genetic code, and combined the qualities that make up our unique personality. He knew us before forming us in the uterus of our mother.

> *For you created my inmost being; you knit me together in my mother's womb* (Psa. 139:13).

God made each one of us to know and to respond to Him in a unique way. He designed us to be receivers and givers of His love.

It is only when God brings humans on the scene that creation is declared to be *very* good (Gn. 1:31). A remarkable creature has been brought into the story, the Creator's crowning work.

> Human uniqueness consists not simply in the fact that we converse with each other, but rather that God talks to us and invites us to respond. In other words, we are invited to become part of that conversation which is the divine life.[1]

Human beings have the capacity of being addressed by God and making a response to God. "That indeed," points out Old Testament scholar Chris Wright, "is the very essence of what it means to be human, in God's image. We are creatures who know of our origin in God . . . Human life is God-conscious and God-related in every dimension of our existence."[2]

> *God Himself is man's birthplace.*
> —George MacDonald

The Bible, in effect, announces to each person: "You exist because God wanted someone just like you. He came up with the idea of you, and He loved the idea. You are a unique creation, born in the heart of God. A one-of-a-kind person deliberately planned and designed by the Master Craftsman for purposes that are glorious and great. You are alive because God wanted a world with you in it."

To exist in this Story is a greater gift than any of us can imagine. N. D. Wilson writes,

> Understand this: we are both tiny and massive. We are nothing more than molded clay given breath, but we are nothing less than divine self-portraits, huffing and puffing along mountain ranges of epic narrative arcs prepared for us by the Infinite Word Himself. Swell with pride and gratitude, for you are tiny and given much. You are as spoken by God as the stars. You stand in history with stories stretching out both behind and before.[3]

Valued by God

God is not in the process of making up His mind about the human race. The value of each person is not in the balance. We were made *"by Him"* and *"for Him"* (Col. 1:16; Heb. 1:3). We are His work of art. His image and likeness are upon us—we are self-portraits of God. He purposed we would be His treasure. He knows our name, and values us more than we can imagine.

"People only truly matter if they matter to Someone who matters," pointed out one writer.

We have not been given the burdensome task to impress God, or to convince Him to look favorably upon us. Our value has been determined by our Maker, and it does not fluctuate like the stock market.

A man in southern California had a wife who loved garage sales. They were not his idea of fun, but one Saturday he decided to accompany her. At one sale, he noticed a rusty old motorcycle covered up in a garage.

"How much do you want for it?" he inquired.

The owner thought for a moment, "I'd let it go for $35."

The motorcycle changed hands and ended up in the new owner's garage. Some time went by and the man's wife said, "If you don't do something with that old motorcycle, I'm going to get it hauled away." So the man went into the garage to see what it would take to make the old bike run.

He wrote down some parts numbers and called Harley-Davidson. After a long silence, the parts department man said he would call back in about an hour.

Harley-Davidson finally returned the call and asked the man to check if there was anything written under the seat of the motorcycle. When he reported what he'd found, Harley-Davidson offered the man a six-figure sum for the bike.

Why would a rusty old Harley-Davidson be worth that much money? As it turns out, the garage sale motorcycle had been made for Elvis Presley. Its worth was not in the bike, but in the person for whom it was made.

Some people question whether this is a true story. Regardless, the point is well taken: People are valuable because they were made by God and for God. We were created to belong to Him. This confers extraordinary worth to human beings.

It is not our efforts or our exploits that give us value—*it is our origin*. It is our Maker who establishes our worth. We may be messed up, damaged and in disrepair, but we need to lift the seat of the bike and see what's written underneath. We have an owner. We are His special treasure.

A False Narrative

We live in a world where many have chosen to believe the false narrative of secular atheism. This worldview states that we are descendants of primordial protoplasm that washed up on a beach billions of years ago. We are no more than the arbitrary product of blind chance, a vast amount of time, and natural forces. We are a mere grab-bag of atomic particles existing in a pointless universe.

Doesn't that make you feel great about yourself?

Tragically, once we remove God from the story, the value of human life plummets. Francis Schaeffer writes:

> If man is not made in the image of God, nothing then stands in the way of inhumanity. There is no good reason why mankind should be perceived as special. Human life is cheapened. We can see this in many of the major issues being debated in our society today: abortion, infanticide, euthanasia, the increase of child abuse and violence of all kinds, pornography.[4]

If God is eliminated from the equation, where does one find the sandbags to stack against the rising tide of degeneracy and barbarism?

Could the denial of God also explain the escalating rates of depression and suicide? Is the growing disenchantment with life a logical result of a worldview that states, as one prominent atheist put it, "there is, at bottom, no design, no purpose, no evil and no good, nothing but blind, pitiless indifference"?[5]

Who Are We Really?

What a refreshing and radically different viewpoint we get when we turn to God's Word! It leads us to a perspective that is heartwarming and breathtaking. It sheds light on the true story...

In the beginning, before time began, there was the great dance of life, a rich fellowship of togetherness and intimacy, an unfettered interchange of love and delight . . . a circle of glory we refer to as God. The stunning truth is that this Father, Son and Holy Spirit, in astounding and lavish love, purposed to widen the circle and include others in this communion of overflowing joy. This God of goodness and glory chose to create human beings in His image and likeness, and share the Trinitarian dance with them.

It was in the midst of this eternal fellowship of love that the idea of you and I came into being! We were conceived in the heart of God before the Milky Way Galaxy was ever heard of. In an act of unexplainable grace and goodness, our existence was determined by Him. And *that* is why we are on the stage of history.

The Author of the universe purposed to make us a part of a love story. He planned a cosmic romance that would play out on Planet Earth and extend into eternity. It was a Story in which love overcomes insurmountable obstacles, pursues relentlessly to the point of death, and triumphs gloriously. It is the ultimate romance.

Admittedly, there are many subplots woven into this divine drama, but this is the overarching Story.

When Coins Get Lost

A parable found in Luke 15:8-10 helps to illustrate the remarkable drama we are immersed in.

> *Or what woman, having ten silver coins, if she loses one coin, does not light a lamp and sweep the house and seek diligently until she finds it? And when she has found it, she calls together her friends and neighbors, saying, "Rejoice with me, for I have found the coin that I had lost." Just so, I tell you, there is joy before the angels of God over one sinner who repents.*

God is presented as a housewife, desperate to find a lost coin. She turns the house upside down in her relentless search for the missing piece of money. Her persistence finally pays off. She finds the coin, and is so elated that she throws a party. Her neighbors and friends join her to celebrate the recovery of the coin.

> *Sin does not make us worthless, but lost.*
> —Dallas Willard

This is the story of our world in a nutshell. We are the lost coin, and God is the seeker.

We got hopelessly lost. We took a lot of wrong turns, got into messy situations, and brought great sorrow to the heart of our Maker. The divine image upon us was tarnished and soiled.

And all that messy stuff? That is *not* who we are. That is not the real us. That's the grime on the outside. Who we are—*is the coin*.

The coin may have fallen into the dirt, but the dirt on the coin doesn't alter the value of the coin. It continues to be valuable. Its value is such that the Sovereign Lord moved heaven and earth to recover it. If market value is determined by the price someone is willing to pay, then what happened at the cross makes a huge statement. We may have doubts about the value of our life, *but God never has.*

The sin we have fallen into does not define us. Our waywardness does not define us. Our failure does not define us. What defines us is that we were made by God, and made *for* Him.

Our sins are not powerful enough to shut down His love. They are abhorrent and destructive, but are not strong enough to turn Him away, or to deter Him from loving us.

"After ten thousand sins, He loves you as infinitely as ever," stated the famous preacher Charles Spurgeon.

He came for us, and He wants us back. What an amazing God He is!

- Coins do not lose their value—even if they are lost.
- Coins have value on the basis of the image they bear.
- Lost coins are the object of an intense search.
- When coins are found—a celebration takes place.

Our True Identity

German theologian Helmut Thielicke points out:

> [Mankind's] greatness rests solely on the fact that God in his incomprehensible goodness has bestowed his love upon him. God does not love us because we are so valuable; we are valuable because God loves us.[6]

We may be confused about our identity, but our Maker has never lost sight of who we are. Man began in God. No matter how far mankind has strayed from His original place of innocence, an undeniable fact remains—we exist because He wanted us, designed us, and in love stamped His own image and likeness on us. We were made to belong to Him.

There are no ordinary people. You have never talked to a mere mortal.
—C. S. Lewis

You have a birth certificate. And it's eternal. It's the deepest truth about you—you carry the *imago dei*—the image of God. When we forgot who we were, when we believed a false story and lived a lie, the Divine Maker did the unthinkable. He came and suffered and died to redeem us. When we wandered away, heaven paid the ultimate price to get us back. Moved by love beyond all measure, the Life-Giver gave His life for us. How astonishing is that!

This is the story our hearts long for.

James Bryan Smith explains,

> The only story large enough for the human soul is the story that stops us in our tracks with wonder; it melts our cold hearts with the warmth of love and goodness; and it is sturdy enough to build our lives on, now and forever.... We need a story that makes us quiver, not with fear but with delight. We need a story so big that we will never be able to grasp it, so vast that it can handle the darkness of evil and suffering...[7]

We find ourselves in that kind of story.

PRAYER

LORD GOD MAKER OF ALL THINGS, we are grateful to know that we are here not by accident, not by chance, but by design, Your design. It is wonderful to know that we can trace our lineage all the way back to Your heart of love. You imagined us. You came up with the code of our DNA. You gave us the unspeakable privilege of existing. Thank You for granting us the gift of life, and for making us a part of Your story. And thank You for loving us in our brokenness. We are grateful that You are not finished with us, and that Your purposes for us are full of goodness, mercy and blessing. You are not only in the business of creating, but also of redeeming. We give You thanks, oh Lord, our God. Amen.

*When Jesus said He was
the light of the world He wasn't
just claiming to be brighter than the sun;
he was claiming to be the source
of the universe.*

—D­AVID A. B­AYLISS

CHAPTER NINE

THE GIVER OF LIFE

*In him was life, and that life was
the light of all mankind.*
JOHN 1:4

TRAVELERS ONCE CAME UPON an island inhabited by a tribe of moon-worshippers. The visitors remarked, "This is strange. If you are going to worship something in the sky, why don't you worship the sun rather than the moon?" They were told, "It's very simple —the sun only comes out during the day, when it's light and we don't need it; but the moon shines at night when it's dark and we cannot see!"

Something is wrong with the logic!

The light-source that provides our planet with light and heat is a glowing sphere of hot gas that blazes in the sky almost 93 million miles away. The sun makes life possible on our planet. Without it the Earth would be a frozen rock floating in space. The sun illuminates our world, warms our oceans, generates weather systems, and gives energy to plants that provide food and oxygen. Without the sun's light and heat, we would not exist. The sun's crucial role for earth has even caused some civilizations to look upon it as divine.

However, this remarkable ball of fire has no divine power of its own. It is a lamp hung in the sky by someone called the Logos. It is dependent upon and sustained by Him. He is the One who started the fire, and turned on the light. He is the real source of light and life.

The Life Giver

That life was the light of all mankind (Jn. 1:4).

What is John saying?

Created beings have life, but this life does not exist on its own. Life is derived from the Logos—and it *depends* on Him. The eternal Word creates and also *sustains* all things (Col. 1:17). If He distanced Himself from creation, all life would be extinguished, and the whole universe would disintegrate into nothingness. The in-breaking of death and chaos is averted only because He upholds all things *"by his powerful word"* (Heb. 1:3).

Martin Luther stated,

> The sun would not long remain in the heavens giving light, no child would be born, no ear of corn, blade of grass, or anything else would grow on earth or renew itself were not God continually at work.

We are not autonomous, self-sustaining, self-determining beings. Our continuing existence is dependent upon Him. Whether we are believers or blasphemers, God-lovers or God-deniers, the Divine Logos is the sustainer of every human life.

He gives life, breath, and everything else to all people (Acts 17:25 CEV).

He sustains both saints and sinners. Displaying astounding humility and grace, the Word continues to be the source of every person's existence.

The Light of Life

The apostolic writer, however, is not thinking merely of physical life—the Son of God is *"the light of men"* in the spiritual realm. Our inner life was meant to be illuminated and invigorated by Him, even as our world depends on the Sun to sustain life. We were made to live in the joy of His presence.

This was the original arrangement.

Humanity was wired to receive light and life from the Divine Logos. We were created to experience life in fellowship with God and in the knowledge of His delight and pleasure. Our hearts were made to bask in the light of His love, rejoice in it, and reflect it. It is in this light we flourish; it enables us to live out of an inner wholeness and fullness that overflows into our relationships with others. *We were meant to live loved.*

This was the Creator's blueprint for human life.

This is how life was lived in the Garden of Eden, when our Maker rejoiced in His world and delighted in mankind (Prov. 8:31). Our first parents lived in an enviable heart-to-heart conversation with the divine Giver of life and love. They reveled in His goodness. They lived in the wonder of a story where God's love flows unstoppable and His extravagant favor abounds. They found in Him their source of life—their worth, their significance and sense of completeness.

Anselm of Canterbury, a Christian thinker of the eleventh century, concluded that man "was created for the purpose of being happy in the fact of God's delighted approval." Could greater bliss be imagined?

This was our original habitat.

And it was unspeakably glorious.

The Original Plan

Our life was meant to thrive on a heavenly source of energy. We were made to live connected to divine light and life and love. The original intention was for people to be filled with God's unfailing love, and overflow with love back to God (worship), and to their fellow man (love for neighbor). This is what the Great Commandment is all about (Mk. 12:30,31)—God's love poured out on people, generating love for God, and for others.

This is the original game plan.

In *Mere Christianity*, Lewis states:

> God made us: invented us as a man invents an engine. A car is made to run on gasoline, and it would not run properly on anything else. Now God designed the human machine to run on Himself. He Himself is the fuel our spirits were designed to burn, or the food our spirits were designed to feed on. There is no other... God cannot give us a happiness and peace apart from Himself, because it is not there. There is no such thing.[1]

The vacuum at the core of human beings was designed to be filled with the love of the triune God. Psychologists tell us that people have a fundamental need for security, affirmation, affection and purpose. These basic needs were intended to be met by the inflow of divine love that would allow us to live from a place of fullness. We were meant to be receivers and reflectors of the love of God. We were designed to be joyful participants in the life and love of Father, Son and Holy Spirit.

This is what the Bible means when it states our ultimate purpose is to "glorify God" (Ps. 86:9; Isa. 43:7; Rev. 4:11). God's glory is His "spectacularness"—the sheer magnificence of His goodness. When God's goodness is poured out on individuals and flows through them to others, God's gloriousness goes on display. We glorify God—we exhibit His unsurpassable love—by receiving it, enjoying it, and reflecting it back to God, and to each other.

This is the goal of everything.

When the Lights Go Out

A symphonic orchestra was presenting Handel's famous work, *The Messiah*, when suddenly there was a power outage. The concert hall went dark, the music faltered, and very quickly came to a halt. The musicians and singers could no longer play or sing properly, and the presentation stopped. They were unable to continue—because nobody could see the conductor!

A worse blackout happened in the Garden of Eden. As the result of sin, darkness descended on God's world and the original majesty and melody of creation was disrupted. Harmony and beauty gave way to dissonance and clash. When people stopped following the lead of the Divine Conductor, the masterpiece was marred.

"This present darkness" is how the Bible describes the age we live in. A kingdom termed *"the domain of darkness"* (Col. 1:13 ESV) set up operations in this world, and its basic strategy is to keep people blinded to the truth of who God is (2 Cor. 4:4).

Sin robbed our capacity to see clearly. The fall into sin is often seen as a matter of law-breaking—but the problem is much more catastrophic. Sin did more than produce guilt—it left us *"blind."* A profound delusion has overtaken us.

One scholar describes our dilemma like this:

> The deepest problem of sin is that it makes us utterly incapable of knowing the Father. It afflicts us with such a dastardly wrong-headedness; we cannot know the Father's heart. It makes us so blind; it is impossible for us to see the Father's face. And without knowing the Father's heart, we have no basis for real assurance or hope in our lives at all. If we cannot see His face, we have no possibility of living in the freedom of His abounding love, and in the security and joy of His lavish and eternal embrace.[2]

Living in a False Story

If our humanity was made to receive "life" from knowing the Father's heart, hearing His voice of affirmation, and delighting in His strong embrace—then spiritual blindness is the worst thing that could befall us.

WHAT STORY HAVE WE FALLEN INTO?

What happens if we are blind to His love? If we no longer taste and see that God is good? If we no longer live in the assurance and freedom and joy of His embrace?

What happens when we get separated from our true life source? *We look for alternate gods.*

We end up looking for "life" in other places. Often *wrong places.* We struggle to make sense of our existence inside a false narrative where all the ladders we climb are too short, and all the roadmaps fail to get us to where we want to be. All our strategies for getting "life" fail to deliver.

I am using the term "life" to refer to something we all long for—a deep sense of identity, worth, significance and security. This insatiable desire is firmly lodged in every human being; everyone has a hungry heart.

> **As soon as we become spiritually deaf to the voice that calls us the beloved, we are going to look someplace else to make us the beloved.**
>
> —Henri J. M. Nouwen

What we are looking for is a source of love so strong and secure that allows us to relax in the deepest part of our being. That warms our heart, that allays our fears. Failing to find that, we turn to all kinds of destructive substitutes.

Is this not the story of our lives—one confused attempt after another to find something that gives us a sense of being loved, of being valuable, of having meaning in our lives?

The Tree of Life

The human race once had full access to the source of life. At the dawn of history, in a garden called Eden, there was a tree called the Tree of Life. It was one of two trees in the center of the garden; one imparted life, the other, death. Our first parents ate from the second one, the Tree of the Knowledge of Good and Evil. As a result, Adam and Eve were expelled from the garden and denied access to the Tree of Life. To eat from that tree would have been disastrous for them. It would mean to live forever in a fallen state, to be trapped permanently in a life ruled by sin. God wanted to protect them from such a horror, and the way back to the garden was barred.

Since then, the human race has lived with a deep unquenchable yearning, an unattainable longing. We long for a happiness that eludes us. The romance, the car, the house, or the job of our dreams somehow fails to deliver what we had hoped for. These may provide temporary relief, but sooner or later the hunger returns.

C. S. Lewis describes this "inconsolable secret":

> Our lifelong nostalgia, our longing to be reunited with something in the universe from which we now feel cut off, to be on the inside of some door which we have always seen from the outside, is . . . the truest index of our real situation.[3]

What is this restless desire so deeply entrenched in the human heart?

We long to be loved deeply and unconditionally.

And, if the truth be known... we don't just want to be loved. We long for the ultimate miracle. Our deepest desire is to be loved by the most important Person in the universe. Our greatest yearning is to be wanted and loved by the God who made us. If He could possibly love us—that would be the best news we ever heard. Our search for the source of life would be over.

The Life Bringer

John has some earth-shaking news for us. Look again:

> *In him was life, and that life was the light of all mankind* (Jn. 1:4).

Is this not an echo of something mentioned in Genesis? Is this not an allusion to the Tree of Life? John's book is a rewriting of the creation story, and here he declares that in Christ the human race once again is given access to "life." Indeed, this is the central message of the Fourth Gospel:

> Very truly I tell you, the one who believes has eternal life (Jn. 6:47).

Eternal life does not simply mean to live forever; it involves more than the duration of life. There is one place in the Bible where eternal life is defined. Notice how our Lord described it:

> Now this is eternal life: that they know you, the only true God, and Jesus Christ, whom you have sent (Jn. 17:3).

Eternal life entails "knowing" someone; it is a relational matter. It involves an interactive relationship with God and with His Son. It is to be brought into the life and love of the Trinity. Theologians Köstenberger and Swain define it beautifully: "Eternal life… consists in sharing in the gracious overflow of the Father's eternal love for the Son in the Spirit."[4] When Jesus speaks about eternal life —this is what He is talking about.

The Tree of Life turns out to be Christ Himself. He, the Divine Son who dwells in the Father's eternal embrace, came across all worlds to find us in our brokenness and darkness and bring us back into the enjoyment of the life and love of God.

The Joy Bringer

The Son of Abba came to bring us into the joy of God. He announced,

> Let anyone who is thirsty come to me and drink. Whoever believes in me, as Scripture has said, rivers of living water will flow from within them (Jn. 7:37-38).

What is this thirst-quenching water?

It is the love Christ has always shared with the Father. And it is the love He has come to share with us. He does so by giving us His Spirit—the bond of love that unites the Trinity.

John the Baptist declared that Messiah came with a two-fold purpose:

- Take away sin (Jn. 1:29)
- Baptize with the Holy Spirit (Jn. 1:33)

Here is the solution to the human dilemma. It resolves the issue of sin, and restores our connection with God. It is the inbreaking of hope for Adam's family that lives on the wrong side of paradise.

The removal of sin clears the way for free and full fellowship with God. That's what the Holy Spirit is fundamentally about. He is our "reconnection" with God. He brings God's love into our hearts (Rom. 5:5), and causes it to spill over upon others (Gal. 5:22). He leads us into the freedom and joy of our belovedness as children of the Father (Rom. 8:15).

To be know and follow Christ is to come back to the Source. It is to find our "life" in the love God has shown at Calvary.

And so we know and rely on the love God has for us (1 Jn. 4:16).

We were created to drink from that river, to live in the Father's love. When we were lost in the dark, God's Son came for us. He shows us the heart of the Father. He cleanses us from sin. And He shares with all who trust in Him the overflowing and unstoppable Niagara of love that flows between Father, Son and Holy Spirit (Jn. 17:26). He brings us back to the Real Story.

He brings us back to the river—our true source of life.

No Other Stream

In C. S. Lewis' book, *The Silver Chair,* Jill is in a Narnia adventure. She walks into the forest, grows thirsty, and hears the sound of running water. She discovers a stream, but is startled to see that beside the water is Aslan, the huge, golden lion. Jill waits, hoping he will go away. Aslan finally speaks: "If you are thirsty, you may drink." Jill is startled and holds back.

WHAT STORY HAVE WE FALLEN INTO?

"Are you not thirsty?" said the Lion.

"I am dying of thirst," said Jill.

"Then drink," said the Lion.

"May I — could I — would you mind going away while I do?" said Jill.

The Lion answered this only by a look and a very low growl. And as Jill gazed at its motionless bulk, she realized that she might as well have asked the whole mountain to move aside for her convenience.

The delicious rippling noise of the stream was driving her nearly frantic.

"Will you promise not to — do anything to me, if I do come?" said Jill.

"I make no promise," said the Lion.

Jill was so thirsty now that, without noticing it, she had come a step nearer.

"Do you eat girls?" she said.

"I have swallowed up girls and boys, women and men, kings and emperors, cities and realms," said the Lion. It didn't say this as if it were boasting, nor as if it were sorry, nor as if it were angry. It just said it.

"I daren't come and drink," said Jill.

"Then you will die of thirst," said the Lion.

"Oh dear!" said Jill, coming another step nearer. "I suppose I must go and look for another stream then."

"There is no other stream," said the Lion.

PRAYER

GOD OF MERCY AND GOODNESS, You are the Light Giver, the Life Giver, the Joy Giver. I confess that, instead of living in the light of your love, I often find myself stumbling in the dark. Instead of drinking from Your river, I turn to other streams that fail to bring the joy that I seek. I end up confused and frustrated. Lord Jesus, open my eyes to the emptiness of life apart from You. Find all my broken parts and bathe them with Your Father's love. Captivate and teach my restless heart to live in the freedom of Your endless love and in the safety of Your embrace. Teach me to find my joy in You, oh Lord of my heart and God of my salvation. Amen.

> "Let there be light," He still says,
> and will continue saying, till there is
> no evil of Darkness left in all that
> is Nature and Creature.
>
> —WILLIAM LAW

CHAPTER TEN

DISPELLING THE DARKNESS

*The light shines in the darkness, and
the darkness has not overcome it.*

JOHN 1:5

WITHIN THE FIRST MINUTES of most movies, an "inciting incident" takes place. The princess is kidnapped. An airplane is hijacked. A ring is discovered. A conspiracy is launched. An unforeseen event upsets the applecart. This crisis snags the viewers' attention and sets the stage for the rest of the story.

In the Bible, the inciting incident takes place in the third chapter. Forbidden fruit is eaten and the hope of God is gone. A box is opened and all evils swarm out. A line is crossed and mankind is plunged into darkness.

Why is our world filled with both beauty and tragedy? Why is joy interwoven with sorrow? What has gone wrong? The biblical answer is that God's good creation was hijacked and has fallen under the sway of a Dark Power. This evil spirit is behind death, disease and sin in this world. We now live in a part of the universe in the grip of the enemy.

WHAT STORY HAVE WE FALLEN INTO?

We've got a real story happening here!

Genesis 3 chronicles the great crash of creation. This event called the Fall is crucial for understanding the drama of our world. C. S. Lewis referred to the Fall as "the key to history." It is how we got into this mess. It is why every human solution for making things better breaks down. The biblical narrative is the record of what God is doing about it—and it is the most amazing story of all.

It is a story of light overcoming darkness, beauty vanquishing brokenness and grace triumphing over sin.

> *There cannot be any "story" without a fall— all stories are ultimately about the fall.*
> —J.R.R. TOLKIEN

A Cosmic Conflict

We only take a few steps into the Fourth Gospel when we run smack into this matter of "darkness." John is giving us a replay of sorts of the creation account. The first words spoken in the Genesis narrative, *"Let there be light,"* put darkness to flight. However, darkness made a comeback and engulfed our planet. John informs us that into such a world, "the light of the cosmos" now shines— and the darkness is powerless to stop it.

The Apostle John is clearly setting up his book as a new Genesis, a new creation story. The one who spoke the universe into existence comes to speak again. He is the Word who makes everything new. He is the *"Light of the World"* who has come to drive back the darkness.

In His presence, sickness flees, storms are calmed, demons take flight and death releases its prey. At His word, the hungry are fed, blind eyes are opened and hearts are healed. When He comes, darkness retreats. "The darkness should be afraid of the light," writes Christine Caine, "because the light of Christ will eat it up."[1]

He will continue to declare *"let there be light"* until no darkness remains, and the kingdom of this world becomes the kingdom of our God (Rev. 11:15). It is the pushback of the kingdom of heaven, the counterattack of light against the domain of darkness. It is the undoing of the tragedy that took place in Genesis chapter three.

One Day in the Garden

Our first parents were granted the privilege of living in an idyllic paradise surrounded by beauty, abundance, goodness and splendor. It seemed inconceivable they could be persuaded to turn away from the Giver of such extravagant gifts. What could possibly cause them to distrust their Benefactor?

Could these favored humans be made to think they would be better off *without* the One who had lavished such goodness upon them? Could they be tricked into believing there was a better story than the one they were living?

It would require extreme craftiness. Someone devilishly evil.

Enter the serpent.

It looked like a serpent, but make no mistake—this was the Prince of Darkness.

> *Now the serpent was more crafty than any of the wild animals the Lord God had made. He said to the woman, "Did God really say, 'You must not eat from any tree in the garden'?"* (Gn. 3:1).

The deceiver cleverly drew Eve into his trap. An expanded version of the conversation might read like this:

"Is it true what I've heard that you've not been given the freedom to eat of all the trees of the garden? Just as I suspected! God puts this perfectly good tree in front of you, and then He tells you you're not to enjoy its fruit. That's just like God! Restricting people's freedom and enjoyment!

As someone who has been given 'dominion' over all of creation, do you not have the right to enjoy everything in the garden? You must not let God violate your freedom and impinge on your rights. It's dreadfully selfish of Him. And, if I were you, I wouldn't put up with it."

Eve responded, *"But God said if we ate from the tree—we would die."*

WHAT STORY HAVE WE FALLEN INTO?

"God said . . . ? My, you really are behind the times! Nobody is paying much attention to what God says anymore. We have come up with better ways of looking at things. People no longer believe those ridiculous ideas. You need to break free from such regressive ways of thinking.

Listen, if God were truly good and kind, he wouldn't be placing such unreasonable limits on your freedom. He wouldn't be laying unfair burdens on you. If you allow Him to dictate your life, I'm afraid you will live to regret it. It's time you started enjoying life. It's time you wrote your own story."

Adam and Eve took the bait. They swallowed the lie. They swallowed the forbidden fruit. Doubting God's goodness and love for them, the first humans stepped out of the Creator's story into the deceiver's narrative.

> Satan's first attack upon the human race was his sly effort to destroy Eve's confidence in the kindness of God.
> —A. W. Tozer

And now... everything was about to unravel.

A Clouded Vision of God

Adam and Eve started to tell themselves a different story about God—a false story. And very soon they found themselves cowering in the bushes of Eden. They now viewed the Almighty through the filter of their fallenness, and were filled with anxiety and fear. They hid from their Creator and hid from each other. No longer able to perceive the unsurpassable goodness and love of the Father, they withdrew into a self-protective world of concealment, brokenness and frustration.

Of all the devastating results of the Fall, the fundamental problem is this—*we no longer know God.* Christ stated,

> *No one knows the Father except the Son* (Mt. 11:27).

These are stark words about the spiritual blindness of Adam's race. Humans have a flawed perception of God and of life. The

Enemy's lies about our Maker have become our default setting. We have embraced distorted ideas about God.

The Reformer Martin Luther points out that before the Fall, Adam was "drunk with joy towards God." Afterward, he believes lies, flees and avoids his Maker.

What prompted him to hide?

Had God changed? Had He stopped loving them? Had the Giver of every good gift turned against them?

It was not the Creator who had changed—it was Adam. God continued to be steadfast in love, abounding in mercy, overflowing with grace. Sin did not cause God to turn from humanity; it caused humanity to turn from God. Sin is man separating himself from God. Separation was man's decision. The exclusion from paradise merely put into effect the choice Adam had made.

When Darkness Reigns

Having turned from life and light and love, a profound blindness overtook the human race. *This is the tragedy of sin.* It brings darkness to our understanding; it hides from view the unwavering, immeasurable love of God. We can no longer see the Father's heart.

Our guilt-ridden mind now reconfigures God in the image of our brokenness. His beauty, His love, His goodness are misunderstood. We perceive Him as a disapproving judge quick to find fault, and eager to condemn—a view fabricated by the darkness that has invaded our minds. This delusion has sunk deep into every human heart.

Several centuries ago, John Owen wrote:

> How easy we find it to think of God as hard, austere, severe, unable to be pleased and fierce, which are the very worst characteristics of men and therefore most hated by God (Rom. 1:31; 2 Tim. 3:3). How easily Satan deceives us! Was it not his purpose from the beginning to inject such thoughts of God into our hearts?[2]

It is a soul-bending falsehood.

It wrecks us on the inside.

How will we ever escape the labyrinth of our benighted minds? How will we ever break out of this dark prison and come to know the heart of the Father? How will we ever see God as He truly is, and live again in the confidence and freedom and joy of His embrace?

This is the human dilemma.

And this is why the Son of God came.

> *The spiritual witchery of the devil creates in the heart a wrong idea of Christ.*
> —Martin Luther

The Light Bringer

Christ came to demolish our false ideas about God. He is the Eternal Word who tells us who God is. He is the Light that drives away the darkness and gives us a true understanding of the Almighty. He overturns the lies, and shows us a God who is infinitely beautiful, wonderful and good.

As we trace the steps of Christ through the Gospels, we are struck with the richness, compassion, fullness, grandeur, beauty of His life. Here is a human life that reflects the heart of God—and the world has never seen anything like it.

E. Stanley Jones wrote:

> Then there quietly appeared, out of the obscurity of a country village, and out of the lowliness of a carpenter's shop, a Man... There was something about the Man that made the best of men feel that they were in deepest need. And yet the worst of men felt drawn to him. Here was goodness attractive, winsome, compelling... Here was goodness that was not meticulous, but merciful, not standing on pedestals to be worshiped, but bending in lowly service over the lost. Here was goodness, not pharisaical, but friendly, not terrible, but tender... Never did majesty and meekness so blend and become so beautiful as here.[3]

The man from Galilee revealed a God who was not ominous, dark, cold and forbidding. He is *all* light. In Him, there is no darkness at all. Like the brilliance of the sun, He radiates life, goodness, truth, warmth—the beauty of God made visible to human eyes.

The great Russian novelist Fyodor Dostoevski declared:

> I believe there is no one lovelier, deeper, more sympathetic and more perfect than Jesus – not only is there no one else like him, but there could never be anyone like him. If someone proved to me that Christ is outside the truth and that in reality the truth were outside of Christ, then I should prefer to remain with Christ rather than with the truth.

Light Rejected

Sadly, not all were attracted to the brightness of this light and to the warmth of His love. Some felt threatened. Others were envious and angry.

> *Light has come into the world, but people loved darkness instead of light because their deeds were evil. Everyone who does evil hates the light, and will not come into the light for fear that their deeds will be exposed* (Jn. 3:19,20).

Unable to argue with such goodness, the Jewish leaders opted to get rid of Him. They conspired to extinguish this bright shining light. Their deadly scheme was carried out. A mock trial was held, and the Rabbi from Nazareth was executed by crucifixion.

Evil triumphed.

The darkness overcame the light.

Or . . . *so it seemed.*

But what appeared to be a humiliating defeat turned out to be quite the opposite. The victim proved to be the victor. The crucifixion turned into an exhibition of the heart of God. The light was not extinguished, but rather shone brighter than ever.

Out of that moment of darkness blazed forth the radiance of self-giving love, unrivaled humility, and unspeakable mercy. God took the moment of greatest evil in history and made it ground zero for the ultimate display of His heart of love. Light prevailed over darkness.

> *But God puts his love for us beyond all doubt by the fact that Christ died on our behalf while we were still sinners* (Rom. 5:8 OEB).

The cross is the ultimate unveiling of God.

> **God does not love us because Christ died for us; Christ died for us because God loved us.**
> —John R. W. Stott

"The cross is the surest, truest and deepest window on the very heart and character of the living and loving God," declared theologian N. T. Wright.[4] Nothing more clearly demonstrates the heart of God as what happened at Calvary. Here is a God who expresses His "God-ness" by laying down His life for us. The cross lets us see how unfathomably generous, othercentered, humble and compassionate God really is.

Brennan Manning put it well:

> Jesus said, "He who sees Me sees the Father." From our brother Jesus, who alone knows the Father, we learn that there is a welcoming love, unconditional acceptance, a relentless and eternal affection that so far exceeds our human experience that even the passion and death of Jesus is only a hint of it. Think on that for a moment: the torn, broken, lacerated, spit-covered, blood-drenched body of Jesus is only a hint of the Father's love. The very substance of our faith is an unwavering confidence that beyond the hint lies love beyond measure.[5]

Revamping Our View of God

If the one nailed to the cross truly was Immanuel—God with us—then everything we believed about the Most High just got flipped on its head. The crucifixion of God forces us to rethink our ideas about the Almighty.

How can the one who occupies heaven's throne be on a cross? How is it possible that the Architect of the universe bleeds and dies to redeem rebels and sinners? We thought the Lord of Heaven was all about glorious majesty and limitless power. But now we see His glorious *humility*. We see His *limitless love*.

"Christianity is the only religion whose God bears the scars of evil," says Os Guinness.

God has been redefined.

"*No one has ever seen God*," declared John.

But now we have seen Him. The light has come, the shadows are gone, the truth about God has been made known. The Son of God has come and has shown us the heart of God. The Lord Almighty who reigns on high is exactly like Jesus. *We have a Christlike God.*

This is the best news we have ever heard.

> *Jesus Christ is what God does, and the cross is where God did it.*
>
> —Frederick Buechner

No Other God

We need to scrap the idea that behind Jesus there is a sinister God who is less loving and compassionate. "There is no other God, no hidden God, no secret God lurking behind . . . Jesus Christ, ready to judge us with law rather than love," writes theologian Andrew Purves.[6] Jesus Christ is one with His Father. He is the "*the exact imprint of his nature*" (Heb. 1:3 ESV). In the words of Luther, Christ is "a mirror of the Father's heart."

S. D. Gordon writes,

> He was the heart of God throbbing love out to man's heart. He was the face of God looking into man's face. He was the voice of God, soft and low, clear and distinct, speaking into

man's ears. He was the hand of God, strong and tender, reaching down to take man by the hand and lead him back to the old trysting-place under the tree of life, down by the river of water of life.[7]

The Sun of righteousness has appeared. The *"Light of the world"* has come. He dispels all our anxious, dark, confused and frightened imaginings of the sovereign Lord. The God of glory has made Himself known in His Son—and He turns out to be more wonderful than we ever imagined.

> *For God, who said, "Let brilliant light shine out of darkness," is the one who has cascaded his light into us—the brilliant dawning light of the glorious knowledge of God as we gaze into the face of Jesus Christ* (2 Cor. 4:6 TPT).

God is like Jesus.
God is better than we thought.
Better than we hoped.
Better than we dared to believe.

PRAYER

LORD GOD IN HEAVEN, it fills our heart with joy to understand that the Author of our existence is not a faceless, nameless, divine abstraction. You are the joyful fellowship of Father, Son and Holy Spirit, a circle of passion and life and goodness and glory. It thrills us to know that God is love. Not a manager, not a bookkeeper, not a power-broker, not a puppet-master, but God is love. Boundless, eternal, bottomless, never-ending love. Love is the foundation, the reason, the goal, the answer to everything. Such knowledge is too wonderful for us; it is high, we cannot attain it. Shine the light of Your love into our hearts, and dispel the darkness. Teach us that only Your love is better than life. Help us to see Your love as our greatest treasure and the cause for our highest joy. In Jesus name, Amen.

∼

*We see that it is not the task of Christianity
to provide easy answers to every question,
but to make us progressively aware of a mystery.
God is not so much the object of our knowledge
as the cause of our wonder.*

—Kallistos Ware

∼

CHAPTER ELEVEN

A TWIST IN THE STORY

*There was a man sent from God
whose name was John.*

JOHN 1:6

IN ANCIENT TIMES, a peculiar type of individual would occasionally erupt on the scene with a message from another world. They were known as prophets—men with special insight into the true nature of things. Sometimes they were called *"seers"* (1 Sam. 9:9), a term that comes from the Hebrew word "to see." Their eyes had been opened to see visions or images not evident to others. They had caught sight of the Real Narrative in which we find ourselves.

These men, in the words of A. W. Tozer, were "likely to be lean, rugged, blunt-spoken, and a little bit angry with the world." They stood in flat contradiction to the false narratives people had embraced; they debunked the myths. They called people back into alignment with God's Story.

And they stoked the fires of hope. They had a dream that one day heaven would send Someone to make things right. They referred to Him as Messiah, which in Hebrew means "the Anointed One." He would be anointed by God for an enormous task—he would do a remake of the world. Nothing would be the same.

And then suddenly, prophets disappeared. Not one showed up in Israel for four hundred years. Prophets became an extinct species.

And then John arrived.

Called by God

Just five verses into the Fourth Gospel, the writer abruptly switches gears. He leaves momentous topics such as the beginning, Trinity and creation, to speak of a man named John.

Prophetic silence was broken.

John strode out of the desert with a message from God, and began proclaiming it by the Jordan River. Word spread like wildfire. No prophetic voice had been heard for centuries—and when John appeared, people flocked to hear him.

He was a rough-cut outdoorsman who made his home in the wilderness of Judea. His diet was organic—locusts and wild honey. His attire was animal skins. Not your typical preacher.

> *He came as a witness to testify concerning that light, so that through him all might believe* (Jn. 1:7).

When the moment arrived for God's long-awaited intervention in history, the Lord of heaven did not call for a press conference. He bypassed the political and religious leaders. He disregarded all strategies of effective publicity.

He sent John.

The Time Had Come

"The Light" was about to enter the world like the sun breaking over the horizon. This was the Logos, the Author of our Story, the Answer to our questions. He would dispel the darkness.

And John the Baptizer was to herald His arrival. He described himself as a "voice" calling out in the desert. He came in fulfillment of an ancient prophecy of one who would announce the revealing of God's glory (Isa. 40:3-5).

John was that prophet—the last and greatest of the prophets (Lk. 7:27). Unlike those who preceded him, this man from the desert did not simply predict the coming of Messiah. He had the privilege of *presenting* Him. He declared,

> *I testify that this is God's Chosen One* (Jn. 1:34).

John the Baptist introduced the Messiah to the world. He indicated that astounding and earth-shaking events were to take place. As recorded in the first chapter of John's Gospel, the messianic mission boiled down to two key game changers:

- He will *"take away the sin of the world"* (Jn. 1:29)
- He will *"baptize with the Holy Spirit"* (Jn. 1:33)

Sin, the root of all our problems, is going to be removed. It will be "taken away." Darkness will be pushed back, evil will be overthrown. Things have gone wrong in God's creation, and the World-Maker is coming to set things right.

Secondly, there is going to be a "baptism"—not with water but with the Holy Spirit. People will be "submerged" in the Divine Presence, reconnected with God. There will be a restoration of the Creator's original purpose—life will be lived in God.

A brighter chapter for this troubled world was about to begin.

> *The true light that gives light to everyone was coming into the world* (Jn. 1:9).

The world was about to be flooded with the goodness of God. A new day had dawned.

Messiah had come.

And now the prophet's job is done.

Mission completed.

Or was it?

When Prophets Get Perplexed

As time went by, doubts arose. The Messiah identified by the prophet was drawing large crowds, miracles were happening—but it wasn't *all* John had hoped for. His nation had not been freed from the oppression of Rome; crime and corruption had not disappeared.

Christ was doing wonderful things, but what troubled John was what Jesus was *not* doing. Tyranny had not been overthrown. Evil had not been eradicated. By all appearances, the kingdom had not come.

And, to make matters worse, God's prophet landed in prison.

Perhaps he had made a mistake.

He decided to settle the thing once and for all. A couple of his followers were dispatched to ask Jesus if He was really the Messiah or not. They received this answer:

> *Go back and report to John what you have seen and heard: The blind receive sight, the lame walk, those who have leprosy are cleansed, the deaf hear, the dead are raised, and the good news is proclaimed to the poor. Blessed is anyone who does not stumble on account of me* (Lk. 7:22-23).

John the Baptist had hoped for a black-and-white response. Are You the real Messiah? Yes or no.

The answer he got was perplexing.

The blind, the lame, the lepers, the deaf are getting a new lease on life. And even the dead are raised. That's wonderful! But what I wanted to know is: Are you the One we were waiting for?

The question remained hanging.

The prophet was puzzled.

Pondering in Prison

John must have reflected many times on that memorable day at the Jordan River when Jesus stepped forward to be baptized. If there was anyone who did not need a baptism of repentance, it was Him! But the carpenter from Galilee insisted, and He was baptized.

And then it happened. The skies broke open, a voice spoke from heaven, a dove descended on Him. It was precisely what God had told John. The one on whom the Spirit falls and remains—*that was Messiah* (Jn. 1:32-34). The prophet saw it with his own eyes.

It was unmistakable.

But then, the Baptizer began to have second thoughts. The Messiah had very different ideas about things. Their ministries moved in opposite directions.

Where John preached grim justice, Jesus announced extravagant forgiveness. While John lived a frugal life in the wilderness, Jesus enjoyed socializing in Galilean towns and villages. While John lived on locusts and honey, Jesus attended dinner parties. John exuded sternness and austerity; Jesus radiated love and joy.

It is no wonder the prophet was perplexed.

When Dreams Get Shattered

When John was commissioned to prepare the way for Messiah, no doubt he anticipated witnessing the arrival of the kingdom in glory and power. Great things lay ahead! But now, he is baffled. He has met a God he doesn't understand. He has come up against the mystery of God's ways. He is discovering that the Almighty operates on a level far beyond his own.

> *For as the heavens are higher than the earth, so are my ways higher than your ways and my thoughts than your thoughts* (Isa. 55:9 ESV).

No human being has the formula for deciphering the ways of God. Job could not fathom why the Lord had allowed a tornado of tragedy into his life. Mary and Martha were puzzled when Jesus didn't come when they called for His help. When it became clear that Jesus was not the kind of messiah they were looking for, some disciples *"turned back and no longer followed him"* (Jn.

6:66). The Most High regularly works in manners we did not expect. His ways are past finding out.

> *And blessed is he who is not offended because of Me* (Lc. 7:23 NKJV).

When God allows our dreams to shatter, it is because He has bigger dreams for us. We frequently pin our hopes for happiness on illusions and falsehood, which, in God's mercy, often self-destruct. Our Father has something better in mind. Something higher. He knows that nothing outside of likeness to Christ and friendship with God will truly satisfy our hearts. He invites us to trust Him, even when we can't understand.

Chaotic Communication

One day, I received a phone call from a missionary colleague who worked in Sucre, a city four hours drive away. A believer had died, and my friend Phil Train requested I relay the message to Anastacio, the man's brother.

This was before cell phones and internet, and getting messages out to rural villages was not an easy task. I went to a truck stop where vehicles traveled south. Perhaps someone could drop off a message to Anastacio in the village of Tuctapari. However, no trucks were leaving that day.

On my way home, I spotted a Quechua believer, sitting on the back of a truck. I approached him and explained, "Anastacio's brother has passed away and I need to get word to him." The man's Spanish was not very good, and he thought I had said, "Brother Anastacio had passed away." Anastacio was a well-known and beloved servant of God. Thinking this dear man had died, the Quechua man broke down and wept.

Unaware of the misunderstanding, I said goodbye to my mourning friend and went to the telegram office. I dispatched a message to inform that Anastacio's brother had passed away. The telegram was sent to the village of Caiza, from there it was relayed to Vitichi and then a man on a bicycle was sent to take the message to Tuctapari.

Having done what I could, I went home for lunch.

Partway through the meal, I was surprised to get a call from Anastacio. "I have been trying desperately to get in touch with you," I blurted out. "Could you come to the house for lunch?"

Anastacio showed up shortly afterward. As we sat at the table, he told me he had come upon two brothers in Christ, weeping on the back of a truck. Another man had arrived since I left, and now both of them were mourning Anastacio's passing. The weepers were amazed to see their dear friend alive and well, and exclaimed, "We were just told you were dead!"

I was able to explain it was Anastacio's *brother* who had passed away. I then drove my friend to where he could catch a ride to Sucre. Anastacio boarded a truck carrying contraband, and before long the police arrived, and he ended up spending the night in jail!

Upon his release the following day, he was finally able to make it to Sucre, arriving at the cemetery just as they were saying the final prayer.

A few days later, when Anastacio returned to his village, he was handed a telegram—the one I had sent him. It had gotten somewhat scrambled in the process. It read: "Brother Phil Train has passed away in Sucre. Please come to the funeral."

Life can be very confusing at times!

A Twist in the Story

God's prophet was puzzled. The Messiah project was not going as planned. And then, sadly, John the Baptist was executed by King Herod. Had he lived longer, he would have found greater cause for bewilderment. He had rightly identified Jesus as Messiah. He had correctly understood the Old Testament story pointed to and was fulfilled in Jesus. What John didn't realize was the totally *unexpected* manner in which He would complete the story.

Jesus would not only fulfill but *reframe* the whole story.

No doubt, we have all enjoyed the moment in a book or a movie where an unexpected twist happens. Something that changes our understanding of the entire story. The surprising event forces us to rethink everything that took place previously.

The Bible is such a story. It contains a shocking plot twist. Abba's Son completes God's story in such an unanticipated way that those who were awaiting the Messiah ended up rejecting Him. Their king was not crowned—*He was crucified.* His life came to an abrupt and inglorious end.

Instead of putting an end to lawlessness, Christ becomes the victim of massive injustice. Instead of ascending to a throne, He is raised up on a cross! Rather than leading a revolt against the Romans, this Messiah is brutally put to death by them. In place of overthrowing his enemies, He gives his life for them.

He doesn't follow the official script.

No one saw this coming.

The Great Reversal

No one expected the Messiah to be murdered.

But this strange twist in the story turns everything around. Slowly his followers began to see things in a different way.

Athanasius explains, "A marvelous and mighty paradox has thus occurred, for the death which [Christ's enemies] thought to inflict on Him as dishonor and disgrace has become the glorious monument to death's defeat."

As E. Stanley Jones points out, Christ took the worst thing that could happen to Him (the cross) and turned it into the best thing that could happen to the world (redemption). What looked like failure turned out to be success. An apparent defeat resulted in victory.

James Stewart, pointing to Calvary, said,

> He compelled their dark achievements to subserve His end, not theirs... They thought they had defeated God with His back to the wall, pinned and helpless and defeated: they did not know that it was God Himself who had tracked them down.

The whole narrative gets flipped.

Never was there a moment so dark—and yet so full of light. So ugly—and yet so beautiful. So awful—and yet so wonderful.

The crucifixion turns into the supreme example of what love looks like—love is cross-shaped. Calvary becomes the ultimate demonstration of what true power looks like—power is self-sacrificing. The cross is the definitive display of true greatness—greatness lays down its life for others.

And Christ's self-surrender unto death is the final statement of what God looks like—*He is a cross-like God.*

The crucifixion is a stunning revelation of God's true character, a blazing forth of His extraordinary love for rebels and sinners. The horror of the cross reveals the scandalous beauty of God.

The crucified Messiah gives us a counter-intuitive revelation of the Almighty. It tells us how astonishingly humble, totally self-giving and marvelously compassionate He is. Calvary unveils a God infinitely more wonderful than we ever imagined.

> *The riddles of God are more satisfying than the solutions of man.*
>
> —G. K. Chesterton

And it unveils a surprising Deity—one who will never cease to astound us. He is trustworthy, but not predictable.

The Unpredictable God

He is a God who shows up where we don't expect to find Him (Jn. 6:29), He speaks words no one has ever heard before (Jn. 7:46), and does things no one has ever done (Mt. 13:54; Mk. 2:12). He does not operate on our schedule, or fulfill our expectations.

Madame Jeanne Guyon has a word of caution:

> If knowing answers to life's questions is absolutely necessary to you, then forget the journey. You will never make it, for this is a journey of unknowables – of unanswered questions, enigmas, incomprehensibles, and most of all, things unfair.

We love closure, resolution and clarity. Life with God often involves mystery, uncertainty and paradox. The sovereign Lord is utterly uncontainable.

There are those in the Christian church who thrive on certitude. They have downsized everything to non-mystery. They have shrunk divine mysteries down to proof-texts and pat answers. The Lord of heaven and earth has been fenced into a tight theological enclosure. The grandeur of God has been explained, the wonder has been decoded, the mystery has been mastered.

Adherents to this view would do well to pay a visit to the greatest of the prophets as he sat bewildered in a prison cell. They should turn to Paul, who with all the truth revealed to him, admitted that he saw things dimly as if looking in a broken mirror (1 Cor. 13:12). "If God were small enough to be understood, He would not be big enough to be worshiped," Evelyn Underhill reminds us. We don't have the Divine Lord figured out.

> *God thunders wondrously with his voice; he does great things that we cannot comprehend* (Job 37:5 ESV).

> *How unsearchable are His judgements and His ways past find out!* (Rom. 11:33 NKJV).

"Theology is always a 'stammering' in the face of the transcendent mystery of truth," one scholar confessed.

"Mystery is not the absence of meaning," points out one writer, "but the presence of more meaning than we can comprehend."[1]

We are not about to reduce the fascinating, irresistible, unpredictable Christ to an equation. He is bigger than our doctrines and our theological explanations. His Story will continue to surprise us. His goodness, grace and love will never cease to amaze us.

"We can never nail him down," asserted Frederick Buechner, "not even if the nails we use are real ones and the thing we nail him to is a cross."[2]

PRAYER

ALMIGHTY GOD, Your thoughts are higher than our thoughts and Your ways are past finding out. We never know what You are about to do next. Lord Jesus, You made wine at a wedding, overturned tables in the temple, walked on the water, washed the feet of Your followers, filled boats with fish, and made breakfast on a beach. You work in surprising ways and show up where we least expect to see You. We like things to be predictable and the path to be smooth. You prefer to surprise us with twists and turns. We like things to be understandable. You prefer to stretch us with truth that has more meaning than we can comprehend. We are grateful to belong to a God who will never cease to amaze us. A God we cannot fully explain, but a God of Calvary love that we can trust fully and completely. We give you praise, oh Lord our God. Amen.

*Jesus Christ . . . walked into time and quietly
divided it into before and after—B.C. and A.D.
He walked into the realm of thought and altered all
our conceptions about God and life and destiny.
He walked into our moral conceptions and codes,
and now we are good or bad according to
whether we embody His spirit or not.
He walked into our sundered relations
with God and healed them by His cross.
He walked into the chaos of human relationships
and projected a Kingdom which is destined to
gather all our chaos into cosmos, to be the goal
and end of all human history.*

—E. Stanley Jones

CHAPTER TWELVE

THE BIG BLUNDER

*He himself was not the light; he came
only as a witness to the light.*

JOHN 1:8

AN AIRLINE HAD A MIX-UP in its schedule. The passengers waited as the crew met to discuss the matter. There was confusion regarding the destination of the flight. The plane didn't move from the gate, and the travelers sat expecting an announcement.

Finally, a flight attendant came on the intercom, "There seems to be some confusion concerning the destination of this flight. If your destination is Omaha, please remain seated. If your destination is Dallas, you are asked to exit the plane at this time."

The door to the cockpit suddenly opened, the pilot grabbed his flight case, tipped his hat to the passengers, and said, "Sorry, folks—I've got the wrong plane."

Mistakes are easy to make.

A big blunder was made by a group the Bible calls: "the disciples of John the Baptist." Unfortunately, they are not the only ones to make this mistake. In fact, it's become rather common.

John the Baptist came with a mission from God. His job was *"to testify concerning that light, so that through him all might believe"*

(Jn. 1:7). Messiah was coming, and John was commissioned to announce His arrival.

The man from the desert made a huge impact. He became such a powerful "voice" for God, that many thought he was the incarnation of the prophet Elijah, or Messiah Himself.

John flatly denied this. He was simply the forerunner.

> *He himself was not the light; he came only as a witness to the light* (Jn. 1:8).

John was no more than a voice, a signpost directing people to the Light. He went to great pains to set the record straight.

- I am not the Christ (v. 20)
- I am not Elijah (v. 21)
- I am not the prophet (v. 21)
- I am not worthy to untie His sandals (v. 27)

We get it! John is *not* the light. He merely points people to the real Light.

> *I am not the Messiah. I am only here to prepare the way for him* (Jn. 3:28 NTL).

The author insists on rehashing this point.

When Disciples Depart

Simon, Andrew, John, along with many other disciples of John the Baptist, became followers of Jesus. That was the plan. The Baptist's job was to prepare the way, show the way, and then get out of the way. As a forerunner, John was to announce the arrival of another, and then fade out of the picture.

But, why does the writer of this Gospel tell us over and over that the main character in the story is not John but Christ?

There is an important reason:

> *The disciples of John and of the Pharisees were fasting. Then they came and said to Him, "Why do the disciples of John and of the Pharisees fast, but Your disciples do not fast?"* (Mk. 2:18 NKJV)

Notice who the critics are—"John's disciples."
Are we talking about the disciples of John the Baptist?
Yes, indeed.
Well, something is wrong! The disciples of John should have become the disciples of Jesus. But these men never made the transition. Instead of following Messiah, they stuck with the chairman who introduced Him. They were disciples—but they were following the wrong person!

The "John" Movement

Now scroll ahead twenty-five years. The Good News of Christ is spreading across the Roman Empire. In his travels, the apostle Paul runs into a group of "disciples" in a city called Ephesus, and he discovers they are disciples of John the Baptist!

Imagine this. Way off in Turkey, 25 years after the great prophet died, a group of his followers are faithfully holding to the teachings of their spiritual mentor. The "Baptist" movement should have shut down—but it continued. These men are dutifully following John—not realizing it was all about *Jesus!*

Paul explained to them that the whole point of John's ministry was to introduce people to Messiah.

> *On hearing this, they were baptized in the name of the Lord Jesus. And when Paul had laid his hands on them, the Holy Spirit came on them, and they began speaking in tongues and prophesying. There were about twelve men in all* (Acts 19:5-7).

Twelve men converted from John to Jesus.

They finally got the point. Jesus, not John, is the Light of the World.

The Problem Persists

A few more decades go by. Matthew, Mark and Luke have written their books. And finally, as an old man, the apostle John picks up his pen to write the fourth and last Gospel. And in the first chapter, he writes:

> *He himself was not the light; he came only as a witness to the light* (Jn. 1:8).

More than fifty years have passed since John the Baptist's death, yet the apostle still finds it necessary to assert the superiority of Jesus over John. Apparently, there were those who had misunderstood the Good News. They were convinced John was the one to follow. Were these disciples of John creating confusion in the Christian community?

Very likely.

The John the Baptist movement remained alive a long time after it should have been dead and buried.

And the problem didn't die out in the first century. It is an amazing fact that, even to this day, there is a group in Iraq called the Mandaeans who claim John the Baptist as their great spiritual leader. The fascination with John continues!

Getting it Wrong

The question arises: Was John not a prophet sent from God?

He certainly was.

Was he not declared to be the *greatest* of the prophets?

That's right.

Did he not faithfully and fearlessly present the message of God?

Undoubtedly.

But, here's the problem—Great servants of God who impact multitudes run the risk of getting *idolized*. The servant often becomes the celebrity!

When Revivals Get Derailed

When God works mightily through a John the Baptist, a John Calvin, a Martin Luther, a John Wesley, a Charles Finney, a potential danger develops. Those blessed by the ministry become enthralled with the minister. Devotion grows to the man of God and his message.

His followers become attached to his focus, perspective, emphasis, doctrinal framework. They read his books, follow his teaching and become part of a movement.

And they say, I am of Paul, I am of Cephas, I am of Apollos, I am of Calvin, I am of Luther, I am of Wesley, I am of Finney (See 1 Cor. 1:12).

> *I think the minute we begin to get away from Jesus Himself, we begin to cloud our theology.*
>
> —Author unknown

Their loyalty gets deflected from the Lord Jesus Christ Himself. They end up as faithful followers of a great man of God, of a doctrinal emphasis, of certain principles—instead of being followers of Christ. The focus is now on a line of truth, a certain person, a certain perspective. *And Christ-centeredness gets derailed.*

Someone has well stated: Whatever becomes the issue, becomes the *idol*. There is only one issue—*Christ Himself*. He is the center. He is the way, the truth and the life. He is the Light of the world. Following anything or anyone else leads to darkness. Making anything else the issue is idolatry.

> *Now the teaching which has been delivered to you has Jesus Christ our Lord Himself as its center and circumference. Therefore let your life be lived in Him* (Col. 2:6 F.F. Bruce, paraphrase).

WHAT STORY HAVE WE FALLEN INTO?

The Fading of John

When John the Baptist's ministry started to be overshadowed by Jesus, some of his followers felt threatened.

> They came to John and said to him, "Rabbi, that man who was with you on the other side of the Jordan—the one you testified about—look, he is baptizing, and everyone is going to him" (Jn. 3:26).

John, you're losing your congregation. Everyone is following Jesus!

The forerunner knew this was the plan, and he repeats his favorite line, "*Make no mistake. He's the Messiah, not me!*"

John then states these immortal words:

> He must increase, but I must decrease (Jn. 3:30 ESV).

The prophet understands his mission. "I am about to fade out of the picture, but He comes to stay. My task is to say: 'He's the One. Follow Him. And after that—my work is done.'"

John the Baptist got it right. His followers *didn't*.

> **Let Christ be first, last, and everything in between.**
> —Charles H. Spurgeon

A Misplaced Focus

When the president of a nation comes on stage at an important event, the master of ceremonies quckly fades into the background. All eyes are now on the leader of the country. Nobody is focused on the man who introduced him; he is forgotten and the president has everyone's attention.

However, in the case of John the Baptist, *that didn't happen*. He made his announcement, walked off the scene, *and a group of men followed Him!* This makes no sense at all! They should have followed Messiah, but they stuck with the man who presented Him.

A BIG BLUNDER

The person John came to present is not simply an enlightened figure. He is THE LIGHT. He is not a Word; He is THE WORD. He is the center, the first, the foremost, the focal point, the foundation, the goal, the reason, the nucleus of everything.

> *For in him all things were created: things in heaven and on earth, visible and invisible, whether thrones or powers or rulers or authorities; all things have been created through him and for him* (Col. 1:16).

What a stunning affirmation of the incomparable greatness of the Lord Jesus Christ! He towers far above everything and everyone; His importance cannot be overstated. The spotlight of heaven and earth is on Him. He is the central fact of the universe.

Whoever knows Him knows the reason of everything.

—Blaise Pascal

The material world that took shape on the seven days of Creation bears the imprint of its Maker. What came into being on each day is a reminder of Christ Himself.[1]

1. Christ is the light of the world (Jn. 1:9; 8:12).
2. Christ is the water of life (Jn. 4:10; 7:38).
3. Christ is wheat and bread (John 12:24; 6:35).
4. Christ is the sun and morning star (Mal. 4:20; Rev. 22:16).
5. Christ is the Lamb of God (Jn. 1:29).
6. Christ is the model man (Jn. 19:5; Rom. 5:14).
7. Christ is the true Sabbath (Col. 2:16-17).

The Lord Jesus Christ is written into the fabric of the universe. The entire cosmos is a reflection of His magnificent person. "Jesus isn't the vital piece of the puzzle. He's the picture," declares Glen Scrivener. Christ is absolutely supreme, not only in creation, but in God's plan of redemption.

> *There is only Christ: He is everything* (Col. 3:11 NJB).

The story is told that when Buddha was dying, some of his followers asked how they could best perpetuate his memory. He told them not to bother; it was his teaching, not his person that mattered. And such is the case with virtually every religious system; what matters is the message. *Not so with the Christian faith.* Here what matters is the person. Everything centers in the Incarnate Christ. Everything is contingent on who He is, what He has done and what continues to do. He is the pivotal issue.

C. H. Macintosh wrote, "Christ is our rule, our model, our touchstone, our everything."

Campbell Morgan states, "The center and circumference of the Gospel is Christ Himself." The Gospel does not call us to believe something, but to trust Someone. Paul did not say, *"I know what I have believed,"* but rather, *"I know WHOM I have believed"* (2 Tim. 1:12). Christianity is Christ.

Christ or Chaos

In him all things hold together (Col. 1:17).

When we get away from Him, things fall apart. Marriages falter; life unravels. The universe does not function well apart from Him. When we live in Him, by Him, for Him—we live; if we live in any other way, life goes to pieces. The wheels fall off. Only "in Him" do things hold together.

E. Stanley Jones writes,

> A soul finds itself only as it finds itself in Christ. Here it lives. A great flywheel in a factory revolves with tremendous speed and power and yet with perfect silence. Why? It is adjusted, it has found its centre. But take it off its center and make it eccentric, it then shakes itself and the building to pieces. It has become a thing of destruction instead of construction. Life in Christ has found its center, and it silently sings to the music of its found rhythm. But take life out of Christ and it becomes ec-centric, inwardly full of friction and outwardly full of clash.[2]

To live in Christ is to live in tune with the Way, the Truth and the Life. It is to be right with the universe. It is, as George MacDonald says, to be "right with God . . . one with the power, the love, the will of the mighty Father, the cherisher of joy, the Lord of laughter, whose are all glories, all hopes, who loves everything and hates nothing but selfishness."[3]

Discovering Water

Some scientists at Smolensk University decided to develop a fish that could live out of water.

So, choosing some healthy red herrings, they bred, crossbred, hormoned and chromosomed until at length they had a fish that could live—at least exist—out of water.

The local commissar was not satisfied. True, these fish had survived until now on rarefied gas, but what about reactionary tendencies? He suspected a secret yen for water.

"You have neglected education," he said, "Start over, and this time do not neglect education."

So again they bred, crossbred, hormoned and chromosomed, and this time they did not neglect education—down to the veriest reflex.

The result? A red herring that would rather die than get its tail wet. The slightest suggestion of humidity filled the new herring with dread. Thought control had done its perfect work, and with the possible exception of the red herring, everyone was happy. Surely this year's Lenin Prize would go to the scientists of Smolensk University.

But the world must see this triumph of Soviet research. The commissar who had thought of education must take the fish on tour.

Somewhere in Hungary the tragedy occurred. Quite accidentally, according to official reports, the red herring fell into a pool of water. Deep in the green translucent stuff it lay—eyes and gills clamped shut—afraid to move lest it become wetter. And, of course, it could not breathe—every reflex said no to that. Never did a fish so wet feel more like a fish out of water.

But breathe it must, and there was nothing else to breathe. Only water. So the red herring drew a tentative gillful.

Its eyes bulged. It breathed again. Its jaw flew open. It flicked a fin . . . then another . . . and wiggled with delight. Then it darted away. The fish had discovered water!

And with that same kind of wonder, men, conditioned by a world that rejects Him, discover God.[4]

> *For in Him we live and move and have our being* (Acts 17:28).

Finding our True Home

E. Stanley Jones writes, "Life out of Christ is out of its element. It is gasping on the shores of life—gasping for *life*. Christ is its true element. Here it *lives*."[5]

> *Without Christ, I was like a fish out of water. With Christ, I am in an ocean of love.*
> —Sundar Singh

Surrendering to Christ has the feeling of a homecoming. It feels right. It is where we were created to live. Turning away from Him brings feelings of estrangement, of disconnection. The Gospels tell of a rich young ruler who went away from Christ "sorrowful." Everyone does. All departure from Christ is a departure from life. It is to swim against the current of the universe. It doesn't feel right. Life was designed to be centered in Christ. We can't truly live if we center it anywhere else.

Jürgen Moltmann states, "Where Jesus is, there is life. There is abundant life, vigorous life, loved life, and eternal life. There is life-before-death."

Frederick Buechner poses an important question:

> And now, brothers, I will ask you a terrible question, and God knows I ask it also of myself. Is the truth beyond all truths, beyond the stars, just this: that is to live without him is the real death, that to die with him is the only life?[6]

PRAYER

LORD JESUS CHRIST, beloved Son of the Father, You are the way, without You there is no going. You are the truth, without You there is no knowing. You are the life, without You there is no living. We find it so easy to turn the wrong way, to believe the wrong thing, and to live the wrong life. As the songwriter said, "Prone to wander, Lord, I know it, prone to leave the God I love." Strong Redeemer, keep us from being allured by the madness of the world. Keep our feet on Your path, illuminate our minds with Your truth, and warm our hearts with Your love. May we live in the abundance of life that comes from You. May we run the race with our eyes steadily fixed on Jesus, until that day when faith gives way to sight, oh Blessed Lord and Mighty Savior. Amen.

*Faced with the Fall,
God did not step angrily aside.
Instead He personally united
Himself with the race.
Lost humanity has been
called home.*

—Karl Barth

CHAPTER THIRTEEN

THE GOD WHO STOOPS

He was in the world, and though the world was made through him, the world did not recognize him.
JOHN 1:10

THE HUMAN RACE, "to which so many of my readers belong" (Chesterton), makes its home in a tiny suburb of God's creation called "Planet Earth."

Our neighborhood turns out to be a minuscule planet in an immense universe. Our galaxy is so huge that, traveling at the speed of light, it would take about 200,000 years to get from one side to another. This enormous swarming mass of solar systems is like a giant spiral rotating majestically in space, with glowing arms trailing behind it. It makes a complete rotation in 250 million years. Our world is a tiny speck that rotates around our sun—one of 200 billion suns in this massive network of solar systems.

If we took our largest telescope to the nearest star, Alpha Centauri, and looked back, the earth would not be visible—even with the aid of that powerful instrument.

We don't even show up on the map!

The galactic star-cluster closest to us is Andromeda. It dwarfs our galaxy and is home to a trillion stars. To get there you would have to travel at the speed of light (186,000 miles a second) for twenty-five million years. That's our nearest neighbor!

The entire universe is thought to be about 93 billion light-years in diameter. For many years, it was generally estimated to harbor about ten hundred billion galaxies. Recent studies suggest there are probably ten times more than that! It seems science is never "settled" for astronomers. Their calculations are regularly on the increase; things just keep getting more astonishing.[1]

This cosmos is incomprehensibly vast!

Incomprehensible Immensity

A creation of this magnitude showcases a power that baffles our minds and beggars our speech. What kind of energy source fueled all those stars and keeps countless galaxies spiraling through space at speeds of several million miles per hour? Who orchestrated all this enormousness and keeps it running like clockwork? We cannot begin to fathom such bigness. We stutter and stammer in the face of such greatness.

The Gospel of John, in a most unpretentious manner, states regarding the Logos: "The cosmos was made through Him." As if it were a minor accomplishment!

One thing is overwhelmingly clear—the Creator of the cosmos is inconceivably big, and we are ridiculously small.

Once Upon a Planet

"Lost somewhere between immensity and eternity is our tiny planetary home," remarked astronomer and science writer Carl Sagan.

We could easily be overlooked.

However, the Maker of the star fields shows a particular interest in what goes on in this cul-de-sac of His creation. And He scripted a Story for our world that will astonish the entire universe. It is a drama as staggering as the vastness of the cosmos.

Our home address is the Milky Way. On the outer rim of the galaxy, if you look closely, you find our solar system—eight planets orbiting a relatively small star. Around that star circles a little grain of sand—*that's our world.*

On that grain of sand live tiny headstrong humans made from dust, who, according to Scripture, decided to revolt against their Creator. Thinking they would be better off without Him, they mutinied against their Maker.

How ridiculous does it get?

We are inhabitants of a planet in rebellion.

Whatever possessed these dust-people to tell the Most High God to back off? They flaunt their freedom and scoff at His guidelines for living. The High Lord of heaven—snubbed by specks of dust. How absurd is that?

Then the unthinkable happens...

The Visited Planet

The Maker of the galaxies came to our planet disguised as a human.

> *He entered into the world he created, yet the world was unaware* (Jn. 1:10 TPT).

The Creator crosses all worlds to live among us! He touches down on our planet, and takes up residence on this piece of dust called *terra firma.*

And nobody recognizes Him.

He looks like a carpenter—but there is more to Him than meets the eye.

This is the Divine Playwright, the one who crafted the whole narrative. Not content with writing the story—*He steps into it.* The Author of our drama moves into our neighborhood, rubs shoulders with peasants and paupers and lives in anonymity. The One who was always with God, *is now with us.*

Has anything like this ever happened in the history of the universe?

When God Goes Unnoticed

The One who masterminded the cosmos arrived—and the news did not go viral. The media did not cover it. Almost no one noticed!

> *But although he made the world, the world didn't recognize him when he came* (Jn. 1:10 TLB).

The Creator was here—and no one realized it!

If God Almighty should come to our planet, we would expect it to be an earth-shaking event. It would strike fear into every heart. We would tremble before His limitless power, His radiant majesty, His overwhelming greatness. We would be face to the ground, awe-struck and intimidated by His presence.

We would expect Him to take charge. To throw His weight around. To impose His authority. To scatter His enemies. To demand submission. That's how gods operate.

But *not* this God.

This God is not like Zeus.

This God is like Jesus.

The Lowliness of the Most High

He comes among us incognito and becomes a part of our world. He works as an artisan in an obscure country village (Jn. 1:46). He goes about ministering to the sick, the needy, the outsiders. He never uses His miraculous power or genius of wisdom to acquire wealth, influence or social status. He feeds the hungry and eats with sinners. He identifies with the broken, the burdened, the vulnerable and the weak. He does things we never expected God to do.

E. Stanley Jones writes,

> He did not merely bend over to hand out, he bent over to get under. He stooped under the poverty and the toil, the sin and

the shame, the troubles and the toil—under the very lives of fallen men, and when there was nothing left to get under, he got under the cross and bore that for them.[2]

He is a God who stoops.

A God Like No Other

We have already discovered a unique feature about God in John's Gospel—He is a Trinity. And here we find a second aspect that distinguishes the Christian view of God from every other religion—*His humility.*

> **Loving humility is a terrible force: it is the strongest of all things, and there is nothing else like it.**
>
> —Fydor Dostoyevsky

> *Though he was God, he did not demand and cling to his rights as God, but laid aside his mighty power and glory, taking the disguise of a slave and becoming like men. And he humbled himself even further, going so far as actually to die a criminal's death on a cross"* (Phil. 2:6-8 TLB).

The Almighty is humble.

Humility and divinity seem contradictory. We associate God with irresistible power and indisputable authority. He is high and mighty—not meek and lowly. He is a king—not a servant.

Gods are not known to be humble. They come to take charge—not to work as a common laborer. They come to be worshipped—not to be scorned! They come to give orders—not to give their life! To be God means you call the shots. You are the undisputed boss.

However, the man from Galilee overturns all our notions about Deity. He redefines God for us. He showcases the incomparable beauty of God. In the human life of Jesus, God's stunning humility is seen in high definition. When we grasp that Christ is the true revelation of God (Jn. 1:18), we begin to perceive more clearly the majestic tenderness, the unspeakable goodness, the heart-grabbing loveliness of God.

WHAT STORY HAVE WE FALLEN INTO?

Os Guinness writes,

> The Word became flesh and spoke in a human form as one of us, though incognito and in a disguise that fooled us and made fools of us... The God of all power chose to become weak to subvert our puny power, the God of all wealth chose to become poor to subvert our meager wealth, the God of all wisdom chose to become foolish to subvert our imagined wisdom, and the God who alone is the sole decisive one chose to be a nobody to subvert us when we stupidly thought we were somebody.[3]

Problematic Power

A never-to-be-forgotten event took place on the Master's last night with His disciples. They met in a borrowed second-story room to celebrate the Passover feast.

John prefaces the account with these words:

> *Jesus knew that the Father had put all things under his power, and that he had come from God and was returning to God...* (Jn. 13:3).

Authority over the entire universe had been given to Jesus Christ. It was granted to Him to be Lord of all. Absolute supremacy. And, at this moment, Jesus was conscious of that fact.

> *If you want to test a man's character, give him power.*
> —Abraham Lincoln

Power is no easy thing to handle. "Power tends to corrupt and absolute power corrupts absolutely," observed a famous historian. Power poisons people, and can make a despot of most any man.

History is replete with leaders who were corrupted by power. We have seen countless tyrants like Herod, Cesar, Hitler, Stalin and Chairman Mao who made ruthless, cruel and shameless abuse of their power.

Who can hold power and not be corrupted by it? Even a minor position of authority can cause one to become conceited and arrogant. The intoxicating influence of power is insidious.

How many could become mayor, governor, or senator and remain humble? Who could become the head of a great nation or empire, and not succumb to pride? But, let's notch this up even more—What would it be like to have the *entire* universe under your command? Who could handle absolute power over *all* creation?

That's what was given to Christ—*and He was well aware of it.*

Redefining Power

And what does the Lord of the universe do?

> *He got up from the meal, took off his outer clothing, and wrapped a towel around his waist. After that, he poured water into a basin and began to wash his disciples' feet...* (Jn. 13:4-5).

No servant was present in the upper room to perform the customary foot-washing procedure. There were thirteen pairs of dirty feet, and no one to carry out that humble service.

And so the Owner of the galaxies gets up—*and takes care of it.*

The Sovereign Lord gets down on His knees, and redefines greatness.

The hands into which the entire universe had been placed were now washing grimy feet. The Lord Most High was doing the work of the most lowly servant. Humility reached a new high-water mark.

> *We are at the feet of the God who washed our feet.*
> —E. Stanley Jones

"We value big. God became little. We value recognition. He was despised. We value beauty. He was marred."[4]

Our concept of God was turned on its head.

Radically reconfigured.

WHAT STORY HAVE WE FALLEN INTO?

A World Where God Was Not Welcome

Not only was the Author of the Cosmos not recognized when He came into His world, John states he was *"not received."*
That is putting it mildly.
What happened was this...
They conspired against the Son of God, impeached Him, tortured Him and brutally terminated His life. They murdered their Maker.
A crucified Christ—how can we make sense of that?
From the perspective of the Roman Empire, His death was simply another execution, an example of Roman power and brutality.
From the perspective of the Jewish leadership, the death of Jesus of Nazareth was a moment of victory. The elimination of a threat to their religious power and prestige.
From the perspective of the disciples, the death of the one they believed to be Messiah was a moment of profound horror and grief. Their hopes were dashed. Their world collapsed.
Three days later, Jesus came back, risen from the grave.
And everything changed.

> *Christ lifted the gate of the centuries off its hinges with His bleeding hand.*
> —German Historian

The Magnificent Defeat

In the light of the resurrection, the disciples looked back and suddenly realized that when Jesus died on the cross something earth-shaking had taken place. What happened on Calvary's hill was so huge, so vast, so far-reaching, they couldn't begin to get their minds around it.
It began to dawn on them that the death of Christ was, in fact, the event of all events. It was the pivotal moment of history. The whole scheme of things shifted on its axis. It was ground zero for the transformation of the cosmos. The Cross of Calvary decisively and profoundly altered everything.

THE GOD WHO STOOPS

Richard Crashaw, a seventeenth-century poet, wrote:

Christ, when he died,
Deceived the cross;
And on Death's side
Threw all the loss:
The captive world awaked and found
The prisoner loose, the jailer bound.

The New Testament is the record of the apostle's joyful attempt to come to grips with the immensity of what had taken place.

What looked like defeat had turned into a victory. The Crucified One had triumphed—overwhelmingly. Death was conquered, sin was purged, hell was plundered, the law was fulfilled, evil was dethroned, Satan was vanquished, the curse was annulled and darkness was driven back.

> **At the cross God wrapped his heart in flesh and blood and let it be nailed to the cross for our redemption.**
> —E. Stanley Jones

He forgave us all our sins, having canceled the charge of our legal indebtedness, which stood against us and condemned us; he has taken it away, nailing it to the cross. And having disarmed the powers and authorities, he made a public spectacle of them, triumphing over them by the cross (Col. 2:14-15).

"The cross cannot be defeated, for it is defeat," wrote Chesterton. The weakness and foolishness of God turned out to be stronger and greater than the devices of men. This was the mystery of God's plan, mapped out by divine wisdom before the world began.

None of the rulers of this age understood it, for if they had, they would not have crucified the Lord of glory (1 Cor. 2:8).

Glen Scrivener put it like this: "In becoming man, Jesus stepped into the cockpit of this world and through His death and resurrection, turned the whole thing around."

WHAT STORY HAVE WE FALLEN INTO?

"He is sold, and cheap was the price," says Gregory of Nazianzus, "yet He buys back the world at the mighty cost of His own blood."

We live on a planet where something astonishing took place:

> The Creator was crucified.
> The curse was crushed by a cross.
> The serpent was smashed by Roman spikes.
> The victim became the Victor.
> The narrative of sin and death was reversed.

Our world was invaded by the bleeding love of God. It was a most daring rescue operation! A stunning conspiracy of grace!

We are still trying to come to terms with what took place.

But one thing is clear. We are in a Story more amazing than fiction.

PRAYER

MAKER OF HEAVEN AND EARTH, You tossed trillions of galaxies into unending space, and You know every star by name. You are the Author of bewildering vastness. Who can begin to fathom Your wisdom, power and greatness? The heavens declare Your glory, oh God. We stand in awe before You, Creator of the worlds. But what amazes us even more is that "God so LOVED the world." Your love and goodness are what astonishes us most of all. You sent Your Son to find us in our lostness, our blindness, our brokenness. And He laid down His life to bring us back to the Father's embrace. How can we ever begin to fathom that? You are the Maker of the stars and the Seeker of the lost. You are wonderful beyond description, and we praise Your Holy Name. Amen.

*To become a child of God
is the only solution
of the world's enigma.*

—Helmut Thielicke

CHAPTER FOURTEEN

THE GOD WHO IS ABBA

*Yet to all who did receive him, to those who believed in his name,
he gave the right to become children of God.*
JOHN 1:12

FABIOLA IS A MOTHER of two daughters. Her husband is serving time in prison and Fabiola struggles to make ends meet. She often gets behind in her rent, and resorts to all kinds of tricks to avoid running into the landlady. When a knock is heard at the door near the beginning of the month, she and her daughters regularly go silent and lie low. Sometimes they quietly tiptoe out very early in the morning. Other times the lights are left off and no music is played. They have learned to come up with creative excuses for their delay in paying the rent. It's awkward to have someone at your door wanting rent-money when you are unable to pay.

The Gospel of John depicts God as coming into our world and knocking on our door. John 1:11 could be paraphrased thus: "He came to his own home and we slammed the door in his face." The Maker of the Cosmos was rejected in the world He had made.

Did people think He had come to collect the rent?

In the minds of many, God is an overbearing, bothersome landlord who makes unreasonable demands. He comes to make life difficult for people. In the words of H. G. Wells, many see

Him as "a harsh implacable hostility." And, He won't stop knocking on the door.

It comes as no surprise that some hang a "Do Not Disturb" sign on the door. They have enough issues to deal with.

What they fail to understand is *why* He is knocking. They have no idea what prompted Him to come, and what He purposes to do.

They think He has come to collect the rent, when in actual fact, *He has come to pay it.*

This awful blindness has afflicted humanity since the Fall in the Garden of Eden—an event more devastating than the Chernobyl disaster. Our default setting was corrupted. Our mind became clouded and unable to perceive the truth about God. The reality of His overwhelming goodness has been eclipsed by the idea He only comes to collect the rent.

We think of God as the Landlord.

We fail to understand He is a Lover.

And in our blindness we turned Him away.

The Reason He Came

Of course, we had good cause to think God had it out for us. Human hands had put heaven's Beloved Son to death in the cruelest manner imaginable.

We turned on Him like a pack of wolves and hounded Him to Golgotha. We maligned, cursed, mocked, and condemned Him to death. We flogged His back and spat on His face. We spiked His hands and feet and speared His side. We crucified our Maker, and hurled insults at Him as He writhed in agony and shame.

Does it get any uglier than that?

For God so loved the world He gave His only begotten Son— *and we killed Him.*

How would heaven respond? We might expect:

- The fierce wrath of Almighty God
- Fire and brimstone

- Destruction into oblivion
- Everlasting torment

That's *not* what happened. The very next verse in John's Gospel gives us God's response. This is the most staggering part:

> *But whoever did receive Him, those trusting in His name, to these He gave the right to become children of God* (Jn. 1:12 TLV).

Who has ever heard of such a thing?

God's Son didn't come as a rent-collector, He came as redeemer. He came to *give,* and not to take. He came to set people free, not to enslave them.

He came to bring us into a Story whose dimensions are wider, deeper, higher and richer than anything we ever imagined. He came to bestow upon rebels and sinners the highest privilege in the universe—He came to make us children of the Most High God.

This Story will stun the entire cosmos.

Shocking Grace

Here we come face to face with something so huge, so inconceivable, that we are baffled and bewildered. It is indeed, as one scholar put it, "a glorious, uproarious, absurd generosity." Well might we say with an ancient poet, *"Such knowledge is too wonderful for me; it is too high, I cannot attain to it"* (Psa. 139:6).

When John presents the Good News of the Gospel to his readers, he doesn't highlight aspects such as forgiveness, redemption, salvation, reconciliation. These privileges are indescribably wonderful. Words cannot be found to adequately praise God for them. However, the beloved disciple draws our attention to the highest privilege of all (Jn. 1:12; 20:17). It is the ultimate circuit blower—*we are granted the gift of sonship.*

And here we stand speechless.

Is there anything that tops that?

In his book, *Knowing God*, theologian J. I. Packer points out that the climax of the Bible is the revelation to the believer of God as his Father. Packer argues that adoption is the crowning privilege the Gospel offers. Justification is the fundamental blessing; it provides peace with God. But adoption is the *highest* blessing; it leads us into the Father's embrace.

Justification is a forensic concept that views God as the judge who declares us righteous. But adoption is a family idea that sees God as Father who brings us into a deep relationship with Himself. This high privilege takes us beyond freedom from guilt to fellowship, closeness and affection. "To be right with God the judge is a great thing," states Packer, "but to be loved and cared for by God the Father is a greater."[1]

> **Being able to say, "Abba! Father!" is the heart of Christianity and our greatest privilege.**
> —Derek W. H. Thomas

The most exciting part is not what we are redeemed from, but what we are redeemed into. It is marvelous that Jesus Christ, the Lamb of God, takes away the sin of the world. But more marvelous still is the fact that He baptizes us in the Spirit—the Spirit of adoption (Jn. 1:29-33; Rom. 8:15). The removal of sin and corruption is crucial, but the larger purpose is *that we would know His Father as our Father.*

The ultimate reason for Christ's coming is not salvation—*it is adoption.*

Who Is Eligible?

Notice to whom this high and holy privilege is offered:

> *Yet to all who did receive him...* (Jn. 1:12)

The phrase "as many as" means: whoever, whosoever, anyone without exception. It throws the door wide open to every person no matter who they are, or what their past might be. John loves to emphasize the inclusiveness of the invitation, and the words "whoever," "everyone," "anyone" and "all" crop up all through his Gospel.

There is a glorious "wideness" to this invitation. No one should feel excluded or beyond redemption. You don't have to be good. You don't need a good credit rating. You don't have to be smart. You don't have to be anything... you just have to be lost. That's it.

Your sins do not disqualify you. Your lifetime accumulation of lies, lusts and lunacies does not exclude you. All the blunders and badness of humanity were resolved by the One who came "*to take away the sin of the world*" (Jn. 1:29). It has all been put away, disposed of, carted off, finished, discarded, done with. The whole wretched mess, in the words of Robert Capon, has been dropped down the black hole of God's forgetfulness. That is the Gospel, the Good News, without which we would all be in the soup.

The only thing that can stand in anyone's way is their non-acceptance of God's gift of grace. Nobody misses eternal joy because of his sins, but because of rejecting Christ. And we have yet to find one good reason why such a choice would make any sense.

Predestined for Adoption

Believers in Christ are the receivers of the most preposterous gift ever offered—the right to become children of God. When we stood guilty before God, the judge declared, "Pardoned!" He also announced: "We just adopted you." The Supreme Judge becomes our Father. The Son of God becomes our brother in the family of God (Heb. 2:11-12). And the Holy Spirit unites us to this eternal celebration of love and glory.

How amazing is that!

> *But when the set time had fully come, God sent his Son, born of a woman, born under the law, to redeem those under the law, THAT WE MIGHT RECEIVE ADOPTION TO SONSHIP* (Gal. 4:4-5).

WHAT STORY HAVE WE FALLEN INTO?

The Son of God was sent to bring us into the life and love of God. The High King of heaven, it appears, did not want to be God without us. He purposed to expand the circle of eternal joy and include countless others in it. This was not an afterthought—*this was the original plan*.

Look what Paul says in Ephesians 1:

> *Praise be to the God and Father of our Lord Jesus Christ, who has blessed us in the heavenly realms with every spiritual blessing in Christ. For he chose us in him before the creation of the world to be holy and blameless in his sight. In love he predestined us for adoption to sonship through Jesus Christ, in accordance with his pleasure and will—to the praise of his glorious grace, which he has freely given us in the One he loves* (Eph. 1:3-6).

The apostle has seen something breathtaking and glorious. He is overcome with astonished wonder, and his words tumble out in joyful profusion as he attempts to describe what he has seen. He writes the longest sentence in the New Testament without taking a breath. He wants to wake us up to the glory of it all.

What is Paul so excited about?

Notice what he is saying. He talks about the creation of the world—not the fact that it was created by God, but the *why* of its creation. Paul points out that there was a plan formulated before anything else existed. This eternal plan is the key to our story.

The divine plan centers in "adoption." This eternal purpose, born in God's heart of love, involved creating us, making us *"holy and blameless in his sight"* (mending all our brokenness), and adopting us into His family. Before the universe came into existence, Father, Son and Holy Spirit purposed with boundless delight that we should participate as beloved children in the love and joy of the Trinity.

The original plan, the mystery, the secret of the universe has to do with *adoption*. This is the reason we are here. This is what our story is all about. *We were predestined for adoption*. Paul is telling us why God created us. Adoption was not an idea the Creator came up with after giving us existence. It was not even God's forethought; it was His eternal thought.

The Story of our adoption predates the existence of the cosmos.

The Eternal Plan

Why would God do something like this?

Paul gives us the answer—it was done *"in love"* (Eph. 1:4). There is no explanation for it outside of the lavish, relentless, unshakeable, uncontainable love of God. It is a love beyond reason and beyond measure. There is more than enough love in the triune God to flood an entire universe—*and He decided to create one.*

The apostle declares the adoption plan was done *"in accordance with his pleasure and will."* God absolutely loved the idea! He was delighted with the thought of having us in His family. Can you wrap your mind around that?

The Eternal God makes this astounding assertion:

I have loved you with an everlasting love (Jer. 31:3).

Every love has a starting point—except for this one. It existed before time began. Here is love beyond comprehension. "Our sonship rests on a love that never began as well as a love that will never end," writes Michael P. V. Barrett.[2]

A Dutch theologian famously said, "The best proof that He will never cease to love us lies in that He never began."[3]

> **To be adopted as children of God is surely to be at home in the most profound sense.**
>
> —BARRY L. CALLEN

Adopted and Begotten

John states that our sonship is not based merely on a legal transaction, but on *procreation*—by being *"born of God"* (Jn. 1:13). The Bible distinguishes between *"bios,"* biological life inherited from our parents, and *"zoe,"* spiritual life only Christ can impart. *"In him was life* [zoe]*,"* (Jn. 1:4), and *"whoever* believes in him may have eternal life" [zoe] (Jn. 3:15). Every child of Adam is born into this world with *"bios."* However, there are those who have received *"zoe"*—and they are children of God.

John marvels that we have truly become sons and daughters of the Father.

> *See what great love the Father has lavished on us, that we should be called children of God! And that is what we are!* (1 Jn. 3:1; see also 1 Jn. 4:7; 5:1).

In 2 Peter 1:4, we find the stunning statement that believers *"share in the divine nature."* We have His DNA.

C. S. Lewis suggests that the difference between the *"bios"* and *"zoe"* is the difference between a statue and a real man. Statues are created objects, while men are procreated beings. "This world is a great sculptor's shop," says Lewis. "We are the statutes and there is a rumor going round the shop that some of us are some day going to come to life."[4]

Our True Identity

One day, at the Jordan River, when Jesus was baptized, His Father announced from heaven, *"This is my beloved Son in whom I am well pleased."* We are given a glimpse of the outpouring of love that goes on between the Father and His Beloved Son.

The miracle of the Gospel has widened the circle. The Father now turns to each believer in Christ and declares, "You are my beloved son, you are my beloved daughter, in whom I am well pleased."

Define yourself as radically loved by God. This is your true identity.

Sadly, this marvelous "you are mine" often gets drowned out by the voices of our unworthiness, guilt and doubts. Why do we listen to these imposters? Why give them any credence? The Lord of heaven and earth has spoken. We must listen to Him.

What was the greatest concern of the apostle Paul? Martyn Lloyd-Jones, a respected Bible teacher of the 20th century, gives this answer: "that we should know and realize that we are sons of God." The profound and vital truth that God is our "Abba" is what the Spirit of God longs to reveal to us (Rom. 8:16).

His Love is Firm

John Owen, one of the greatest puritan theologians, wrote,

> The love of the Father is unchangeable. Though we change every day, yet his love does not change. If anything in us or on our part could stop God loving us, then he would long ago have turned away from us. It is because his love is fixed and unchangeable that the Father shows us infinite patience and forearance.[5]

Prominent New Testament scholar, Gordon Fee, after completing a masterful commentary on 1 Corinthians, was giving a lecture on this epistle. He came to chapter 13, the love chapter, and read these verses:

> *If I speak in the tongues of men or of angels, but do not have love, I am only a resounding gong or a clanging cymbal. If I have the gift of prophecy and can fathom all mysteries and all knowledge, and if I have a faith that can move mountains, but do not have love, I am nothing. If I give all I possess to the poor and give over my body to hardship that I may boast, but do not have love, I gain nothing.*
>
> *Love is patient, love is kind. It does not envy, it does not boast, it is not proud. It does not dishonor others, it is not self-seeking, it is not easily angered, it keeps no record of wrongs. Love does not delight in evil but rejoices with the truth. It always protects, always trusts, always hopes, always perseveres.*
>
> *Love never fails. But where there are prophecies, they will cease; where there are tongues, they will be stilled; where there is knowledge, it will pass away.*

WHAT STORY HAVE WE FALLEN INTO?

Dr. Fee commented that, when he was working on his commentary, he arrived at this chapter, and sat lost in thought. What could he possibly say about it? Has a more sublime piece of poetry ever been written? What could a theologian possibly add to it?

And then God spoke to him: "Gordon, do you understand, this is the way I love you?"

"Yes, Lord."

"Gordon, what if it were not so?"

And Gordon Fee, a large outspoken man, cried like a baby for an hour.

What if it were not so? What if God loved as we did—within limits, reluctantly sparingly, sporadically. When prompted by a sense of obligation. When it was convenient.

What if it were not so? What if God's love were like ours?

His love is *not* like ours. It is Calvary-like. It is unshakeable, immeasurable, unending, unwavering. Humanity did everything possible to persuade God to stop loving us—and we failed miserably. Here is love that even crucifixion cannot quench.

> *We need to open the eyes of faith and see the smile of our heavenly Father.*
> —Tim Chester

Being the Beloved

Brennan Manning writes,

> Living in awareness of our belovedness is the axis around which the Christian life revolves. Being the beloved is our identity, the core of our existence. It is not merely a lofty thought, an inspiring idea, or one name among many. It is the name by which God knows us and the way He relates to us.[6]

No longer need we build our sense of worth on the shifting sands of what we can acquire or achieve. Our identity is anchored in the God who says to us, "You are my child, my beloved one."

The riddle of our story has been cracked open—a better story could not be imagined.

PRAYER

HEAVENLY FATHER, it may strike some as presumptuous to address the Lord God who reigns on high as "Father," but we dare to use the word—because this is what Your Beloved Son taught us. "Our Father…" This word is music to our ears. And, if that were not enough, the Holy Spirit teaches us to cry, "Abba." What an unspeakable honor, what a shocking privilege has been granted to us! Open our eyes to perceive the wonder of it all! Not slaves but sons! Knowing that we are cared for, loved, delighted in by the Father fills us with great joy. It spurs us to be steadfast in running the race—to serve, to love, to give of ourselves. It gives us a song to sing. It compels us to praise and honor the God who dares to call us His children. We give glory to Your Name, oh God our Father. Amen.

The incarnation is the universe-sundering, history-altering, life-transforming, paradigm-shattering event of history.

—Timothy Keller

CHAPTER FIFTEEN

THE HUMAN FACE OF GOD

The Word became flesh and made his dwelling among us.
JOHN 1:14

ONE OF THE ENIGMAS that has puzzled scientists for many years is the exact nature of light. Is it a wave or a particle? Some experiments demonstrate the wave-like nature of light, others show it acts like a particle. Light behaves both as waves and particles at the same time.

Confusing?

Welcome to the mysterious world of quantum mechanics!

Danish physicist, Niels Bohr declared, "If quantum mechanics hasn't profoundly shocked you, you haven't understood it yet."

The wave-particle debate has compelling evidence on both sides. This finally led scientists to the conclusion that *both* theories are correct. At the same time.

Is light a wave or a particle?

It's both. Sort of.

Albert Einstein wrote, "We are faced with a new kind of difficulty. We have two contradictory pictures of reality; separately neither of them fully explains the phenomena of light, but together they do."[1]

The Dual Nature of Light

Two thousand years ago, Jesus identified Himself as *"the Light of the World."*

And, interestingly enough, the exact nature of who He really is became an enigma. Listen to comments made about Him in the book of John:

> *Rabbi, you are the Son of God* (1:49).
> *Are you greater than our father Jacob?* (4:12).
> *Could this be the Messiah?* (4:29).
> *You are the Holy One of God* (6:69).
> *Some said, "He is a good man." Others replied, "No, he deceives the people"* (7:12).
> *Surely this man is the Prophet* (7:40).
> *Are you greater than our father Abraham? . . . Who do you think you are?* (8:53).
> *This man is not from God* (9:16).
> *If this man were not from God, he could do nothing* (9:33).
> *You, a mere man, claim to be God* (10:33).

Conflicting opinions abounded. What John said was true:

> *And the light shines in the darkness, and the darkness did not comprehend it* (Jn. 1:5 NKJV).

Is He God? Is He a man? There were people on both sides of the debate.

Are we back to quantum mechanics?

The Man Who Was God

Many centuries before scientists discovered the dual nature of light, the apostle John spoke of the dual nature of the Light of the World. He was two millennia ahead of his time.

The Word became flesh and made his dwelling among us (Jn. 1:14).

Is He God or man?

Both. In Jesus, God took on humanity. To say He is a man does not explain Him. Neither does it suffice to say He is God. We must affirm *both*. He is the God/man. Fully God and fully man—in one person. Deity and humanity have come together. Jesus is the human life of God.

The Word became tangible, physical, vulnerable.

And admittedly, the mystery of godliness is great: God was manifested in the flesh (1 Tim. 3:16 RGT).

To paraphrase Niels Bohr, "If the incarnation hasn't profoundly shocked you, you haven't understood it yet."

"The more you think about it, the more staggering it gets," writes J. I. Packer. "Nothing in fiction is so fantastic as this truth of the Incarnation."[2]

The Central Miracle

In John 1:14, we come to the center-piece of John's prologue. The previous verses move toward it, and the following ones flow from it. "It might well be held that this is the single greatest verse in the New Testament," suggests Scottish theologian William Barclay.[3]

This text refers to the Incarnation, the staggering reality that the Almighty became a mortal man. Here we are confronted with the astonishing descent of the Holy One who came to us in our fallenness, weakness and estrangement. He immersed Himself in our humanity. The Most High became the Most Near.

The cosmic gap has been closed.

The Incarnation means that a card-carrying member of the Holy Trinity is now part of the human race. He bridged the uncrossable divide between Creator and creation, between Divinity and humanity. He became our blood relative, our next of kin. A member of the Godhead has a body of flesh and bone—just like ours.

He is one of us.

Literally.

Down-to-Earth Spirituality

This foundational fact of the Christian faith—*the Word became flesh*—clobbers the Gnostic idea that the material world is somehow evil or illusory. It also overturns the tables on those who subscribe to a world-denying spirituality.

The Incarnation forces us to rethink our ideas about nature and matter and the physical world. It shipwrecks the false separation of "sacred" and "secular."

The "Word made flesh" is thoroughly human. He grew, breathed, walked, ate, drank, worked and wept. He experienced working with wood, eating dried figs, basking in sunshine, cooking breakfast on the beach and laughing with friends. The Creator, who at the beginning of time looked upon his creation and declared it to be good, now tasted, touched, smelled and felt its goodness.

It is often heard in wedding ceremonies that, by His presence in the wedding at Cana of Galilee, Christ blessed and sanctified marriage. However, a wedding was not the *only* place He showed up: He toiled at a carpenter's bench, strolled through markets and meadows, went boating on a lake, enjoyed meals in the homes of friends and hiked up mountains. The unavoidable conclusion is this—Christ sanctified *every* sphere of human activity.

Jesus of Nazareth is our most compelling evidence that "spiritual" and "material" are not to be separated. Supernatural and natural belong together. The fact that Holiness took on humanity forces us to reconstruct our understanding of "spiritual."

The duties and delights of daily human life are not obstacles, but opportunities for spirituality. We can honor God as we cook, paint, dance, write novels, compose music, fly kites, run a business or grow orchids. In Christ the joys, pains, pleasures and struggles of earthly living are the very context of godly living and worship.

We are not called to take flight into some spiritual stratosphere of mystical experience. We are called to live in a physical body in a physical world—to the glory of God.

Christian spirituality is not an other-worldly affair. It is about becoming truly human—like Jesus. It entails embracing the miracle of God's real presence in our life, in our work, and in our world. It involves celebrating sunsets, roses, coffee, family and all of God's good gifts with gratitude and joy.

So slow down. Stop. Look. And, like Moses, take off your shoes because holy is all around us in the common stuff of everyday life. "Earth is crammed with heaven, and every bush is aflame with the glory of God," wrote Elizabeth Browning.

Spirituality is a down-to-earth matter.

If God truly became human—how could it be otherwise?

A Redemptive Connection

God and man are now inseparably connected. The Lord of the universe has become a part of our story. And a part of our predicament. He has thrown His lot in with us. *Immanuel* turns out to mean—we are in this together. He has joined our ranks to such a degree that our dilemma has become His dilemma. Our misfortune has become His.

> *The Incarnation is proof that God is not against us.*
> —Martin Luther

He got embroiled in our brokenness—more than any self-respecting God ever should have.

Immersed in our mess.

He was not about to abandon His fellow humans to their plight. He embraced our burden. He shouldered our cause.

We are no longer alone in our distress. Hope has come.

We have a Redeemer.

Quantum Spirituality

Normally, when the author of the play walks on the stage, you know the play is over.

But not in this story.

The Story Writer crossed over into our world, not to be applauded, *but to be an actor in the drama.* Not to be told what a fine story He had written, but to salvage a story that had gone off the rails. The Alpha and Omega of the whole project came to rescue it from ruin, and steer it towards a glorious finale.

This is either the most ridiculous thing we ever heard, or the best news that has reached our world.

John dares us to believe that the Creator actually stepped inside His creation. The One who scripted our existence showed up incognito and became part of our world. He immersed Himself in all the "down-to-earth" realities of human life. He was known as Jesus of Nazareth. He so identified with our world that no one suspected He was from another one.

The drama of our planet has taken a fascinating twist.

Scholarly men of ancient times once declared, *"gods don't live among mortals"* (Dn. 2:11). That sounds like a reasonable claim, but the Gospel dares to counter it. It declares that an "incarnation" has taken place. That among the many humans who live on this planet—*one of them is God!*

> **The Incarnation is the central fact of the entire history of the world.**
> —Herman Bavinck

And it dares to say that *this is the main event in the whole Story.*

How could the Author of our Story possibly move into our neighborhood? We were invented; He is the Inventor. We have life, He is the Life-Giver. We were scripted, He is the Script Writer.

Has anything like this ever happened in the universe?

The Ultimate Mystery

The Incarnation, according to one theologian, is "the most profound mystery in all the universe." Here is, as an ancient prophet said, water that not only comes to your ankles, your knees, or your waist, but water to swim in (Ezek. 47). We are never going to get to the bottom of this, but let's dive in and reflect on this magnificent mystery.

The One who joined Himself to our humanity, is, of course, the One who is eternally joined to the Trinity. Verse fourteen needs to be read in the light of verse one.

> *In the beginning was the Word,*
> *and the Word was with God,*
> *and the Word was God.*

With these three statements, the apostle turned everything we knew about Deity on its head. He opened a window into the wonder, the mystery and the profound beauty of the Trinity. He pointed us to an understanding of God as "a perichoresis of love, a dynamic coinherence of the three divine persons, whose life is eternally one of shared regard, delight, fellowship, feasting and joy.[4]

The Matrix of Reality

Long before anything else existed, the great dance of Trinitarian life was going on. It is the eternal celebration of life-giving love and unfettered joy of the Father, Son and Holy Spirit. Three Divine Persons whose love for each other is so rich, so strong, so deep they actually become ONE.

What does this have to do with the Incarnation?

> The amazing truth is that this Triune God, in staggering and lavish love, determined to open the circle and share the Trinitarian life with others. This is the one, eternal and abiding reason for the existence of the universe and human life within it. There is no other God, no other will of God, no second plan, no hidden agenda for human beings. From the beginning, God is Father, Son and Spirit, and from the beginning, this God has determined not to exist without us.[6]

This is the mind-boggling meaning of the Incarnation. This is why the *"Word became flesh."* The One who lives in the Father's eternal embrace came into our world in order to bring us into

His. He became human in order to share this life with us. He came, not merely to fix the Fall, He came to elevate us to the status of sonship in the family of God. "Atonement" was the first step; the final goal was ADOPTION.

The Incarnation forged "at-one-ment" with us in order to bring us to "at-one-ment" with God.

> *He became what we are that He might make us what He is.*
> —Athanasius

Heavy Lifting

Years ago, a bridge was being built over the Hudson River when a problem arose. In the very spot where one of the pilings was to be located, they found a sunken ship at the bottom of the river. Crews were brought in to remove the wreck, but the old ship was lodged deep in the mud and could not be budged.

A man showed up who claimed he could do the job. A large barge was towed to the spot, and when the tide was at its lowest, he sent down divers with chains and cables and attached them to the sunken ship. Then the man sat down to wait.

After a while, the tide began to rise. As the barge rose, the cables tightened. The water level continued to rise and the sunken ship was lifted off the bottom and successfully moved to another location. What motors and pulleys could not accomplish was achieved by the silent rise of the tide.

Not unlike that shipwreck, humanity had sunken into the mire of sin, and all attempts to raise us up had proved unsuccessful. We were "stuck" in a bad place.

Then God surprised us.

He came into our world, and by becoming a man, He connected Himself to our humanity. The taking-on-of-flesh was the forging of an unbreakable link between God and man, between heaven and earth. He became one of us with a view to lifting us up. He entered our place of death and darkness, and was then raised back to life. And not only did He rise—so did all those who believe in Him.

Paul describes it like this:

> *But because of his great love for us, God, who is rich in mercy, made us alive with Christ even when we were dead in transgressions—it is by grace you have been saved. And God raised us up with Christ and seated us with him in the heavenly realms in Christ Jesus* (Eph. 2:4-6).

Lifting us up out of the mire is wonderful enough—but it doesn't end there. God had greater plans. He lifts us up from "muddy places" to "heavenly places." We are brought from death to life, from "wreckage" to glory, from fallenness to exaltedness. Believers end up seated with Christ in the highest possible place of honor in the universe.

That's a circuit-blower if there ever was one!

Mission Accomplished

Please notice that this "lifting up" was entirely God's doing. It was determined before the foundation of the world that God's Son would take on the responsibility to carry out this plan. He is the One who would bring it to pass.

We were chosen "in Him," predestined to adoption "through Him," accepted "in Him." The entire responsibility for our redemption was placed into His hands. He accomplished it—*and finished it.*

The Incarnate Christ crossed all worlds and plunged into the midst of human brokenness and alienation. Through His death and resurrection, sin was cancelled, death was defeated and the Fall was undone. His ascension to glory was our ascension—our inclusion into the circle of the Father's fellowship and joy.

The Gospel showers a colossal volume of spiritual blessings upon believers (Eph. 1:3). Those who by faith are "in Christ" (as opposed to being "in Adam") are made holy and blameless, they are adopted and accepted. Christ's righteousness becomes their righteousness. Christ's acceptance is their acceptance. They have eternal life, which consists in sharing in the overflow of the Father's boundless love for the Son in the fellowship of the Spirit.

Notice what Christ shares with those who belong to Him:

- His peace becomes our peace (14:27)
- His love becomes our love (15:9)
- His joy becomes our joy (15:11; 17:13)
- His glory becomes our glory (17:22)
- His Father becomes our Father (20:17)
- His mission becomes our mission (20:21)

We have been given a staggering gift, the gift of participating in the shared life and love of the triune God.

This is the secret of our story.

This was the plan from eternity. The life, death and resurrection of the Logos turned it into an accomplished fact. It has taken place.

Stop and take this in.

We are not called upon to repair our relationship with God or regain His favor. Nor could we. That task was given to someone else —and He carried it out perfectly. This is wonderful news. *It is done.*

The Incarnate Christ is the strong basis of our confidence before God. He is our reconciliation, our acceptance, our belovedness. He is our assurance of sonship and eternal glory. "Jesus was God and man in one person, that God and man might be happy together again," stated George Whitefield.

> *And you yourselves, who were strangers to God ... he has now reconciled through the death of his body on the cross, so that he might welcome you to his presence clean and pure, without blame or reproach* (Col. 1:21 PHLP).

Our wrongness has been made right.

In Christ we are ransomed, healed, restored, forgiven.

The Father now says to us, "I have embraced you and adopted you. You are mine."

It doesn't get any better than that.

PRAYER

BLESSED GOD AND FATHER, it fills us with amazement to think that Your Son, who was eternally connected with the triune God, through His incarnation, has become connected to the human race. Bone of our bone, flesh of our flesh. It was not a visitation, but an incarnation. The Creator acquired kinship with His creatures. No longer is God simply God, He is also man. No longer is deity separate from humanity, they have become one. The Most High has become the Most Near. He is Immanuel—God with us, unalterably, unashamedly, unmistakably with us. God is with us, God is for us. We praise You, our God, for this marvelous fact. Our hearts sing with gratitude that You came to us in our lostness and in our fallenness. What a wonderful God You are! We honor You and bless your Holy Name. Amen.

*God is better than we thought.
Much better than we feared.
Better even than we dared
to believe.*

—John Eldredge

CHAPTER SIXTEEN

THE STORY OF HIS GLORY

We have seen his glory . . .
JOHN 1:14

TWELVE MEN WERE GRANTED the high privilege of accompanying the Rabbi from Nazareth for three years. John was one of them. It was an unspeakable honor. Sixty years later, as the aged apostle reflects on that unique experience, he sums it up with one concise phrase:

We saw his glory (Jn. 1:14).

What did he mean by that?

We use the word "glory" to speak of magnificence, splendor, grandeur or exceptional beauty. It describes something stunningly spectacular, that snags our attention, that makes us catch our breath. Most often it is used with reference to God—the overwhelming splendor of His excellence, His superlative praiseworthiness.

When John searched for a word to describe Jesus the Messiah, the best term he could find was: "glory."

There was something strikingly beautiful about this man from Galilee. There was a wise and majestic gentleness, an exquisite attractiveness and goodness about His life. It was so compelling, so captivating, that as a young man, John had left everything—his boat, his business, his buddies—to follow the Master.

Glory Displayed

We get helpful insight into the idea of "glory" in an event that took place on Mount Sinai. Moses had witnessed a spectacular series of miracles during Israel's exodus from Egypt, but he had one special request: "Please, show me Your glory" (Ex. 33:18). How would the Divine Lord answer? By displaying His power? His holiness? His majesty? Notice God's response:

> *And the LORD said, I will cause all my GOODNESS to pass in front of you* (Ex. 33:19).

God *switched* the word! Instead of glory, He used the term "goodness." This is significant. Everything about God radiates perfection and beauty. But there is one aspect in particular to which the term "glory" points—*His overflowing goodness.* His magnanimous generosity, His boundless benevolence. God is indescribably good. Here lies the essence of His splendor.

The glory of God is radiant and outgoing. As the sun never ceases to give light and heat, so God's glory is relentlessly outward-focused and self-giving. Divine glory is not about taking, but *giving.* It is the shining forth of goodness, favor and love.

The other-centeredness of divine glory is rooted in the triune identity of God. Father, Son and Holy Spirit interact in a self-giving relationship of love and joy. In the New Testament, and particularly in the book of John, we see each member of the Trinity loving, delighting in, giving to and honoring the other. They do not hoard glory, they deflect it. The persons of the divine community are so deeply and fully other-focused—*that they are one.* It is here we find the basis for affirming that God is *one* and God is *love.*[1]

The Bible declares: "*No one should seek their own good, but the good of others*" (1 Cor. 10:24). The triune God is the supreme example of this other-centered love. His glory does not consist in self-promotion but in self-giving. He is so overflowingly complete in Himself that He finds His greatest joy in spreading goodness, in transmitting blessing, in extending favor.

> *God is like the sun at high noon, always giving all he has.*
> —A. J. Gossip

God's glory is lavish self-giving benevolence.

And never was the glorious radiance of God's love seen more clearly than when *"the Word was made flesh and made his dwelling among us."*

When Glory Came Down

John uses the word "glory" more than all the other Gospel writers combined. He tells us that the divine glory, once centered in the tabernacle (Ex. 40:34), has come out into the open. The glory that could not be seen by Moses has become visible. On Sinai, the Lord declared that no one could contemplate His glory and live (Ex. 33:20), and yet now humans gaze upon it and they do not die. As a matter of fact, as John points out all through his Gospel, it is only by looking upon the glory of God in Christ *that we truly live.*

N. T. Wright points out,

> John invites us to be still and know what God is like. He invites us to look into the human face of Jesus of Nazareth, until the awesome knowledge comes over us that we are looking into the human face of the living God.[2]

Jesus is the glory of God in human form.

This is the theme of John's Gospel. The Gospel of Matthew points to Jesus as the King of Israel. Mark shows us the Perfect Servant ministering to the needy and the lost. Luke sees Christ as the bringer of salvation. But, John has a unique focus—*he wants to show us the glory of God.*

What Glory Looks Like

The Fourth Gospel is wrapped around seven miracles or "signs" that put the glory of God on display; they are miracles with a message. Not unlike the seven days of creation, these are seven signs of the new creation. The One who made all things by the power of His word speaks again—He now speaks words of joy, hope, renewal, liberation and life.

In John 2, Jesus is present at a wedding. He does not simply turn water into wine, but into *Cabernet Sauvignon* of superb quality. And, plenty of it! It signaled the joyful abundance of His kingdom. We are told this is the "first" sign (2:11). Clearly there's more to come. This is only the beginning. It only gets better— and the best wine is yet to come.

Next, the Master performed two miracles of healing. He restored to health the son of a royal official from over 20 miles away, and then raised up a man who had been bed-ridden for thirty-eight years. Now His glory dispels illness and paralysis. It fixes what's wrong. It will ultimately restore all that is damaged, twisted, broken, wounded and ravaged. It makes all things new.

The fourth sign comes in chapter six. Five barley loaves and two fish were turned into a feast for 5,000. The supply was greater than the need, and the crowd was unable to finish all the food. When they could eat no more, twelve baskets of leftovers remained. Jesus explained the sign by identifying Himself as the Bread of Life. Here is a Christ abundantly able to satisfy the hunger of human hearts—and in Him there is inexhaustible fullness.

In chapter 9, a man born blind recovers his sight. It is a delightful story that dramatizes the Lord's claim to be the Light of the World. We were not made to live in darkness, and Someone has come to bring us back into the light. This glorious Christ brings light into darkened hearts and into a benighted world—and the darkness cannot overpower it.

Then, in chapter 11, a man who had died and been buried for four days is called back from the dead. Jesus did not do funerals —He did *resurrections*. He said to the man's sister:

> *Did I not tell you that if you believe, you will see the glory of God?* (Jn. 11:40).

Quite a display of glory! It is the glory of the life-giving, death-vanquishing Christ. He came so that we may have life. (Jn. 10:10).

That makes six signs. Six dramatic demonstrations of Christ's power to put right what has gone wrong in our world. But, where is number seven? Chapter two gives us a hint:

> *The Jews then responded to him, "What sign can you show us to prove your authority to do all this?" Jesus answered them, "Destroy this temple, and I will raise it again in three days"* (Jn. 2:18,19).

What is He talking about? He is speaking of His death and resurrection. The entire book of John points to Sign Number Seven. The writer is inviting us to see Christ's death at Calvary as the greatest manifestation of God's glory.

But, how could the cross be a place of glory? Nothing is as inglorious as dying on a cross. Crucifixion is as far removed from glory as you can possibly get. What is John saying to us?

Redefining Glory

The apostle forces us to rethink our understanding of "glory." After declaring at the beginning of his book, *"we saw his glory,"* John then uses the term increasingly as Jesus approaches the cross. He refers to "glory" in a most unusual and disconcerting manner. He turns our concept of this word on its head.

Notice what Christ says as He anticipates His death on a cross:

> *The hour has come for the Son of Man to be glorified. Truly, truly, I say to you, unless a grain of wheat falls into the earth and dies, it remains alone; but if it dies, it bears much fruit. . . . Now is my soul troubled. And what shall I say? "Father, save me from this hour"? But for this purpose I have come to this hour. "Father, glorify your name." Then a voice came from heaven: "I have glorified it, and I will glorify it again"* (Jn. 12:23,24,27,28 ESV).

Jesus opens and closes this section with the word "glory." It appears that "glory" has something to do with what is about to happen at Calvary. It is connected with the cross.

Here we run up against an understanding of glory that baffles us. It has nothing to do with glamor and elegance. There is nothing glitzy about it. Nothing ostentatious. *Glory is getting redefined.*

On three occasions Jesus speaks of His imminent death as the hour of His "glorification" (Jn. 12:23; 13:31; 17:1). Our Lord is clearly referring to the cross, and He makes a puzzling connection between death and glory. In John's Gospel, the cross, the ultimate symbol of "shame"—turns out to be "glory." The cross is not the humiliation of the Son of God. *It is His glorification.*

The death of Christ on a cross caused God's glory to shine forth as the crushing of a rose releases its fragrance.

"Glory" has taken on a deep mysterious splendor.

Two Moments of Glory

In contrast to the other Gospel writers, John makes no mention of Christ's glorious appearance on the Mount of Transfiguration. Although the Beloved Apostle witnessed that mystical moment of glory, in the Fourth Gospel the "glory" of God's Son is put on display on a different mountain—Mount Calvary. Here it is not Moses and Elijah who accompany Jesus, but two robbers. On this occasion, His face does not shine "like the sun," rather the sun hides its face and leaves the world in darkness. Here no voice from heaven is heard to declare the Son's belovedness. Rather Jesus tastes utter forsakenness—the place of forsakenness where our sins were dragging us. It is to that place that we were headed —*but Someone went there in our stead!*

What a staggering contrast there is between these two moments of "glory." In the first instance, our Lord was *"transfigured,"* in the second He was *"disfigured,"* as Isaiah said, and *"marred beyond human likeness"* (Isa. 52:14). In the Transfiguration, we see the splendor of His majesty. In the crucifixion we see *the splendor of His love*—the greater glory of His grace.

The Glory of the Cross

It is the supreme paradox that Christ never was so glorious as when He became horribly inglorious. It was in the moment of greatest ugliness His beauty shone most brightly. It was in the place of utmost shame that His splendor blazed forth. The crucifixion of the incarnate God did not extinguish His glory—*it revealed it.*

"Glory" was nailed to a cross and lifted up for all to see. It was the glory of His self-giving, self-sacrificing, redeeming, restoring love.

The inglorious cross is the final, supreme and shocking revelation of the glory of God, the unveiling of His heart of love for a lost and rebellious world. The cross is God loving a world gone wrong, and coming in person to take its agony and brokenness upon Himself. The cross is God's Son drinking a cup brimming with the bitterness of human sin.

Charles Spurgeon said it well: "It seemed as if hell were put into His cup; He seized it, and at one tremendous draught of love, He drank damnation dry."

The cross is God spelling out the meaning of our story with wood and spikes. It was where God's only Son was broken for the love of you and me. The meaning of the Story is a Calvary kind of love. A love that *"bears all things, believes all things, hopes all things, and endures all things"* (1 Cor. 13:7 NKJV).

The glory of God turns out to be the love of God.

Unveiling the Glory

At the moment of Christ's death, the curtain in the temple that concealed the glory of God's presence was ripped open. And rightly so. God's glory was no longer hidden. It had come into plain view through the crucified Christ.

John Calvin writes:

> In the cross of Christ, as in a splendid theatre, the incomparable goodness of God is set before the whole world. The glory of God shines, indeed, in all creatures on high and below, but never more brightly that in the cross…[3]

WHAT STORY HAVE WE FALLEN INTO?

"*We saw His glory*" ultimately turns out to mean, "we saw Him lay down His life for us on a cross."

> *The cross, that terrible gallows, had become a tree of glory.*
>
> —Tom Holland

The darkness of our world was pierced by the light of His love. A love greater than our sin and stronger than death. A love that reveals the exquisite beauty of God.

Alexander MacLaren points out that it is not in the "majestic attributes" that we find the true glory of God's character. There is something more godlike in God than the fact that He is all powerful, all knowing, all wise, omnipresent. McLaren says, "Not in any or in all of these lies the glory of God, but in His love. These are the fringes of the brightness; this is the central blaze."[4]

Glen Scrivener writes:

> Wind the clock back all the way through time, before creation, back and back and back into the depths of eternity and you will find Jesus with His Father loving and serving each other in the power of the Spirit. That's what the Trinity has ALWAYS been up to. That IS the eternal life of God. So on the cross, when we see Jesus giving Himself up to the Father we see the eternal glory of God. At the cross when we see the Father GIVING His Son to the world, we see the eternal glory of God. The cross *is* God's glory. And it's the glory of infinite SELF-GIVING love. God's glory is His grace. It is His very "Godness" to give Himself away to us and for us.[5]

Love is not one of His many attributes—*it is His identity.* It is the essence of who God is. It is what makes God glorious and supremely beautiful. God is love—*and that is His glory.*

Crucifixion had always been about torture and shame. It was the ultimate disgrace. No one ever dreamed a Roman cross could be glorious. Until God got on one.

He makes all things glorious.

Even a shameful cross.

Such is the greatness of His glory.

PRAYER

LORD OF GOODNESS AND GLORY, You sent your Son and gave us a close-up glimpse of Your glory—and we stand amazed. Everything about Him is stunningly beautiful—His compassion for the hurting, His friendship for the fallen, His love for the unlovely. We cannot but admire His unpretentious humility, His overflowing goodness, His limitless wisdom. But when we get to the cross of Calvary, we are left without words. The Beautiful One is disfigured, the Holy One is put to open shame, the sinless one is crucified with criminals. And it is in the blood and tears and grief of Christ that we see the shocking beauty of God's "glory." Indeed, "here is love, vast as the ocean." Here is mercy in an overwhelming flood. We can only bow in grateful worship before You, oh God of our salvation. Amen.

*The most striking thing
about our Lord is
the union of great ferocity
with extreme tenderness.*

—C. S. Lewis

CHAPTER SEVENTEEN

GRACE AND TRUTH

We have seen his glory ... full of grace and truth.
JOHN 1:14

VEDRAN SMAIJLOVIC, the lead cellist of the Sarajevo Opera, took his place. In full formal attire, he grasped his bow and began to play Albinoni's Adagio in G Minor.

He was not in a concert hall.

He sat amidst the devastation of his city Sarajevo. The noted musician was playing his cello in the very place where a bomb had fallen killing 22 people who were lined up to buy bread at a bakery. The Bosnian war was bringing death and destruction to his city. But now, in the midst of the rubble, Vedran played his cello.

Many people expressed their appreciation for the unexpected concert. The cellist went back the next day and continued to play his instrument. He did so for 22 days—one for each person killed at that location.

He went to play in other sites where mortar shells had claimed the lives of Sarajevo's citizens. In the midst of the wreckage and ugliness, beautiful music was heard. No one knew where he would play next, but wherever Vedran went, crowds would gather to listen.

His music was a gift to all the grieving and suffering people of his city. It sent a message of hope and healing to hurting hearts. It inspired people all around the world. The cellist of Sarajevo became a symbol of how beauty stands in resistance to the horrors of war.

Music From Afar

The Maker of all things took on a similar role. The One who had composed "the music of the spheres," who scripted all beauty and goodness and harmony in the universe, did something very audacious. He came into a world shattered by discord and sin. He brought a piece of heaven into a world filled with chaos and confusion. He brought beauty from afar into the shattered streets of our world.

He set up to play music in a scorned village called Nazareth—an unlikely location for a concert from the Creator. *"Nazareth! Can anything good come from there?"* blurted out one man (Jn. 1:46). It was far from being a prestigious concert hall—but it was the place where the highest good and the greatest beauty began to shine.

> *The light shines in the darkness, and the darkness has not overcome it* (Jn. 1:5).

Light came into our darkness. The transcendent symphony was heard amidst the dissonance of a world ruined by the Fall. Beauty came into our brokenness.

Grace and Truth

Unlike Moses who caught a glimmer of the glory of God from behind a rock, John the apostle had a front row seat. He heard, saw and touched the glory of God in human form (1 Jn. 1:1-3). The stunning beauty of that life caused John to exclaim, *"We beheld His glory . . . full of grace and truth."* With these two words, "grace" and "truth," he sums up the delightful blend seen in Jesus of tenderness and truthfulness, of kindness and candor.

> Grace by itself might easily lead to weakness and mere sentimentality. Truth by itself might easily be expressed in rigor, sternness, severity. But when grace is strengthened by truth, and truth is mellowed by grace, we have the perfect character and the true life of man. It is the union of these opposites in Jesus Christ in perfect balance and consistency that demands our attention. Other men are only fragmentary, one-sided, biased. He is complete, balanced, perfect.[1]

Never did grace and truth harmonize as they did in Him. They combined like the words and music of a song. His grace was consoling, captivating, heart-warming. His words of truth were ground-breaking, enlightening, revealing. Grace gushed forth like a spring from a hillside. And truth shone like the morning sun that constrains darkness to pack up and leave. He abounded in grace and truth.

> *"Truth" without grace is not really truth, and "grace" without truth is not really grace.*
>
> —Timothy Keller

Throughout his Gospel, the apostle John shares the stories— the events that transpired when grace and truth walked among us. He helps us hear the music and bask in the beauty of that heaven-sent melody.

Finding More Than Water

John tells of a night-time conversation with a bewildered scholar named Nicodemus. The Master treated him with deep respect and sympathy, and granted him the honor of hearing the richest and most profound presentation on record of the Good News of God's love in John 3:16.

The apostle tells of Jesus sitting by a well where He strikes up a conversation with a woman who has come to draw water. Her life is scarred by multiple broken marriages, and she is living with a man who is not her husband. She has known plenty of rejection, heartache and scornful stares.

Jesus ditches social convention by addressing her in public, and by drinking water from her jug. The woman is blown away by the fact that this stranger knows all about her past, yet treats her with kindness and respect. Forgetting her water pot, she dashes back to the village to tell everyone about the One who had said to her:

> *Whoever drinks of the water that I will give him will never be thirsty again. The water that I will give him will become in him a spring of water welling up to eternal life* (Jn. 4:14 ESV).

The woman arrived with a water jar and went away with a spring of living water. She came with her brokenness and found wholeness. She came with her rejection and found acceptance. She came with questions and went away sharing answers. Her life had been full of quiet desperation. She ran back overflowing with hope.

Christ has tireless concern for those who are floundering. Never do we see Him belittling, ridiculing or mocking anyone. He has genuine respect for each person. His grace and truth reveal both our brokenness and belovedness. When it comes to healing wounded hearts, He has no equal.

"God does not love people because they have sorted themselves out," says Michael Reeves. "He loves failures. And that love makes them flourish."

Astounding Truth

A group of temple guards is dispatched to apprehend this "disruptive" Rabbi from Galilee. The armed men draw near to where the Master was teaching and stop to listen. Among other things, they hear Him say:

Let anyone who is thirsty come to me and drink. Whoever believes in me, as Scripture has said, rivers of living water will flow from within them (Jn. 7:37-38).

The temple police had heard countless sermons—*but never words like these!*

E. Stanley Jones comments,

> His words had the ring of reality about them. Others quoted authorities; he taught with authority of his own insight. Others came seeking truth; he came proclaiming it... and men listened to these words as if they were hearing some long-lost chord, something that belonged to them, that belonged to the very structure and make-up of their being. They felt that this was the soul's homeland.[2]

Unable to comply with their orders, the guards returned empty-handed. "Why didn't you bring him?" demanded the religious leaders. The guards responded sheepishly, *"We never heard anyone speak like this!"* (Jn. 7:46 NLT).

It was impossible to apprehend one so full of grace and truth.

Astonishing the Stone-Throwers

Then, a woman caught in the act of adultery is dragged before Him. It's a cleverly planned trap. The adulteress is thrown at the feet of the Master, where she weeps, head bowed, shame-ridden. The Lord stoops and writes in the sand, refusing to gaze on her shame and add to her anguish. The woman's accusers challenge Christ, and ask if He respects the law's demands for stoning people guilty of this kind of sin.

Pompous and smug, they wait for an answer.

When it finally came, they were flabbergasted: "Let any one of you who is without sin be the first to throw a stone at her."

The faultfinders were thunderstruck. One by one, all stones were dropped. The debate was over.

Jesus had one more thing to say—a word of grace and truth for the woman:

> *Neither do I condemn you . . . Go and leave your life of sin.*

Then Jesus wrapped up the whole affair by declaring:

> *I am the light of the world. Whoever follows me will never walk in darkness, but will have the light of life* (Jn. 8:12).

There was no reason to doubt what He said. The brightness of His light and the warmth of His love was undeniable.

Opening Sightless Eyes

A blind man gets mud smeared on his eyes, and when he washes it off, he sees the light of day—for the first time. He not only regained his sight, but quickly gained spiritual understanding. He recognized Jesus as a "man" (9:11), a "prophet" (9:17), the "Son of God" (9:35) and finally as "Lord" (9:38). Grace and truth turned the man into a worshipper. The religious leaders threw Him out of the temple, but the One who had opened his eyes, took him in.

The more we trace the steps of Jesus the Messiah, the more we are filled with admiration at the stunning beauty of His life. The world has never seen such extravagant goodness, unfaltering tenderness and extraordinary humility. The man from Galilee brought music from a heavenly source and shed light from another world.

> There was something about the Man that made the best of men feel that they were in deepest need. And yet the worst of men felt drawn to him. Here was goodness attractive, winsome, compelling... Here was goodness that was not meticulous, but merciful, not standing on pedestals to be worshiped, but bending in lowly service over the lost. Here was goodness not pharisaical, but friendly, not terrible, but tender... Never did majesty and meekness so blend and become so beautiful as here.[3]

Blending Grace and Truth

Our Lord is a startling synthesis of both grace and truth. He attracts children and frightens demons. He is the friend of sinners, and the enemy of hypocrisy. He lifts the lowly, and blasts the lofty. He sheds tears at a tomb, and then speaks a word that brings the occupant back to life. With tender grace He cleanses a leper; with blistering truth He cleanses the temple.

His words not only give life (Jn. 6:69) and heal bodies (Mt. 8:8), they stifle storms (Mk. 4:39), cause demons to panic (Mk. 1:23), and can wreak havoc on fig trees (Mt. 21:19).

Grace and truth, like the rod and staff of the shepherd, provide protection and correction. The Master, in His wisdom and love, makes optimal use of both. He knows when to prod and when to protect. He knows us, He loves us, and His dealings of grace and truth are exactly what is needed. He's got the balance just right.

Grace in the Garden

On the night of His betrayal, religious leaders arrive in Gethsemane with a detachment of soldiers. They come to apprehend the Rabbi from Nazareth. When He responds, *"ego eimi"*—"I am"—a phrase He used repeatedly, the whole contingent stumbles back and tumbles to the ground (Jn. 18:6). Two words sufficed to leave them flat on their backs. They never could have led Him away had He not allowed it.

And then, as if the Master needed help, Peter springs into action, draws his sword and severs the ear of Malchus, a servant of the High Priest. The Lord graciously reattaches the fallen ear to the man's bleeding head—His last act of healing. The wrong is righted. Any notion of bringing justice to the sword-swinging disciple was effectively derailed. Malchus's superiors would be unable to find any evidence the attack had ever taken place. The incident was erased from history.

The Savior of the world works in a similar manner on behalf of those who turn by faith to Him. By His grace, transgressions are blotted out as if they had never existed. Guilt is gone. He

causes sins to be "remembered no more"—even by an all-knowing God. It appears He causes what took place to have *never* taken place. Expunged from the universe.
Full of grace, indeed.

The Shocking Beauty of God

The exquisite melody of grace and truth was heard wherever He went. But, it was when Christ was falsely accused, condemned, scorned, spit on, flogged, mocked and crucified that the beauty and richness of the music reached new heights. Grace and truth shone as never before.

Mahatma Gandhi recognized the magnificence: "A man who was completely innocent, offered himself as a sacrifice for the good of others, including His enemies, and became the ransom of the world. It was a perfect act."

At Calvary, Christ faced the fierce and full measure of sin's cruelty and animosity. This onslaught, however, was unable to bring to light any weakness or flaw in His character.

> *When he was maligned, he did not answer back; when he suffered, he threatened no retaliation* (1 Pet. 2:23 NET).

The test only served to underscore the untarnished beauty of His goodness, grace and truth.

Admittedly, there's nothing attractive about a man dying on a cross. But there is a strange, hideous beauty about *this* crucifixion.

Look closely. This is the crucifixion of God! The execution of the High King of heaven. It is Abba's Only Begotten who is impaled and suffers in bloody disgrace.

Stand and watch as He refuses to call on heaven's armies to mete out justice on His torturers. Listen as insults are hurled, but no threat is made, or unkind word spoken. Look as He lavishes forgiveness on those who called for His blood. Observe as He agonizes to redeem those who celebrate His suffering.

> This is the gospel of grace. A God, who out of love for us, sent the only Son He ever had wrapped in our skin. He... sweated blood in the night, was lashed with a whip and showered with spit, was fixed to a cross and died whispering forgiveness on us all.[4]

Has there ever been anything so ugly and so beautiful? So hideous and so wonderful?

This is the awful attraction of the cross.

The shocking beauty of God.

The scandalous glory of His grace.

The cross is where God's love and man's sin met head-on. It is the intersection of divine grace and human depravity. It is where earth's cruelty and heaven's mercy collided.

And mercy won.

Love prevailed.

The Power of Love

When Christ declared before Pilate that He had come into the world to testify to the truth, the Roman governor responded cynically, "What is truth?" Never did Pilate imagine that the truth in person was standing right in front of him.

For Pilate, truth was *power*. The power to crucify. The power of violent force that Rome was so good at exercising. This, for Pilate, was ultimate truth—power to crush your enemies, to impose your own agenda. Power enforced by violence.

Jesus understood ultimate reality to be radically different. In his book, *Beauty Will Save the World,* Brian Zahnd comments on the deep irony that Pilate and Christ could both have made the statement, "The cross is truth," and by that mean opposite things. For Pilate, ultimate reality meant power, and ultimate power is the power to kill.

And Jesus could have replied, "Yes, the cross is truth." But *not* in the way Pilate had in mind. The cross is truth, not in the power to kill, but in the choice to love. *Ultimate truth is not the power of violence, but the power of love.*

WHAT STORY HAVE WE FALLEN INTO?

Zahnd writes,

> The Prince of Peace… [made] the most astounding and subversive claim of all: *I am the truth.* In making the ultimate claim—the claim to be truth itself, Jesus was announcing that He was about to re-center the world. The world would no longer be centered around the truth of violence; it would now be centered around the truth of forgiving love—a truth to which he would bear witness all the way to the cross. Jesus was going to re-center the world around an axis of love![5]
>
> —Brian Zahnd

Pilate bore witness to the truth of power. Christ bore witness to the truth of love.

The terrible beauty of the cross broadcasts the rich melody of grace to a world where "might makes right." It proclaims to a world devastated by sin that "goodness is stronger than evil, and love is stronger than hate." It brings salvation, forgiveness and hope. It has power to restore heaven's harmony to human hearts.

"Truth is a person and He is telling a love story," writes Mike Maeshiro.

And when at last the sublime symphony of redemption is fully assembled and reverberates throughout creation, the universe will be witness to the most beautiful music ever heard.

It was Dostoevski who argued, "Beauty will save the world."

I think he's right.

The "terrifying beauty of the cross" is a light that shines in the darkness, and the darkness can not overcome it.

When beautiful music is played among the ruins—anything can happen.

PRAYER

LORD GOD OF GLORY, You sent your Son to live among us, and what magnificent music was heard when He was here! The quiet rich beauty of His life shone in everything He said and did. He is so full of grace that hearts couldn't help but be healed, lives couldn't help but be transformed, and reconciliation couldn't help but happen. He is so full of truth that hypocrisy, falsehood and injustice couldn't help but be exposed. Never was there a life so beautiful or goodness so compelling. His grace and truth blended like the words and music of a song. We stand amazed at His exquisite tenderness, His splendid truthfulness, and we know that He is the answer to the longing of our hearts. He is the Healer and Helper that we need. We bring the discord of our lives to You, oh God, and ask that You tune our hearts to the harmony of Your will, and make our lives a hymn of praise. We ask in the Name of our Mighty Redeemer, Amen.

*The King's grace
is greater than
you know.*

—J. R. R. Tolkien

CHAPTER EIGHTEEN

OUTRAGEOUS GRACE

Out of his fullness we have all received grace in place of grace already given.
JOHN 1:16

NINETEENTH-CENTURY Bible teacher, John Nelson Darby, was once giving a series of lectures in New England. A Methodist theologian, who greatly admired Darby, would go to hear him, although he disagreed with his colleague on a number of theological issues. He had misgivings about Darby's understanding of grace.

On one occasion, Darby was speaking of the fellowship we enjoy with God as we walk in the light—the light of the Gospel. The Methodist scholar reacted to his interpretation, and interrupted with a question, "Brother Darby, if a Christian turns his back on the light, what happens then?"

Darby replied: "In that case—the light shines on his back."

A brilliant response! Grace is outrageously gratuitous. It is overwhelmingly generous. It shines on the evil and the good.

Grace is extreme goodness lavished upon undeserving people. It is being loved when you are unlovable. It does not look for suitable candidates. It pays no attention to entitlement. It refuses to be tethered to our ideas of fairness or propriety. It seeks you out when you have nothing to give in return. As one writer put it, "grace is both un-earnable and un-repayable."

"Grace is wild," pointed out one theologian. "Grace unsettles everything. Grace overflows the banks. Grace messes up your hair. Grace is not tame... Unless we are making the devout nervous, we are not preaching grace as we ought."[1]

Glorious Grace

We are prone to underestimate the grace of God, and John's prologue comes to our aid. The word "grace" appears only four times in the Gospels—and all four instances are in the opening section of John's book. In just four verses, the apostle expands our understanding of the riches of divine grace.

The first thing John does is to connect grace and glory.

> *We have seen his glory . . . full of grace and truth* (Jn. 1:14).

What makes the Lord Jesus Christ supremely glorious is the extravagant outpouring of unwarranted favor. Herein lies His glory—*the splendor of His grace.*

There is, however, a widely held idea that God's glory is self-absorbed, that He does all things for the glory of Himself. That this Sovereign Lord relentlessly pursues the goal of self-exaltation.

Is God an attention seeker who craves recognition?

It is indisputable that we cannot ascribe too much greatness to God. He is worthy of highest praise and honor. It is also true, as the famous catechism declares, that God's glory is the chief end of everything.

Glory is a word that easily slips out of our grasp. What does glory look like when we let the Lord Jesus Christ define the term for us? If He is *"the radiance of the glory of God"* (Heb. 1:3), He is our best definition of glory. He shows us what glory truly looks like.

The glory of Christ is not seen in parading strength, or asserting power. Rather, it is seen in the beauty and perfection of His grace. *It is the lavish display of His goodness.*

How is God glorified? It is *not* by demanding worship. It is not by forcing people to bow, as King Nebuchadnezzar once did in Babylon. Rather, it is by pouring out His goodness and grace in such extravagance that rebels are turned into amazed lovers and worshippers of God. He conquers through a blood-stained cross. He overpowers us with His love. This causes knees to bow and tongues to sing. *This is ultimately how God gets glory.*

One writer put it like this—God does not do all things for the love of glory, He does all things for the glory of love.[2]

If God is love (1 Jn. 4:8,16), and love *"is not self-seeking"* (1 Cor. 13:5), we must conclude that God is not turned in upon Himself, but is turned outward. His glory is not self-exalting, but self-giving; it is not self-centered, but other-centered.

The Glory of His Grace

Glen Scrivener explains:

> Whatever glory we ascribe to this God, it cannot be the glory of self-exaltation... It is the *"glory of His grace, with which He favored us in the Beloved"* (Eph. 1:6 NASB). What we will praise into all eternity is the grace of a Father who from eternity past has determined to do all for the glory of love. The repetition of the phrase "to the praise of His glory" (Eph. 1:12 and 21) can only be understood in the context as a short-hand for this lavish, other-centered benevolence.[3]

"Glory" and "grace" show up repeatedly in Paul's magnificent letter to the Ephesians. Notice how the apostle uses these two words interchangeably:

- *"to the praise of His glorious GRACE"* (1:6)
- *"for the praise of His GLORY"* (1:12)

The apostle loves to intertwine these two terms:

- *"the riches of His GRACE"* (1:7)
- *"the riches of His GLORY"* (3:16)

So what is the supreme glory of Christ?

It is the glory of His grace.

It is the unexplainable, unfathomable, unsurpassable generosity of His goodness to the undeserving. It is the *"pressed down, shaken together and running over"* nature of His benevolence. God is beautiful in every possible way. But nowhere does His beauty shine more magnificently than in the unrestrained outpouring of grace.

> **Infinite sharing is the law of God's inner life.**
> —Thomas Merton

It is a misunderstanding to think of God as a glory grabber and not a glory giver. He does all things—not for the glory of His glory, but for *the glory of His grace*.[4] The Sovereign Lord is not like a heat-seeking missile anxious to find worshippers. He is an other-centered God who delights in exporting and spreading goodness. He is in the business of lavishing grace in relentless extravagance.

This is the glory of God.

And this turns the wayward into worshippers.

There's No One Like Him

The prophet Isaiah declared that a God of such generosity was unprecedented. Only in the Bible does one hear of such a deity.

> *Since ancient times no one has heard, no ear has perceived, no eye has seen any God besides you, who acts on behalf of those who wait for him* (Isa. 64:4).

Isaiah points out three significant facts:

1. No one has ever heard of a God like this.
2. Here is a God whose goal is to benefit and bless people.
3. He only asks that we "wait" or trust in Him.

This God is a *giver*. False gods grant favors to those who work for them. The true God is radically different. *He works on behalf of those who trust in Him.* He is well described by the words of Christ: *"It is more blessed to give than to receive"* (Acts 20:35). His blessedness lies in His infinite willingness to give. "God is other-centred, to the depths of eternity and to the core of His Being," states Glen Scrivener.

Jeremiah adds these words from God Himself:

> *I will rejoice in doing them good . . . with all my heart and all my soul* (Jer. 32:41).

Notice two more remarkable facts about God:

- He finds great joy in working for the good of people.
- He will give Himself to this task with total abandon.

What an astonishing God! He delights in lavishing goodness in reckless abundance. He is so complete in Himself that nothing brings Him greater joy than giving. There is no emptiness in God that needs filling, only fullness which He delights to share. A psalmist rightly asks: *"Who is like the Lord our God?"* (Psa. 113:5).

The Fullness of His Grace

The grace of Christ is not only glorious, *it is abundant.*

> *Out of his fullness we have all received...* (Jn. 1:16).

The abundance of grace is underscored by the use of the word "full" (v. 14), and "fullness" (v. 16), indicating a profuse bountiful provision. There's lots of it! Regardless of our massive need for grace, the supply is greater.

And then John takes it to a higher level still, and adds the phrase *"grace upon grace."* The best translation is probably "grace on top of grace."

This expression reminds one of waves crashing relentlessly on the ocean shore. When you stand on the beach and watch, the waves keep coming—one after another. Nothing deters them. One wave follows another; they don't quit. Wave upon wave—*just like the grace of God.*

"God never seems capable of moderation," mused N. D. Wilson.

WHAT STORY HAVE WE FALLEN INTO?

God gives grace, and then, on top of this grace, He gives more grace. And, if that weren't enough, He gives a further supply. And when we have exhausted this measure of grace, there is more grace to follow. The waves keep coming. It's grace upon grace.

Abounding Grace

How wonderful to know the grace of Christ is not about to run dry. There is no scarcity. There is no limit to the supply. It is not an intermittent trickle. It is an endless ocean. Here is grace in inexhaustible plentifulness!

Christ will never say, "Look, you have already had more than your share of grace. You've exceeded your limit. Your quota of grace has run out." No, it's grace heaped upon more grace.

Perhaps we haven't responded to His grace as we should. We said we would change, and we didn't. We purposed to be faithful, and we weren't. We failed to live as we should.

> *In matters of God's grace, hyperboles are understatements.*
> —Eugene Peterson

Christ does not say, "That's it—there's no more for you."

When we fail miserably, and we turn to Him with our sin, head down and full of shame, He does not give us a tongue lashing. He does not demand we grovel. He gives more grace. We can expect Him to enfold us in His strong embrace and say, "Nothing that you can ever do will alter my love for you. I am going to keep loving you and holding you until all that is twisted and damaged and debased is made whole. I'm not going to stop until you are filled to over-flowing with the light of my goodness and love."

C. J. Mahaney words are timely:

> Don't buy the lie that cultivating condemnation and wallowing in your shame is somehow pleasing to God, or that a constant, low-grade guilt will somehow promote holiness and spiritual maturity. It's just the opposite! God is glorified when we believe with all our hearts that those who trust in Christ can never be condemned. It's only when we

receive his free gift of grace and live in the good of total forgiveness that we're able to turn from old, sinful ways of living and walk in grace-motivated obedience.[5]

"Grace is for the desperate, the needy, the broken, those who cannot make it on their own," points out Philip Yancey. "Grace is for all of us."

The High Calling of Grace

The extreme extravagance of grace brings great comfort, *but it does not encourage complacency.* Quite the opposite. It calls for a response of radical obedience that takes us *beyond* the demands of the law. The law requires that we love our neighbour as ourselves. Under grace, the bar is set higher—*"Love each other as I have loved you"* (Jn. 15:12). The law empowers us to assert our rights; grace teaches us to give up our rights. The law demands much; grace demands more. It is no longer a matter of seeking to keep the letter of the law but of having fulfilled in us the spirit of Christ.

Grace does not mean—"anything goes." Rather, as Paul wrote to Titus, "Grace teaches us to say no to ungodliness" (Titus 2:11-12). Notice, it is *not* the law that teaches us this lesson. It tries, but fails. This saying no to ungodliness is something we learn from grace. The fact that we are loved, accepted and forgiven is the springboard toward turning from ungodliness.

We should not make the mistake of taking sin lightly. Sin wreaks havoc on our lives. It is toxic and devastating. We should not be deceived in thinking otherwise. Sin blinds, enslaves and destroys. But thankfully—it is no match for grace.

> *Sin increased, but grace surpassed it far* (Rom. 5:20 MOF).

John points out four things about the grace of Christ:

- The gloriousness of His grace - *"glory... full of grace"*
- The abundance of His grace - *"full of grace"*
- The wideness of His grace - *"we have all received"*
- The relentlessness of His grace - *"grace upon grace"*

Rediscovering Grace

Periodically in history, spiritual revivals break out as the free gift of God is discovered afresh. The Spirit moves, lives change. Men such as Augustine, Francis of Assisi, the Reformers or John Wesley spread the word. Multitudes rejoice in the abundance of God's grace, love and forgiveness. There is an outburst of infectious joy and faith as people find freedom from guilt and peace with God.

It is marvelous.

But then gradually, over time, the freeness of salvation is replaced by an insistence on outward markers of piety. A more austere environment emerges. Moralism, pettiness and hypocrisy grow. What was a spontaneous, joyful surrender to God, turns into burdensome obligation. Love grows cold. The need arises for a rediscovery of the freeness and plentifulness of divine grace. That it is not calculating and cautious, but unrestrained, inexhaustible, flood-like. Greater than all our sin. It provides both pardon and power. Grace upon grace.

> *Grace has about it the scent of scandal.*
> —Philip Yancey

Edward Judson wrote,

> It is thought that unconditional grace is unsafe. Man will feel free to go on sinning. On the contrary, unconditional forgiveness is the only rope that is long enough to reach to the bottom of the pit into which we have fallen.[6]

Robert Capon reminds us:

> Grace . . . is the only thing that will work on the world as it so sadly is. "An eye for an eye" won't work because all it does is double the number of eyeless people. Retribution won't take evil out of the world; it will simply perpetuate it . . . punishing sinners and rewarding the righteous produces all hell and no kingdom: there are just too many sinners, and there are no

righteous. The only thing that's going to get evil out of the world is for him to take it into himself on the cross—to drop it down the black hole of his death—and to make a new creation by the power of his resurrection.[7]

Saved by Grace

Grace is the only real hope for bruised, broken and bankrupt people. It finds us in our lostness, lifts our burden and heals our hearts. It lavishes unearned and unexplainable love and forgiveness that sends us to our knees in gratitude, wonder and joy. It is not what we deserved—but it is what we desperately needed.

Yancey again:

> Grace means there is nothing I can do to make God love me more, and nothing I can do to make God love me less. It means that I, even I who deserve the opposite, am invited to take my place at the table in God's family.[8]

Lewis B. Smedes writes,

> A first experience of God's grace could feel as if we have landed in a world where 2+2 might knock at our door and introduce herself as 5, where when a wrench falls out of our hand, it rises to the ceiling. There is a weightlessness about grace. It has the feel of a fairy tale; what makes it a very special fairy tale is that it is true.[9]

Wondrous grace.

> *Grace has a grand laughter in it.*
> —Marilynne Robinson

Grace for Grumblers

The surplus of grace is beautifully illustrated when Christ caters for a hungry multitude in the wilderness. It's His fourth miracle in John's Gospel. He provides a meal for an enormous, hungry crowd of five thousand empty stomachs—with barely enough to fill a small grocery bag.

This miraculous feeding of a multitude in the wilderness is reminiscent of what took place in Exodus 16. A daily provision of bread from heaven called "manna" was provided to a group of grumblers on their way to the Promised Land. Grace for grumblers! And the manna kept coming down for forty years.

In John 6, once again we have grumbling Israelites. They are in a desert place and they're hungry. It's déjà vu. Once again, food is generously provided, as much as they wanted—and more than they could eat. And then Jesus announces,

> *I am the bread of life. Whoever comes [constantly, continually] to me will never go hungry, and whoever believes in me will never be thirsty* (Jn. 6:35).

Twelve large baskets of bread were left over—one for each of the disciples. Each man heads home with a basket on his shoulder—a basket loaded with a spiritual lesson. A lesson about the all-sufficiency of Christ. A lesson about His limitless grace.

In Christ there is *fullness* of grace and truth—even for grumblers like us. There is plenteousness that delights to give, abundance that overwhelms our need.

> The Lord Jesus . . . is the bread we need to eat, the water we need to drink, the light we need to see, the way we need to walk, the truth we need to believe, and the life we need to have.[10]

Spurgeon said it well, "I have a great need for Christ; I have a great Christ for my need."

PRAYER

GOD OF GRACE AND MERCY, our foolish hearts have so often turned from You to travel on forbidden paths. If Your grace were not so abundant, if it were not so much greater than our stubbornness and failures, we would be without hope. If it were not so extravagant and free, we would be utterly lost. When we run from You in guilt, You run to us in grace. We bless You, oh God our Father, for mercy that overwhelms our need, for grace that is greater than all our sin. Capture our hearts again with the rich extravagance of Your goodness, with the unwarranted abundance of Your mercy. Dumbfound us, spellbind us, flat out fry the circuit boards of our hearts with the lavishness of Your grace. We pray in the wonderful Name of Jesus. Amen.

*Christ is no Moses,
no exactor, no giver of laws,
but a giver of grace, a Savior;
he is infinite mercy and goodness,
freely and bountifully
given to us.*

—MARTIN LUTHER

CHAPTER NINETEEN

STEP ASIDE, MOSES

For the law was given through Moses;
grace and truth came through Jesus Christ.
JOHN 1:17

MOSES WAS THE GREATEST spiritual leader in the history of Israel. He led his people out of slavery. He brought God's law down from Mount Sinai, and built the tabernacle where the Lord dwelt among His people. He brought Israel into a covenant relationship with God. He wrote the Torah, the first five books of the Bible. There was no one like Moses.

The Scribes and Pharisees proudly identified as disciples of Moses; he was the leader they revered and trusted in (Jn. 5:45; 9:28). The law of Moses was their ultimate guide and point of reference. Moses was their mentor.

John has shocking news for them: *The law-giver has been eclipsed.* Someone infinitely superior has come on the scene.

Moses has been superseded by Jesus the Messiah.

We have come to an overlap of the ages. God is fulfilling His promise to bring a new covenant, a new way of living and relating to God (Jer. 31:31-34). The grace given in the old covenant was being replaced by the fullness of grace of the new covenant. God is doing something new.

This was a hard pill to swallow.

The guardians of the "old way" don't like the idea, and Jesus runs into stiff resistance from the religious leaders. Throughout the entire book of John there is a growing tension between Moses and Christ, between the law-giver and the grace-bringer. The followers of Moses are not about to abandon the old covenant program.

Greater Than Moses

John goes to great lengths to spell out the overwhelming superiority of Jesus. Notice the contrast...

Moses freed Israel from slavery in Egypt, but Jesus frees people from slavery to the world and to sin (Jn. 8:36). Moses provided bread from heaven called manna. Jesus came down from heaven to be the bread of life (Jn. 6:32-33). Moses struck the rock and water flowed for the people to drink. Jesus took the blow of our sins, and he now provides living water (Jn. 7:37-39). Moses lifted up a bronze serpent on a pole in the desert and dying Israelites were healed. Jesus would be "lifted up" to provide eternal life to the entire world (Jn. 3:14-15).

Moses came down from Sinai with the tablets of the law. Christ gives us His Spirit and writes His law in our hearts (Jn. 20:22; Heb. 10:16). Moses built the tabernacle, the dwelling place of God. Jesus turns us into living temples and sends the Holy Spirit to dwell in our hearts (Jn. 14:16-17). Moses' request to see the glory of God was denied. In Christ the glory of God is revealed (Jn. 1:14). Allusions to Moses are scattered all through John's book.

No Help From the Law

In John 5, the Lord came upon a disabled man in Jerusalem by the pool of Bethesda. The numbers in the story are significant. The man had waited for a miracle of healing for thirty-eight years in a place with five porches. Those numbers are very "Jewish." Thirty eight years was the time it took Moses to lead Israel from Sinai to Canaan. Five books make up the Torah, the law of Moses. Here is a paralyzed man in the heart of the holy city, unable to find healing or help—for almost four decades. A word from Christ was all that was required. The man picked up his mat and walked. He typifies the incapacity of the law of Moses to meet our need, in contrast to the all sufficient power of Christ.

A well-known poem sums it up well:

> *"Do this and live!" the law commands,*
> *but gives me neither feet nor hands.*
> *A better word the gospel brings,*
> *it bids me fly and gives me wings.*

A greater than Moses is here.

Shadows and Substance

The religious system Moses brought down from Sinai was merely a "copy and shadow" of spiritual realities (Heb. 8:5). The tabernacle and its sacrifices were a foreshadowing of Christ and His perfect sacrifice that would truly remove sin and bring peace with God. The offerings of the old covenant did not actually "do the job." They served as symbols. They pointed to the final and sufficient sacrifice of Christ (Heb. 10:1-14).

Symbols are not "the real thing," they are mere representations. Compare, for instance, a statue of Christopher Columbus to the real, living, breathing man from Spain who discovered the Americas. One is a mere representation, the other is the reality—the *truth,* if you will.

The Sinai system was like a statue that pointed to another reality. That reality was Christ. This is what John is talking about when he writes of "truth" coming through Jesus Christ. He is not simply speaking of that which is not false. He is speaking of that which is not merely *symbolic.* He is talking about "the real thing" as opposed to an illustration.

"Truth" is one of John's favorite words and one of his great themes. He uses the word more than anyone else in the New

Testament. He highlights the fact that we are no longer dealing with mere symbols—the *truth* has come. A new age has arrived.

Moses brought types and symbols—Jesus brought the reality. Jesus is the "true" light, the "true" bread, the "true" vine. He is the way, the truth and the life.

> *The law is only a shadow of the good things that are coming —not the realities themselves* (Heb. 10:1).

In Christ, the "good things" have come. The shadows have given way to substance.

However, the teachers of the "Torah" were not open to the arrival of the "Truth." The followers of Moses were not about to become followers of Messiah. And sparks began to fly.

Which is God's True House?

When John says in verse 14 of his prologue that the Word made His "dwelling" among us, he uses an interesting word. It literally means to pitch one's tent or tabernacle. The apostle is saying He "tabernacled" among us.

Clearly this word was chosen to draw a connection with another tabernacle—the one Moses built at Mount Sinai. This was where God dwelt in the midst of His people. The portable sanctuary was later replaced by the glorious temple built by Solomon in Jerusalem.

This new house of worship was magnificent. Many tons of gold and silver were used to build it. It was probably the most costly and majestic temple the world has ever seen. The most remarkable feature, however, was not the outer splendor, but the fact the God of heaven put His presence there. The glory of the Lord filled the inner sanctuary known as the Holy of Holies and this temple became the most sacred place on earth.

Through a tragic sequence of events, Solomon's temple was destroyed by the Babylonians six centuries before Christ. A new house of worship was finally erected in its place by King Herod the Great. He created one of the most glorious buildings of his time.

When we open the pages of the New Testament, this impressive structure is at the center of Israel's spiritual life. It symbolized God's presence on earth. Eighteen thousand Levites and priests served there, and people from all over the world came to worship. This glorious temple in Jerusalem was the joy and pride of the Jewish people.

But things are about to change.

Drastically.

John tells us that the God of heaven came into the world (Jn. 1:9). But here's the twist. He came to dwell—not in the temple, but in the body and life of a carpenter from Nazareth. A new tabernacle is here—*not a building but a Person.* The hidden Shekinah glory of God has come into view—and it has a human face. *His name is Jesus.*

An intriguing scenario! We have a structure in Jerusalem which is believed to be God's temple, and we have the living, walking, *true* temple of God in the person of Christ. A clash is inevitable.

For centuries the Jewish temple had fulfilled a vital role in the spiritual life of Israel. John is telling us that things are about to change. No longer will we need to go to Jerusalem—we now need to go to Jesus. The man from Galilee is about to overturn the whole temple system.

Notice how He goes about it.

When Temples Get Toppled

In John 2, Jesus makes a daring move. The temple had become a marketplace, and it was time for spring cleaning. He tosses out the tables, and turfs out the merchants. He scatters the coins, the sheep and the goats, and sends the pigeons back into the sky. Christ goes in with a whip and closes down the whole operation. Never do we see Him taking such drastic measures. The Owner has arrived, and He is rearranging the furniture in the House of God.

And this is only the beginning.

When He gets done, the entire temple system will be dismantled. Messiah has not come to correct some glitches; He is going to overthrow the whole religious program. One by one, every one of the temple tables will be thrown out of the door.

When the Jews demanded an explanation, Jesus responded:

> *Destroy this temple, and I will raise it again in three days* (Jn. 2:19).

John explains that Christ was referring to the temple of His own body (Jn. 1:21). It was a bold statement: "When you destroy me, your temple will be destroyed. When you put an end to my life, I will put an end to all the sacrifices, offerings and ceremonies of this religious system. Getting rid of me will backfire, because in the process, I will get rid of the temple."

That was quite a bombshell!

Jesus had not come to improve the system. He had come *to shut it down*. He had come to replace it, and to bring that which the temple failed to deliver—a true connection with God.

There is a new temple in town.

A new chapter has opened in the divine drama.

Where Does God Live?

In a conversation with a woman from Samaria in John 4, the question came up about the right place to worship. Jesus told her the moment had arrived when worship would no longer be tied to Jerusalem or any other city (Jn. 4:21-24). The time for sacred spaces and sacrifices had ended. The time to find God in a certain location was over. The religious system centered in the temple was about to become obsolete.

The spiritual landscape is getting altered.

The prophet Ezekiel was given an intriguing vision of the temple of God (Ezek. 47). He saw water flowing out from under the threshold of the temple. The water flows east and turns into a river whose waters bring life, healing and blessing to many places.

A river flowing out of a temple? A bizarre phenomenon! What does it mean? In John 7, during a religious feast in Jerusalem, Jesus gives a surprising interpretation to this vision.

The harvest festival, also known as the Feast of Tabernacles, was celebrated every year. It was a moment to thank God for the gift of rain and the fruit of the ground. A priest would carry water from the Pool of Siloam and pour it out by the altar in the temple. This ritual was performed every day for a week. However, on this occasion, the festival ended on a surprising note. The crowd in the temple must have been dumbfounded when, on the eighth day, the man from Nazareth stood up and announced:

> *Let anyone who is thirsty come to me and drink. Whoever believes in me, as Scripture has said, rivers of living water will flow from within them. By this he meant the Spirit, whom those who believed in him were later to receive* (Jn. 7:37-40).

The ritual was about to become reality.

Ezekiel saw waters emerging from the temple, but Jesus gives the vision a new twist and speaks of water flowing from human beings. The house of God gets redefined! Now the Spirit's place of residence will not be a building in Jerusalem—but the body of believers. God would now dwell, not in a *"house made by human hands,"* but in human hearts. Not only Christ Himself, but those who believe in Him would become the new temple of the living God (1 Cor. 3:16; 6:19; Eph. 2:20-21).

God's New Address

The night before His death, the Master declares these memorable words.

> *My Father's house has many rooms; if that were not so, would I have told you that I am going there to prepare a place for you? And if I go and prepare a place for you, I will come back and take you to be with me that you also may be where I am* (Jn. 14:2-3).

Our Lord intends to take His followers to His Father's house, and what usually comes to mind is—heaven. This is true, and it is a wonderful hope. But, as is typical of John's writing, there's another level of meaning here.

Later on in the chapter Jesus expands the meaning of "rooms" (sometimes translated dwelling places):

> *Jesus replied, Anyone who loves me will obey my teaching. My Father will love them, and we will come to them and make our HOME with them* (Jn. 14:23).

This is not about believers going somewhere else, it is about the Father and the Son making their "home" in those who love and follow Christ. This, as the context indicates, is achieved by the Spirit. It does not refer to heaven, it is about life here and now —a life infused by God's presence.

The Spirit and Christ

Two main themes in John 14-16 are the sending of the Holy Spirit and the fact Jesus is going and is coming back.

> *And if I go and prepare a place for you, I will come back* (14:3).

> *I will not leave you as orphans; I will come to you* (14:18).

> *In a little while you will see me no more, and then after a little while you will see me* (16:16).

Christ is leaving but He promises to return. We might ask: "Is He talking about the Second Coming, or the descent of His Spirit at Pentecost?"

The answer is—*yes*.

Theologian F. F. Bruce speaks in his commentary of a "vanishing distinction" in these verses between the two phases of Christ's coming. The Lord is going and coming back *in more than one way*. It will happen at the Second Coming, but it will also happen when the Spirit comes. As is typical of the Fourth Gospel, there is a blending of the two ideas.

On the day of Pentecost is Christ coming back in a different way. It is when our Lord sends His Spirit to indwell the hearts of His people. It is about humans becoming the "home" of God.

When The Curtain Comes Down

At the moment of Christ's death, a shocking event took place in the temple. The curtain that hid the innermost sanctuary from view was suddenly ripped in half. The barrier that kept people out of the holiest place of God's presence was not only torn—it was ripped from top to bottom. And clearly, it was the hand of God.

What was the Lord saying?

- This religious system has become obsolete.
- Access to God is now available to all.
- The hidden glory of God has been revealed.
- The temple no longer is the house of God.

The time had come to close the whole operation down. If any doubts remained, the Romans would come in forty years' time and do the final demolition. This religious system had come to an end.

If God's presence was no longer to be found in a temple in Jerusalem, where could He now be found? Where is His new residence? Hopefully He has left us His address!

Fortunately, He has. Paul informs us in one of his letters:

> *Do you not know that your bodies are temples of the Holy Spirit, who is in you, whom you have received from God?* (1 Cor. 6:19).

God no longer dwells in buildings made of cement and stone. He now lives in human hearts. He resides where He always wanted to be—in the lives of His people. Those who belong to

Christ are the new, living, breathing temple of God. Portable sanctuaries of the divine presence.

The Moses model has been replaced by something unspeakably wonderful.

It Is Finished

The religious system established by Moses was a never-ending attempt to reach an unattainable goal.

> *No matter how many sacrifices were offered year after year, they never added up to a complete solution* (Heb. 10:1 MSG).

There was always more to be done to gain full acceptance with God. It was never enough. In stunning contrast, in John 19:30, we hear the announcement: *"It is finished."*

> *But when Christ had offered for all time a single sacrifice for sins, he sat down at the right hand of God . . . for by a single offering he has perfected for all time those who are being sanctified* (Heb. 10:12,14 ESV).

Mission accomplished.
Atonement made.
Salvation secured.
The work is done.

The Mosaic system has been trumped. The countless, ongoing, repetitious, unavailing sacrifices of the past were rendered obsolete. They were superceded by the once-and-for-all, effectual, definitive, all sufficient sacrifice of Christ.

The first word of the Gospel is not "do this," but *"it is finished."* People are invited, not to behave better, but to believe. Our repentance, faith and obedience do not seek to get God to do something for us. Rather, they are our grateful and glad response to what was accomplished for us.

John is going to take us deeper into this mystery.

PRAYER

LORD GOD OF HEAVEN, we praise You that, at the cross, our Lord and Savior Jesus Christ did the work of reconciling us to God. He put an end to our sins and He put an end to religion. We thank You that through Jesus' death and resurrection every test-passing, point-collecting religious program has been cancelled and declared null and void. We thank You that when neither the Law of God nor our religious devices could get the job done, our Savior fixed the whole mess by Himself without one scrap of human assistance. Help us to understand that everything we ever thought of doing to get right with God is beside the point, and because of the once for all redemptive death of Messiah, we can enjoy Your forgiveness, Your acceptance and Your presence in our lives. We thank You, oh God, for this wonderful and astonishing Good News. Amen.

*In Jesus, God shows us God.
That I believe, is the whole secret
of the Christian faith.*

—BEN MYERS

CHAPTER TWENTY

THE UNVEILING OF GOD

No one has ever seen God, but the one and only Son . . . has made him known.
JOHN 1:18

ON MANY OCCASIONS, I have served as a translator for non-Spanish speakers. I had the language, the other man had the message. I would stand beside him and convey his words to the listeners as clearly and faithfully as I could. I was not at liberty to embellish or to subtract. I was there to transmit as well as possible what the speaker said and how he said it. When he gestured, I gestured. When he spoke with fervor, so did I. When he got quiet, I did too. Translating involves synchronizing with another person in such a way that the audience truly hears what is on his heart.

One time, the well-known speaker Richard Wurmbrand, arrived in Bolivia for a special event. He was a Romanian pastor and author who spent fourteen years in communist imprisonment and torture. For some reason, adequate preparations had not been made for the event, and it had to be cancelled. In its place, a number of services were quickly arranged to take advantage of Wurmbrand's visit. The Romanian pastor was fluent in nine languages, but Spanish was not one of them and I was asked to translate.

A good crowd gathered to hear the visiting speaker. Wurmbrand shared his experiences and gave a powerful message. English, however, was not his first language, and there were moments when it was not clear to me what he was saying. Wurmbrand had enough Spanish to know whether I was translating his words correctly or not. At one point, he stopped me, and said, "That's not what I said." I tried again. "No, you still didn't get it," he responded. I was stumped. Finally, with some help from the audience, we figured it out and the service carried on.

God's Interpreter

Jesus was given the task of "translating" the truth about God into the language of men. His life was a human translation of God. He was making the Lord of heaven known in terms we could understand. And, He did it flawlessly—with no glitches. Word perfect. All He said and did flowed out of a deep connection with His Father (Jn. 5:19; 8:28; 14:24). He was so completely in sync with the Father that He could say, *"Anyone who has seen me has seen the Father"* (Jn. 14:10).

Jesus is God speaking our language.

The Greek philosopher Plato quotes Socrates as saying, "Oh, that someone would come, man or god, to show us God."

The message of John's Gospel is—*Someone came.* The divine Logos crossed all worlds to make God known. He who is the perfect expression of the Father came among us and showed us the essential truth and the unsurpassing glory of the Most High. Abba's Son put God on display.

Nothing in history could be more significant than that.

"No one has ever seen God," John tells us. This is our problem. No one has ever laid eyes on Him. He has been out of reach. Invisible, unknowable, undiscoverable.

But look what happened...

> *The one and only Son . . . has made him known* (Jn. 1:18).

Another translation reads like this:

> *Now he has unfolded to us the full explanation of who God truly is!* (Jn. 1:18 TPT).

The coming of Christ was not just about salvation, it was also about *revelation*. Jesus came so we might know God. He is the self-disclosure of God. The One who eternally lived in the Father's embrace came to open a window into the heart of God.

Some Bible versions say He "declared" God. The Greek word is one from which we get our term "exegesis," often used by Bible scholars. Biblical exegesis is the task of bringing to light the true meaning of a passage. It seeks to dispel faulty interpretations, and explain what the inspired record is really saying. Someone has *exegeted* the heart of God. His true character has been brought to light.

Jesus of Nazareth is the *exegesis* of God. He reveals the true nature of the Most High. He brings out into the open what we could not discover on our own. He debunks the lies about the Almighty. He shows us what God is really like.

William Hoste wrote:

> His every act was the fulfillment of the Father's purpose, every word the echo of His command, every step the effect of His leading, and all His ways the unfolding of God's great heart of love.[1]

The Unseen God

"No one has ever seen God..." is a bold statement.

No one?

What about all those people in the Bible who "saw" God? Did not Abraham, Isaiah, Ezekiel and others see God? Did Moses not catch a glimpse of the Lord on Mount Sinai? Did God not speak to him *"face to face as a man speaks to his friend"* (Ex. 34:11)? How can John say that no one has ever seen the Lord?

Consider carefully what the apostle is saying.

No one in the Old Testament *really* saw God. They were like Moses who had a limited and partial view of God as he peered through a crack in the rock. Those men of the past had remarkable encounters with God. No one can deny that. But what John wants us to understand is this—*it wasn't the whole picture.* Whatever they "saw" of God, when compared to His self-disclosure in Christ, is like "not seeing" Him. A fuller revelation has taken place.

In the person of Christ, God comes into plain view and shows us not His back but His face.

> *For God, who said, "Let light shine out of darkness," made his light shine in our hearts to give us the light of the knowledge of God's glory displayed in the face of Christ* (2 Cor. 4:6).

The Divine Son does not give us another word about God—*He is The Word!* No where else do we get a more thorough, personal and beautiful revelation of God.

The stunning truth we learn from John is this: *You haven't really seen God until you've seen Jesus.*

That's quite a bombshell!

With a few strokes off his pen, the apostle John redefines the entire theological landscape.

Essentially he is saying: "Rethink all your ideas about God. Take all your concepts and views about Him and set them aside, because I am going to tell you what He is really like. I am going to show you the most amazing revelation of God this world has ever seen. The Divine Lord put His glory on display—and His name is Jesus."

Jesus Christ eclipses every other word about God.

The Definitive Revelation

This concept was driven home to John through a mind-blowing experience on the Mount of Transfiguration. Two of the greatest men from the Old Testament—Moses and Elijah—appeared and spoke with Christ. John's fellow disciple Peter was taken aback and blurted out that three shelters could be built for them to camp on the mountain. It was understandable. How often do you get a chance to hang out with Moses and Elijah?

God responded with a sharp rebuke:

> *This is my Son, whom I have chosen; listen to him* (Lk. 9:35).

When the heavenly voice died away, the disciples looked again—Moses and Elijah were gone. Only Jesus could be seen. E. Stanley Jones called this one of the most clarifying moments in the history of the Christian faith. This is not about Moses or Elijah—they are not remotely in the same league. This is all about the Son of God. What God says to us in Jesus takes precedence over all else. All others fade out of the picture, and only Christ remains.

How to Know God

> *Then they asked him, "Where is your father?" "You do not know me or my Father," Jesus replied. "If you knew me, you would know my Father also"* (Jn. 8:19).

> *The Revelation of God is not a book or a doctrine, but a living Person.*
> —EMIL BRUNNER

Jesus is talking to devout Jews who knew the Scriptures. They want to know where Jesus' Father is to be found. Christ's word to them is: "You know neither Me nor my Father. You know much about the book of God, but you don't know the God of the book."

Then, Jesus dares to add,

> *You know my Father as little as you know me* (Jn. 8:19 Weymouth).

An astonishing claim! To know Jesus is to know the Father. If you haven't come to know Jesus, you haven't come to know God. A true knowledge of God is only possible through Christ. It is only when you've seen Christ, that you know what the Father is *really* like. In other words... *What you see in Jesus is what you get in God.*

WHAT STORY HAVE WE FALLEN INTO?

What is God Like?

One of the pressing questions of our times is not, "Is there a God?" but, "What kind of God is there?"

Dorothy Sayers wrote: "The God of the Christians is too often looked upon as an old gentleman of irritable nerves who beats people for whistling."

Others view the Most High, as one writer put it, as "the faceless, nameless, omni-being who watches us from the infinite distance of a disapproving heart."

The word "god" has become almost meaningless. It is a malleable term that can convey a multitude of conflicting ideas. The word needs content put into it. It requires definition.

Jesus is that definition.

That is the message of John's book.

The man from Galilee has made God known.

The Human Face of God

Watch Him as He hugs lepers, opens blind eyes, blesses children and feeds hungry crowds—*because that's what God is like.* Notice as He lifts up the wayward, the weak and the wounded. Observe as He brings healing and hope to those who have lost their way —*because that's what God is like.*

> **Christ is the visible expression of the invisible God.**
> —Colossians 1:15 (Phlp)

Look at Him calm stormy seas and troubled hearts. See Him blessing the broken and blasting the hypocrites. View Him weeping over Jerusalem and washing His disciples' feet. And above all, gaze at Him bleeding and dying as He lays down His life for His enemies—*because that's what God is like.*

The incomparable life of Jesus is a perfect reflection of the heart of the Father. He is the *"flawless expression of the nature of God"* (Heb. 1:3 PHLP). One writer stated, "Jesus is not a kindly moment in the life of an otherwise capricious God. Jesus embodies the eternal posture of God toward sinners."

Spurgeon writes,

> If you reject Him, He answers you with tears. If you wound Him, He bleeds out cleansing, if you kill Him, He dies to redeem. If you bury Him, He rises again to bring us resurrection. Jesus is love manifest.[2]

The Lord who reigns on high is just as compassionate, holy, humble, good, approachable and delightful as Jesus. He declared,

> *Anyone who has seen me has seen the Father* (Jn. 14:9).

There is no other God in heaven, there is no other Sovereign Lord, but the one who has revealed Himself in Jesus of Nazareth.

- Jesus shows us the face of God.
- Jesus shows us the truth of God.
- Jesus shows us the love of God.

The Truth About God

No longer do we need to speculate. The Sovereign Lord has made Himself known. When you have seen Jesus—*you have seen God.* As the living "Word of God," Jesus Christ is God speaking to us, revealing to us the glory, the beauty, the truth about God.

"This is cosmic news," writes E. Stanley Jones, "—the Good News, that will make every planet, every cell, every thing dance with joy at the wonder of it . . . the only Good News that ever reached our planet."

"God is Christlike, and in Him there is no unchristlikeness at all," said Michael Ramsey.

God is just as beautiful as the Man from Nazareth.

Let this heart-stopping truth wash over you.

Let it take your breath away.

One writer exclaimed, "If this is the Heart of the universe, then He can have my heart."

WHAT STORY HAVE WE FALLEN INTO?

C. S. Lewis states: "We trust not because 'a God' exists, but because *this* God exists." We believe in God because of Jesus.

Correcting Our View of God

A university chaplain named George Buttrick would occasionally have students come into his office and say they no longer believed in God. Buttrick had an interesting way of disarming them: "Sit down and tell me what kind of God you don't believe in. I probably don't believe in that God either." He would then speak to them about Jesus—the one who corrects all our mistaken views of God.

"What kind of God do you *not* believe in?" is a helpful question to ask of non-believers. When pressed to explain, many confess that the God they don't believe in looks a whole lot like Zeus. And frankly, as followers of Christ, we don't believe in that God either. Tragically, many people are rejecting a deity who doesn't exist. If they ever caught sight of what God is really like, they might find it hard not to fall on their knees and like the disciple Thomas exclaim, *"My Lord and my God!"*

> *If you have an interpretation of God that doesn't look like Jesus— it's wrong.*
> —Mark Moore

"All our prevailing images and understandings of God must crumble in the earthquake of Jesus' self-disclosure," insists Brennan Manning.

The apostle Paul challenges us to rethink everything we ever thought about God in the light of Jesus Christ:

> *We demolish arguments and every pretension that sets itself up against the knowledge of God, and we take captive every thought to make it obedient to Christ* (2 Cor. 10:5).

"Anything that one imagines of God apart from Christ is only useless thinking and vain idolatry," declared Martin Luther.

And we know that the Son of God has come, and he has given us understanding so that we can know the true God (1 Jn. 5:20 NLT).

Jesus Christ is the truth about God:

- He is what God looks like (Heb. 1:3).
- He is what God lives like (Jn. 5:19).
- He is what God loves like (Rom. 5:8).
- He is what God has to say (Jn. 14:10).

The Incarnation allows human eyes to gaze into the heart of the One who birthed and ordered and directs the cosmos. It unveils the goodness and beauty of the Author of our story.

Thomas Torrance writes,

> There is in fact no God behind the back of Jesus, no act of God other than the act of Jesus, no God but the God we see and meet in him. Jesus Christ is the open heart of God, the very love and life of God poured out to redeem humankind, the mighty hand and power of God stretched out to heal and save sinners. All things are in God's hands, but the hands of God and the hands of Jesus, in life and in death, are the same.[3]

> *Jesus offered a long, slow look at the face of God.*
> —Philip Yancey

"There is no God but the one who said, 'Father, forgive them for they know not what they do,'" declared theologian Robert Jenson.[4]

S. D. Gordon wrote:

> He was the person of God wearing a human coat and human shoes . . . walking freely amongst us that we might get our tangled up ideas about God and ourselves and about life untangled, straightened out. He was God Himself . . . coming close that we might get acquainted with Him all over again.[5]

A True Picture of God

How do you picture the Lord of heaven? This is a soul-bending issue. Our lives are shaped by our view of God. False ideas about Him sabotage our hearts and disfigure our lives. It's impossible to exaggerate the importance of our mental image of our Maker.

- If He is a dictator, then we are just slaves.
- If He is a mere energy force, then we are on our own.
- If He is an uptight foreman, we will be pressured to perform.
- If He is a fussy moralist, we will be obsessed with rules.

But... *if He is like Jesus?*
That would be massively liberating.

To see God in Christ is to know Him as the joy-bringer, the seeker of the lost, the lifter of the fallen, the healer of hearts, the banisher of blindness, the Lord of laughter, the author of life and goodness and beauty, the hope of glory. Never have we seen anyone as wonderful as Jesus, and if God is like Him—*that is the best news ever broken to the human race.*

A Christ-Like God

"Whoever sees Christ as a mirror of the Father's heart, actually walks through the world with new eyes," said Martin Luther.

To have a Christlike God brings light into our darkness. It puts a song in our heart. It frees us to laugh and to live and to love. It draws us into a giving, sharing, satisfying enjoyment of divine favor. It infuses our lives with meaning. It teaches us to see with new eyes, and to live for God with joy and gratitude.

It fills our bewildering story with joy and hope and wonder.

The poet Byron declared, "If God isn't like Jesus Christ, He ought to be."

God is exactly like Jesus—and that changes everything!

PRAYER

OH LORD OUR GOD, how grateful we are that Someone came to show us the Father. Your beloved, eternal Son lived among us and dispelled our tangled and confused ideas about the God who reigns on high. Instead of demanding worship and submission, He came to serve, to give and to lay down His life for us. He revealed a God who pulsates with goodness and power and love and beauty. He showed us a divine Lord whose blessedness lies in giving rather than receiving, whose essence is an overflowing, unstoppable tsunami of grace. He showed up, not as a powerful monarch, but as a servant and sufferer—and overturned all our notions of deity. He showed us a God more wonderful and beautiful than we ever imagined. The glory of God has been revealed, and we stand amazed. We worship You with joyful hearts, oh Lord, our God. Amen.

"I and the Father are One,"
is the center-truth of the universe.
And the encircling truth is,
"That they also may be one in us."

—George MacDonald

CHAPTER TWENTY-ONE

THE WAY TO THE FATHER

It is God the only Son, who is close to the Father's heart...
JOHN 1:18 NRSV

ATHEIST PHILOSOPHER Bertrand Russell suggested that, if we could penetrate to the very center of all things, we would find a mathematical equation. And this would be the answer to the phenomena of our universe.

Not a heart-warming proposition.

This bleak, impersonal view of things effectively demolishes any thought of our existence having ultimate value or significance.

The Bible paints a delightfully different picture. It affirms that at the heart of the universe exists a relationship of indescribable beauty. John refers to it three times in his Logos-hymn:

- *the Word was with God* (1:1)
- *the one and only Son of the Father* (1:14)
- *the only Son, who is close to the Father* (1:18)

George MacDonald was a man of profound spiritual wisdom whose writings greatly impacted the most influential Christian autor of the twentieth century—C. S. Lewis. Read carefully MacDonald's words on what he termed "the issue of the universe":

> The secret of the whole story of humanity is the love between the Father and the Son. That is at the root of it all. Upon the love between the Son and the Father hangs the whole universe.[1]

Please don't miss what MacDonald is saying.

The marvelous mystery at the core of reality has to do with love. It has to do with the passionate, self-giving love and mutual delight of the Father and the Son. H. C. G. Moule writes, "Nothing shines more radiantly in the New Testament than the eternal love of the Father for the Son." This is the central "issue of the universe." This is the matrix of everything.

It is here we come to the richest and deepest truth at the heart of our Story. Let's delve deeper into the breathtaking vision John opens up for us.

Reality Rests on a Relationship

The Son of God is described as living *"in the bosom of the Father"* (Jn. 1:18 NKJV). John Wesley comments: "The expression denotes the highest unity, and the most intimate knowledge." This is not a relationship of cold, reserved formality. Here is exquisite belovedness and togetherness of profound intensity. The Son lives in the delight of His Father's warm embrace.

The love that flows between the Father and His Son is the underlying theme that pulsates throughout the Gospel of John.

- *The Father loves the Son...* (3:35)
- *For the Father loves the Son...* (5:20)
- *For this reason the Father loves me...* (10:17)
- *You loved me before the foundation of the world* (17:24)

Something stunningly beautiful is going on here.

Within the triune God, there is an outpouring of ecstatic, joyful love. The Father is utterly thrilled with His Son and showers Him with all His affection and gladness. The Beloved Son stands under the Niagara Falls of infinite delight. This torrential interchange of love has been going on forever—and it is the most incredible relationship in the universe.

C. S. Lewis describes it as "the great fountain of energy and beauty spurting up at the very center of reality."

This magnificent choreography of joyful oneness is fired by the other-centered love and mutual delight of the Father, Son and Spirit. It is this trinitarian celebration of glory and goodness that lies at the heart of the universe.

The Trinity Connection

In his Gospel, John speaks repeatedly of how Jesus relates to His Father. He gives us insight into the inner life of the triune God.

> *Very truly I tell you, the Son can do nothing by himself;*
> *he can do only what he sees his Father doing, because*
> *whatever the Father does the Son also does* (Jn. 5:19).

Jesus never acted on His own initiative. On the inside He was always looking into His Father's face. Everything He did and everything He said flowed out of that inner connection.

Jesus followed His Father's lead in everything. Consequently, if we want to see what the Father is like—we must look at His Son. Like Father, like Son. When we see Jesus—we see God. We see the wonder of Father's heart displayed in human form.

> *For the Father loves the Son and shows him all he does* (Jn. 5:20).

Jesus keeps talking about the love of His Father. Here is a relationship of unabashed openness, unreserved sharing and unclouded acceptance. The life of Christ was all about knowing and sharing His Father's love. He referred to it as His "food." He once said, *"I have food to eat that you know nothing about"* (Jn. 4:32). This was the secret of His strength—He lived on Love. He was a receiver and a reflector of God's love.

> *I do nothing on my own but speak just what the Father has*
> *taught me. The one who sent me is with me; he has not left*
> *me alone, for I always do what pleases him* (Jn. 8:28-29).

God's Son lived out of an interactive relationship with His Father. He lived in sync with heaven. His life was so fully connected to God that everything He did was an expression of the Father's goodness, love and joy.

> *Even though you do not believe me, believe the works, that you may know and understand that the Father is in me, and I in the Father* (Jn. 10:38).

The Son of Abba lived "in God." On the outside He walked the dusty roads of Galilee, but on the inside, He lived in His Father's embrace. That's where His heart made its home. That was the inner dynamic of His life. The carpenter from Nazareth lived reveling in and reflecting the love of His Father.

God's Eternal Dream

Let's turn to the best-known verse in the Bible:

> *For this is the way God loved the world: He gave his one and only Son, so that everyone who believes in him will not perish but have eternal life* (Jn. 3:16 NET)

Why did God's Son come to this world?

Notice that He did *not* come so God could love us. Christ did not come to change, but to *reveal* the heart of the Father. He came because the love of the triune God for us was so great He could not rest content until we were included in that circle.

John 3:16 is God saying in effect: "I did not create you so that you would perish. I created you so that you would experience my love and my joy. I made you so that you would be part of the Eternal Dance, and I will not resign myself to having you far from me. I am sending my Son to do whatever is necessary so that you will be brought back into the circle of my love."

More than forty times in John's Gospel, Jesus says He was "sent" by the Father. He came because the Father had a dream—a dream to make us participants of His glory. *God did not want to be God without us.* And, in essence, He says to His Son: "Go and get them back. It doesn't matter what it costs. It doesn't matter what we have to do."

Christ finally agonizes and dies on a cross because *the Father was unwilling to let us go.* He gave His Beloved Son because His heart was set upon us. And there was *nothing* He was not willing to do in order to bring us back in His loving embrace.

This is the God Jesus came to reveal.

When God Speaks to God

> *The Trinity does not wish to live alone in its splendid trinitarian communion.*
> —JÜRGEN MOLTMANN

What would it be like to listen in on a conversation inside the Holy Trinity between Father and Son? That is exactly what we have in John chapter 17. It is one of the most remarkable chapters in the Scriptures. It brings us to the innermost circle. Here the Son opens His heart with His Father.

And what is the conversation about?

Here's the amazing thing—about forty times Christ speaks of those whom the Father has given Him. This heart to heart talk between Son and Father focuses on those who belong to Christ.

> *My prayer is not for them alone. I pray also for those who will believe in me through their message* (Jn. 17:20).

Not only does Christ pray for His group of disciples, but for all those who would trust Him and become His followers.

Pay close attention to the petition of Christ:

> *...that all of them may be one, Father, just as you are in me and I am in you* (Jn. 17:21).

Jesus makes a staggering request.

It has to do with the incomparable love that flows between the Father and His Son. Never has there been an outpouring of love such as exists between them. It is where love hits its high water mark. It is the ultimate circle of glory.

But, here's the astonishing part.

Abba's Son requests that the circle of love be widened to include others. He prays that those who believe in Him be brought into the eternal dance of glory.

The coming of Christ to this world was not just about saving us —but about *sharing His glory with us!* This was God's purpose from before the foundation of the world (Eph. 1:4). He had determined in eternity that we be included in the circle of everlasting joy.

To be taken to heaven to be dish-washers or street-sweepers— that would be a privilege great enough to praise God forever. *But to be sharers of God's glory?* How can we even begin to explain that?

This surpasses by far the deepest longings of our hearts. The wonder of it is enough to blow out all our circuits.

Spreading Glory

Jesus' prayer continues:

> *I have given them the glory that you gave me, that they may be one as we are one—I in them and you in me—so that they may be brought to complete unity* (Jn. 17:22-23).

When a man and a woman unite in marriage, they become "one flesh." A unique oneness happens. Two become one. But Christ is speaking of oneness on a deeper level—spiritual oneness. Human beings united and "one" with the eternal fountain of life and love.

Jesus refers to this connection with God as "glory"—the glory of oneness with the Father. It is the supreme privilege of being enveloped by Infinite Love. It is what God's Beloved Son has enjoyed forever. And this "glory" is what He now shares with us!

Could anything be more amazing than that?

The Gospel turns out to be more fantastic than we dreamed!

> *Then the world will know that you sent me and have loved them even as you have loved me* (Jn. 17:23).

How great is the Father's love for us?

Notice what Jesus said: "*You... have loved them EVEN AS* (not almost as) *you have loved me.*" Let that sink in. The love of God in all its fullness is directed toward you, right here and right now. Not a lesser, watered-down, low octane version. The Father loves each one of His adopted sons and daughters with the *same* fierce intensity of love with which He loves His Only Beloved Son.

Loved with the same intensity of love?

If it were not Christ who said it, we might be tempted to doubt it was true. The eternal joy and delight of the Father has turned toward us. We could not be loved more than we are right now. Is there anything that could possible compare with that?

I don't think we have the foggiest idea of what we, as Christ followers, have gotten ourselves into. We have been included in the eternal circle of glory, brought into Christ's relationship with His Father. This is like winning the biggest lottery in the universe!

We can't fully explain what this is all about. It goes beyond anything we have ever dreamed about. It exceeds everything our heart has ever longed for. This is the Mount Everest of all experiences. This is the ultimate privilege.

The Staggering Gift

One afternoon, a well-known theologian and author was settling down on his couch to watch a football game on television. Out of the corner of his eye, he spotted his seven-year-old son with one of his buddies dressed in pretend army gear. The two young soldiers suddenly leaped into action and launched an attack on the father. Before he knew it, the three of them were rolling on the floor, laughing, wrestling and having fun.

Interestingly, the dad had never met his son's friend who had come in and tackled him. They were complete strangers. But now they were tussling on the floor, having a great time together.

Afterward the father thought: "How fascinating. Here's a boy I don't even know. He came into my house and jumped all over me. We wrestled and played—and I don't even know his name."

How would it occur to a young fellow to do that?

WHAT STORY HAVE WE FALLEN INTO?

The answer is simple. When the son started playing with his dad, his buddy simply joined in. He got to enjoy the special relationship his friend had with his father. The boy was not a part of the family, but his friend drew him in and included him in the fun.

The father gained a profound theological insight. From all eternity God's Beloved Son enjoyed a rich, unfettered, delight-filled relationship with his Father. And in sheer grace, the Son of Abba purposed that this overflowing fellowship of goodness would not be His alone—it would be shared with others. The circle would be widened. The Divine Son says to us, "Come on in, I want you to be a part of this."

Rich biblical truth had been played out before his eyes. In profound simplicity, there it was—*a living parable of the Gospel itself.*

The Lord Jesus Christ came to make us a part of His Story. The Son of God became the Son of Man so that the sons of men could become sons of God. He came to share with us His home-life with His Father. He brings us into the enjoyment of what He has always enjoyed.

- His Father becomes our Father (20:17)
- His joy becomes our joy (15:11; 17:13)
- His peace becomes our peace (14:27)
- His love becomes our love (15:9)
- His glory becomes our glory (17:22)
- His mission becomes our mission (20:21)

Abba's Son gives us the staggering gift of participating in the fullness, the richness, the wonder of His relationship with His Father. This is perhaps the most astonishing miracle of all. This is the highest honor that God, by His grace, could grant to a believer.

Dan Cruver states, "There is no better news in the universe (or outside of it, for that matter) than the news that we are loved by the Father even as the Father loves the Son."

We have been brought into the circle of eternal joy.

This is now our true story.

This is now our heart's true home.

PRAYER

HEAVENLY FATHER, thank You for revealing to us that at the heart and center of universe is the wild extravagance of Your love for Your Son. This almighty interchange of love is the foundation, the focus, the flame, the reason, the nucleus of everything—and it is indescribably beautiful. What we cannot fathom is that You would open up and include us in this circle of glory. "I have given them the glory that you gave me." Could this possibly be true? Could such a privilege indeed be ours? Our minds stagger at the thought, and we dare to ask that your Holy Spirit would reveal this truth to our hearts. It appears that we have come into a story of mystery and glory and beauty beyond our dreams. We have become objects of a love beyond our understanding. We bow and worship You, our God, at the unspeakable wonder of it all. Amen.

*The Spirit… is the matchmaker…
whose role it is to bring us and Christ
together and ensure that
we stay together.*

—James I. Packer

CHAPTER TWENTY-TWO

THE GIVER OF THE SPIRIT

Then John gave this testimony: "I saw the Spirit come down from heaven as a dove and remain on him."
JOHN 1:32

A VISITING SPEAKER FROM ARGENTINA was arriving in our town in the mountains of Bolivia, and I had been asked to meet him at the bus terminal. I was on my way there when I suddenly realized I had been given no details on the man I was to find. The bus station was a busy place. How would I ever recognize him?

I wandered around the crowded terminal looking for this unknown person. I didn't know if he was young or old, tall or short. Speakers come in all sizes.

I finally spotted a traveller looking somewhat lost. Perhaps he was the one. I approached him and asked. His face lit up. He gave me a hug. I had found my visitor from Argentina.

The Unmistakable Sign

For many centuries our world awaited the arrival of someone who would be the secret to our story. The One who would bring light into our darkness. A long line of Hebrew prophets foretold His coming, and John the Baptist was the last of them. John had the privilege of not only predicting His arrival but also of presenting him.

How could the prophet recognize Him when he came?

He was given a sign:

> *The one who sent me to baptize with water told me, "The man on whom you see the Spirit come down and remain is the one who will baptize with the Holy Spirit"* (Jn. 1:33).

John was given a clear sign—the Holy Spirit would visibly descend and remain upon someone. When that happened, the prophet could be sure that the Messiah had arrived.

John probably baptized thousands of people. And each time nothing unusual took place—*until he baptized Jesus*. Then it happened. A voice was heard from heaven, and the Spirit of God came fluttering down in the form of a dove, landed on Him—*and stayed there*.

The Baptizer announced:

> *I have seen and I testify that this is God's Chosen One* (Jn. 1:34).

When the Trinity Comes Into View

There is a special connection between the Son and the Spirit. Jesus is identified by the Spirit, is baptized by the Spirit and His mission is to baptize with the Spirit. A clear understanding of what Christ came to do requires that we pay attention to this one called the "Holy Spirit."

First of all, notice this was a Trinity moment.

Jesus went into the water, the Father spoke, and the Spirit descended. A profound revelation was taking place. The God of heaven was showing Himself as Father, Son and Holy Spirit. Never before had the "threeness" of God been seen so clearly. We are being introduced to the Trinity.

Notice what is taking place. As the Father announces, *"You are my Beloved Son,"* the Holy Spirit comes from the Father and lights upon the Son. Here we have a Father loving His Son—and the Spirit moving between them. Look closely—*this is a fascinating glimpse into the inner life of God.*

We have previously seen that Father and Son live in a relatedness of unsurpassed harmony, love and joy. Now we observe there is someone who moves between them—the Holy Spirit. Is He the bond of love that unites them? In the book of Song of Solomon, the dove repeatedly emerges as a symbol of love and affection (2:14; 4:1; 5:2). Is the dove that descended upon Jesus a visible symbol of the love that flows between Father and Son?

The Spirit of Love

After twenty years of study on the Trinity, Augustine concluded that the identity of the Holy Spirit is best seen in the communion of the Father and the Son as the mutual love that flows between them. This viewpoint is shared by many biblical scholars and writers: Thomas Aquinas, Jonathan Edwards, George MacDonald, C. S. Lewis, and others.

> *The Father loves. The Son is loved. The Spirit is the love that binds them together.*
>
> —KARL BARTH

John Piper states, "The Spirit of God is the river of love and delight flowing between God the Father and God the Son."

In his first epistle, John points out that to have the love of God in us is to have the Spirit in us.

> *If we love one another, God lives in us and his love is made complete in us. This is how we know that we live in him and he in us: He has given us of his Spirit* (1 Jn. 4:12-13).

Paul similarly states:

> *God's love has been poured out into our hearts through the Holy Spirit, who has been given to us* (Rom. 5:5).

Love is not a liquid to be stored in a bottle and spilled out by the liter. How then, does God "pour" His love into people? The answer is clear—*He gives them His Spirit.* Is the Spirit of God synonymous with the love of God? Apparently so.

This leads us to an astonishing conclusion.

At the center of reality, there is a community of love we call God. God is the loving unity of three Persons. The love that flows between the Father and the Son is so powerful, so deep, so rich, that it has a Name. He is a Person. He is Divine. He is called: *the Holy Spirit.* He is the shared love between Father and Son. *The Holy Spirit is the bond of love that unites the Trinity.*

The Divine Connection

A visit to Niagara Falls is an unforgettable experience. The sheer power and volume of water is staggering. It's overwhelming. It's unrestrainable.

Much like the Holy Spirit.

In God, love flows like a mighty unstoppable river. The Father loves the Son and the Son loves the Father, and they share all things in the overflowing love of the Holy Spirit. This relationship is unfathomably deep and rich. It is beautiful beyond words.

Sadly, in the minds of many, the idea of a "Holy" Spirit denotes what is correct and proper and meticulous. Holiness is thought to mean "uptightness." We have some deconstructing to do. Holiness is not the severe side of God. Holiness is what gives beauty to all of His attributes. Holiness means one-of-a kind, incomparable, unlike anything else. It is utter uniqueness that inspires awe and admiration. It is properly understood as something winsome, attractive and delightful.[1]

Holy Harmony

The Holy Spirit does *not* make His home in a court of law. He resides in the intimacy, love and face-to-face togetherness of the Father and the Son. "Holy" involves the incomparable goodness, joy, harmony, wholesomeness, and delightfulness of that relationship. It's what makes God unsurpassably wonderful and beautiful.

This community of ultimate togetherness came into view in a new way that day at the Jordan River. The Father's love was verbalized and simultaneously made visible by the dove descending on Abba's Son. The only topic of discussion was love, and that's to be expected, because that's what this three-in-one Divine Community is all about.

It was revealed to John the Baptist that the one on whom the Spirit descends will be the *giver* of the Spirit.

What's that all about?

A helpful insight is found in Luke 11:13. In this verse, Christ says if bad people are capable of giving good gifts to their children, should we not expect God, who is good to the core, to give *superlatively* good gifts? That's how we *expected* Jesus to finish the sentence. But He says something different: *"How much more will your Father in heaven give the Holy Spirit to those who ask Him!"*

So what is God's superlative gift? *The Holy Spirit.* This is the ultimate gift. Nothing greater could be bestowed upon us. This is the gift that exceeds all others, that includes all others.

It is God's love coming to us.

It is God Himself coming to us.

The Gift of God

Notice how this subject crops up all through the book of John.

- Chapter 1 - Messiah has come to baptize people in the Spirit.
- Chapter 2 - Wine is a symbol of new life and joy in the Spirit.
- Chapter 3 - New birth takes place by a work of the Spirit.
- Chapter 4 - The fountain of living water is the Spirit.
- Chapter 7 - Inner rivers of living water flow from the Spirit.

Christ delves deeper into this subject on His last night with His disciples. The moment has arrived for the Lord to depart, and He makes it clear that He is coming back. This is the repeated theme in chapters 14-17.

The statement of Christ, *"I am going away and I am coming back to you"* (Jn. 14:28) is a double-entendre. Not only will there be a "coming" at the end of the age, there is a "coming" that takes place when His Spirit takes up His residence in the believer. This new reality began on the Day of Pentecost.

> *And I will ask the Father, and he will give you another advocate to help you and be with you forever—the Spirit of truth. The world cannot accept him, because it neither sees him nor knows him. But you know him, for he lives with you and will be in you* (Jn. 14:16-17).

Someone just like Jesus was going to come, not just to be *with* them, but to be *in* them. The disciples had walked with Christ for three years, but something more wonderful was about to take place. The Spirit of Christ would not simply accompany them; He would *indwell* them. Now the divine presence will be on the *inside*. God will be where they most need Him—*in their hearts*.

> *I will not leave you as orphans; I will come to you* (Jn. 14:18).

Right after saying the Spirit will come, Jesus says, *"I will come to you."* Well, which one is it? The Spirit or Christ? *"I will come to you"* must mean that *the Holy Spirit is Christ coming to us in a different form.* The Holy Spirit is the Spirit of Christ, who brings to the believer the presence of the resurrected Lord. Pentecost is Christ returning to reside in His followers by His Spirit.

The Gospel and the Spirit

There are four pillars upon which the Gospel rests:

- The incarnation and life of Christ
- The redeeming death of Christ
- The resurrection and ascension of Christ
- The outpouring of the Spirit of Christ

It is important to notice the baptism of the Holy Spirit is not an optional item for religious zealots, an add-on for the spiritual elite. *It is an essential component of the Gospel.* It is a vital link in the chain of salvation.

THE GIVER OF THE SPIRIT

The Spirit of God comes to make real in the believer all that was accomplished through the life, death and resurrection of Christ.

Without the presence of the Spirit in our lives, all our Saviour did would be little more than wonderful historical events. It is the Spirit who unites us to Christ. He makes us participants of all that the Son of God accomplished for us through His life, death, resurrection and ascension. Thus the redemptive work Christ becomes more than history—*it becomes a present reality.* The "Spirit of Truth" comes to make it real or "true" in the life of the believer.

Now we come to an astounding verse:

> *On that day [when the Spirit comes] you will realize that I am in my Father, and you are in me, and I am in you* (Jn. 14:20).

Here we run into an unusual phrase Jesus often uses: *"The Father is in Me, and I in Him"* (Jn. 10:38; 14:11; 17:21).

How can a person be "in" someone else? What is Christ saying? The word "in" goes beyond the idea of "near" or "with." It suggests a togetherness of uncommon depth and richness. This wonderful inner connection with His Father was the central reality of Jesus' life.

Here's the amazing part—the Spirit will help us to know something remarkable. And it is this . . .

> **We are invited to share in this inner and loving life of God.**
> —N. T. Wright

The connection of unqualified acceptance, affection and delight the Son has always had with the Father, *is now shared with others.* This is the connection believers *now* have with Christ. *You will realize that . . . you are in me, and I am in you.*

The same phrase Jesus uses to describe His relationship with His Father is now applied to His followers.

Stop and take this in.

The life-giving Spirit that unites the Blessed Trinity, now comes into human lives and makes them a part of this fellowship of glory. The Love that flows between the Father and the Son—is now poured into the hearts of those who belong to Christ.

The Spirit comes to lead us into the *truth* (Jn. 16:13). This, as Henri Nouwen points out, does not mean an idea, concept or doctrine, but *the true relationship*. "To be led into the truth is to be led into the same relationship that Jesus had with the Father."[2]

Believers are brought into a deep connection with God. They are included in the Divine circle of love and glory. Immersed into the life of the Father and the Son. Baptized into a belonging, into a belovedness, into a blessedness too wonderful for words.

Living Water

God's original dream for humans is nothing less than for us to be participants in the Niagara of love that goes on inside of God.

Jesus talked about it in John 7.

> *Let anyone who is thirsty come to me and drink. Whoever believes in me, as Scripture has said, rivers of living water will flow from within them* (Jn. 7:37-38).

What is this thirst-quenching water?

> *By this he meant the Spirit...* (Jn. 7:39).

We have come to see that the Spirit is the bond of love between the Father and the Son. By giving us His Spirit, Christ shares this love with us. He places His Spirit within us and says, "Drink from this river of love. It is for you to enjoy."

In Christ we have been brought to a river that is deep and wide. At present we are able to take in so little. But there's a Niagara of love. It defies all imagination.

We were created to drink this water. When sin drew us away, redemption brought us back. This is where we now must live. This is where we find living water for our soul.

We need to drink daily.

This is the only water that truly satisfies thirsty hearts.

PRAYER

BLESSED GOD OUR FATHER, if Your goodness were not infinitely patient, and Your mercy were not so much stronger than our waywardness, we would be hopelessly lost. We thank You that Your love is unfailing, unwavering, unending, and will not let us go. How little we perceive the depth, height, length and breadth of Your love. How blind we are to its reality, its richness and fullness. Our prayer, oh Lord, is that we might receive our sight. Teach us that Your love is better than life. Keep us from seeking life in places where it is not to be found. Only Your love can expose and replace the idols of our heart. Only your love can break the chains of our selfishness, and set us free to love well and live well. Satisfy us with Your unfailing love, that we may sing for joy and be glad all our days. In the Name of Christ our Savior, Amen.

*We have received an invitation.
We are invited to make a pilgrimage
into the heart and life of God.*

—Dallas Willard

CHAPTER TWENTY-THREE

A NEW PLACE TO LIVE

They said, "Rabbi . . . where are you staying?"
JOHN 1:38

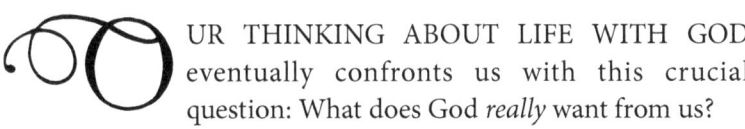UR THINKING ABOUT LIFE WITH GOD eventually confronts us with this crucial question: What does God *really* want from us? Commitment? Holiness? Service? Obedience?

None of the above.

As a matter of fact, *even the question is wrong.* It presupposes God is all about *getting* something from you. That He is a greedy God. A self-serving Deity. A predatory overlord who wants to squeeze everything He can out of your life.

What He *really* wants may surprise you. It might blow you away. It might even turn your life around.

Let's look at John's stunning answer to this question, beginning with an incident found in the first chapter.

Meeting the Messiah

Large crowds are flocking to hear John the Baptist preach at the Jordan River. Many are becoming His followers. The prophet keeps telling them that someone extraordinary is about to appear on the scene.

Expectations run high.

Finally the day comes when the man of God calls out, "Look, there He is!" He identifies the awaited Messiah using an unusual codename: *"Lamb of God"* (Jn. 1:36).

Two of the Baptist's followers look at each other and say, "What are we waiting for?" And they begin to follow Jesus.

> *Turning around, Jesus saw them following and asked, "What do you want?"* (Jn. 1:38).

This catches them off guard. What do you say when you come face to face with God's Messiah? The two men are stuck for words, and they quickly try to think of something to say. Finally, one of them blurts out, "Where are you staying?"

It was a flimsy attempt at getting a conversation going. Small talk of no particular importance. Like talking about the weather.

Jesus diffuses the awkward moment and responds:

> *"Come, and you will see." So they went and saw where He was staying, and they spent the day with Him. It was about four in the afternoon* (Jn. 1:38).

Andrew and his friend were invited to Messiah's place. We are not told what His living quarters were like, but the two men got a chance to hang out with Jesus. That's what they really wanted.

This incident seems rather mundane and unimportant. Hardly worth mentioning. Why does John insert this seemingly inconsequential story into his first chapter? Was it simply to fill up the page?

No, John never wastes words. He never adds irrelevant details.

Far from being a pointless anecdote, this incident has enormous significance. It sums up the message of the *entire* book of John. It takes us to the heart and essence of the mystery and wonder of why Christ came. There is rich spiritual meaning here.

Where the Heart Has its Home

Where does Jesus live? The Greek verb *"meno"* used here is a loaded word in the book of John. He uses it more than any other

New Testament writer. It means to reside, dwell, abide, or remain. It carries the idea of a permanent residence, the place we call "home."

Where was "home" for Jesus?

He was known as *"Jesus of Nazareth"* (Jn. 1:45)—that was His hometown. Later on, He centered His ministry in Capernaum. This is where He slept at night, where He lived geographically.

But, as usual in this Fourth Gospel, there is another level of meaning here. John uses the word *"meno"* not just to speak about a physical address but a spiritual address. Where a person lives on the inside. Where the heart makes its home.

The apostle has already commented on Jesus' heart address in verse 18—"*the only Son, who is in the bosom of the Father.*" This is where God's Son dwelt on the inside. He enjoyed a unique free-flowing togetherness with His Father. He lived in His Father's warm embrace. This was his *real* home. Jesus lived in God.

> *Do not believe me unless I do the works of my Father. But if I do them, even though you do not believe me, believe the works, that you may know and understand that the Father is in me, and I in the Father* (Jn. 10:37-38).

The last phrase is a fascinating one: *"the Father is in me, and I in the Father."* This is a togetherness so profound and complete that the best way to describe it is that they are "in" one another. Some refer to this as "mutual indwelling." One writer described it like this: "By virtue of their eternal love they live . . . and dwell in one another to such an extent, that they are one."

A Profound Theological Question

When the two disciples asked, "Rabbi, where are you staying?" Jesus could have said, "I am so glad you asked that question. As it turns out, I live in the most wonderful place in the universe. I live in the abounding fullness of my Father's love. I make my home in the divine circle of passion and goodness and wonder and joy. That's where I live—and I'd love to take you there."

That was too much theology to unload at one time.

It would take some time before they could process the magnitude of what the Master wanted to teach them. He would have to take them there, step by step, and gradually unfold this mystery to them: *Rabbi, where do you live?*

The answer to this question is what John's book is all about. Jesus responds, *"Come and see,"* and throughout the rest of this Gospel, He is taking them on a journey—*a journey into the Father's heart.* He is leading them to the place where He dwells. He is taking them back to the Source of life and joy. He knows humans have been orphaned since Eden, *and He has come to bring them home.*

Where Jesus really unpacks this topic is on his final evening with His disciples. John dedicates several chapters to this farewell conversation—far more than any other Gospel. Let's go there.

A Very Big House

The Lord is about to leave His disciples and then return in a different form. From then on, He is not going to be "with" them—He is going to be "in" them by His Spirit. His relationship with them is about to take on a new dimension. The Lord is preparing them for that moment.

> *Do not let your hearts be distressed. You believe in God; believe also in me. There are many dwelling places in my Father's house. Otherwise, I would have told you, because I am going away to make ready a place for you* (Jn. 14:1-2 NET).

Christ plans to take His followers to His "Father's house." Earlier in this book we mentioned that this is not merely about heaven. It's also about a relationship in the present—a spiritual abode for homeless human hearts.

The term "The Father's House" suggests intimate kinship. It denotes a place of security, of belonging. It is where sons and daughters are not just acknowledged, but also welcomed, accepted, cherished, embraced and delighted in. In short, this is where Jesus lived. And the wonderful news is this—*this is where He wants to take us.*

In one short phrase, the One who lives in the Father's embrace sums up the purpose of His coming: *"That where I am, you may be also."* This is the eternal plan.

This is what our story is all about.

George MacDonald wrote, "This is and has been the Father's work from the beginning—to bring us into the home of his heart ... This is our destiny."[1]

The Lord is saying something like this: "Where my Father lives is a big, big place. There's lots of room for more people. There's lots of love to go around. There's more than you can even imagine. I have been living there forever. All this time that I have been walking around Galilee with you, on the inside I have been living in my Father's embrace. It's where my heart lives. And, what's more—it is where I want you to live."

> *Jesus answered, "I am the way and the truth and the life. No one comes to the Father except through me"* (Jn. 14:6).

The Master is not simply talking about where we go when we die. He's speaking about getting connected to the Father *while we live.* And Christ came to establish that connection.

- He is the WAY to the Father.
- He is the TRUTH about the Father.
- He draws us into LIFE with the Father.

> *Believe me when I say that I am in the Father and the Father is in me* (Jn. 14:11).

Don't rush past this verse. It takes us to the pivotal issue of the universe. At the center of everything is found the ultimate togetherness of the Father, Son and Holy Spirit. They are caught up in a heavenly dance of goodness and delight. This is where God's Beloved Son lives. And here's the staggering part:

WHAT STORY HAVE WE FALLEN INTO?

> As the Father has loved me, so have I loved you; abide in my love (Jn. 15:9 NRSV).

Not only does Jesus live in the Father's embrace—*this is where He wants us to live.*

A New Address

Abba's Son lived receiving, enjoying and sharing the love of His Father. His life was rooted in that love. It was where He lived and moved and had His being. Now we are called to abide, remain, reside in this love. It's the same verb *"meno"* used in chapter one, when the disciples asked where Jesus lived. The place where Christ lives is now where His followers are to live.

The Master is saying, "My life has been a living demonstration of my Father's love. You have seen it, you have tasted it, now I want you to live there. I want you to stay there. Build your house there. It's where I live—it's where I want you to live."

> **There is rest in this world nowhere except in Christ, the manifested love of God.**
> —Frederick W. Robertson

I have told you this so that my joy may be in you and that your joy may be complete (Jn. 15:11).

What "joy" is Jesus referring to?
Listen to Charles Spurgeon:

> The joy of Jesus is, first, the joy of abiding in His Father's love. He knows that His Father loves Him—that He never did anything else but love Him… Now that is the joy which Christ gives to you—the joy of knowing that your Father loves you!

The Son of Abba is saying: "My joy is to live in my Father's love. It's what makes my heart dance. And I want you to live where I live, and I want my joy to be your joy. This joy is for you—not partially but in full measure."

The Father's Plan

What does God want from you?

This was the question posed at the beginning of this chapter. The message of John's Gospel leads us to the following conclusion:

God wants us to live in His love.

Does this surprise you?

This is what God wants—because this is the launching pad for everything else. This frees us to run the race with joy. To love and serve and forgive. It enables us to bear the fatigue of sacrifice. It gives us a firm foundation for living. The Father wants us to know we are accepted, embraced and loved. *He wants us to live there.*

> *Live on Christ's love while you are here, and all the way.*
> —Samuel Rutherford

Fourteenth century writer Julian of Norwich wrote, "The greatest honor we can give to God is to live gladly because of the knowledge of his love."

Many of us find it hard to believe God could look at us and smile. Abba's Son dares us to believe it. He calls us to rest in the Father's love, enjoy it, respond to it and share it with others. That's how Christ lived His life. *That's how we are to live ours.*

One of the two disciples who spent that first afternoon with Jesus was Andrew (Jn. 1:40). The second one remains anonymous. We suspect it was John, the writer of the Fourth Gospel, but we are not given his name.

There's a reason for that...

Each one of us should place himself in the sandals of the unnamed disciple. We too need to respond personally to Christ's invitation to "come and see." We are called to live where Jesus lived.

It's not about straining to be "spiritual." It's not about memorizing Genesis to Revelation. It's not about mystical flights to the stratosphere.

It's about relaxing in the Love of Abba.

Fellow believer, you are not ignored, neglected or overlooked. You are not "one in a crowd." You are called by name. You are welcomed, acknowledged, accepted and embraced by the Father. He is

WHAT STORY HAVE WE FALLEN INTO?

not going through the motions, or fulfilling some divine obligation. You are His treasure, prized and cherished. He looks upon you with undiluted affection and delight and says, "You are mine. This is where you are to make your home."

T. Austin-Sparks writes:

> The one object the Devil has in view is to raise a question, nay, to establish in you a question, as to God's love and your belovedness to God—that is, personally. If we have any doubt about that, we are finished. This sense of what I have called 'belovedness' is essential . . . To go on quietly, persistently, assuredly, in peace, all rests upon this—the recognition that . . . I am beloved of God.[2]

> *Be always under the sunshine of the gospel.*
> —Richard Sibbes

I'm not very good at this, but I'm learning that I am valued and loved despite my failures. I'm learning there's nothing I can do to deserve His embrace—but it's mine. I have trouble wrapping my brain around that. However, it's where I'm learning to live—*and it's a wonderful place.*

E. Stanley Jones states: "We . . . have one business in life and only one business: to live inside the love of Christ, in union with Him."

If you are a believer in Christ, you have been embraced by the love of the Father. His favor rests upon you fully and permanently.

- He doesn't love us because we're lovable.
- He doesn't love us because we're faithful.
- He doesn't love us because we're useful.
- He loves us—because He loves us. Period.

It makes no difference if you don't understand it. It makes no difference if you cannot feel it. The fact remains: *You are loved by Abba.* If you are a believer, you are His precious child. He wants you to know that. He wants you to live in the enjoyment of that.

You have a new home, a new zip code.

Can you think of a better place to live?

PRAYER

HEAVENLY FATHER, we have hearts that are fearful, anxious and needy. Hearts that are hungry for a place of belonging, a place of acceptance and affection. We are thrilled to discover that we have been welcomed into "the Father's house"—a place where we are valued, cherished, desired and treasured. A place of warmth and safety and joy that we thought only existed in our dreams. God of glory, it is beyond our understanding that You should call us by name, that You would make us the objects of Your lavish, unwavering affection. May Your Spirit let our hearts know that it's true. Dispel our doubts and fears. Teach us to live in the calm assurance of Your unfailing love. We bow and give You thanks, oh God our Father. We honor and praise Your wonderful Name, through Jesus Christ our Lord. Amen.

*In Jesus, God has put up a 'Gone Fishing' sign
on the religion shop. He has done the whole job in Jesus
once and for all and simply invited us to believe it . . .
no fasting till your knees fold, no prayers you have
to get right or else, no standing on your head with
your right thumb in your left ear and reciting
the correct creed... The entire show has been set
to rights in the Mystery of Christ.*

—Robert Farrar Capon

CHAPTER TWENTY-FOUR

A LADDER TO HEAVEN

He then added, "Very truly I tell you, you will see heaven open, and the angels of God ascending and descending on the Son of Man."
JOHN 1:51

ONE OF THE IMPORTANT RELICS found in Rome is *The Scala Santa*, or The Holy Stairs. These are set of 28 white marble steps that lead up to the Church of St. Lawrence.

According to Catholic tradition, Jesus walked on these stairs on His way to trial in the praetorium of Pontius Pilate. It is believed they were brought from Jerusalem to Rome in the fourth century.

The church taught that if you climbed the 28 stone steps on your hands and knees, saying an "Our Father" on each one, when you reached the top, you would have released a soul from purgatory.

In the 1500s, Martin Luther visited Rome and prayed his way up the stairs on his hands and knees. When he arrived at the top, he looked back and asked himself, "What if it's not true?"

Luther returned to Germany, delved into the book of Romans, and discovered what started the Reformation. The Highway to Heaven was not a set of stairs in Rome. It wasn't even climbing up some ladder of moral perfection. He discovered that *the ladder was Christ.*

WHAT STORY HAVE WE FALLEN INTO?

The "ladder" analogy shows up in the first chapter of John. A fellow named Philip was called to follow Christ, and he quickly finds his friend Nathanael to tell him about it. Nathanael is skeptical that the Messiah could possibly come from a town with a bad reputation like Nazareth, and he is invited to see for himself. Here's what happened:

> *When Jesus saw Nathanael approaching, He said of him, "Here truly is an Israelite in whom there is no deceit."*
> *"How do you know me?" Nathanael asked.*
> *Jesus answered, "I saw you while you were still under the fig tree before Philip called you."*
> *Then Nathanael declared, "Rabbi, you are the Son of God; you are the king of Israel"* (Jn. 1:47-48).

They had never met, but Christ knew all about Philip's friend. That was proof enough for Nathanael, and he became a believer.

Now, pay attention to this verse:

> *He then added, "Very truly I tell you, you will see 'heaven open, and the angels of God ascending and descending on' the Son of Man"* (Jn. 1:51).

Open heavens, angels ascending and descending. What is that all about?

A Jewish person would immediately be reminded of an incident in the life of the patriarch Jacob. The story is vital for understanding what Christ was saying.

A Man on the Run

Jacob had deceived his father and cheated his brother Esau to get the rights of the firstborn and become the heir. This did not sit well with his brother who now wanted to kill him. Jacob decided it was a good moment to leave town. He quickly said goodbye and made his getaway. He had made a mess of things, and now he was running away.

What a good picture of humanity's plight!

We too have blundered badly. We once made our home in a wonderful paradise; it was heaven on earth. We decided not to pay attention to a "Thou shalt not eat" sign—and that ruined everything. It brought about a spiritual disconnection between the human race and God. As a result, we are not doing well on Planet Earth. We have played the role of Jacob, and things are a mess.

The deceiver was now on the run. One night, as he camped under the open sky, Jacob used a stone as a pillow and went to sleep. It is here we come to the verse picked up by Jesus in John 1.

> *He had a dream in which he saw a stairway resting on the earth, with its top reaching to heaven, and the angels of God were ascending and descending on it* (Gn. 28:12).

In his dream, Jacob saw angels moving up and down on the ladder that reached from earth to heaven. In the verses following, God repeats the promises that He had made to Jacob's grandfather, Abraham. Jacob is promised a land with numerous descendants and a blessing for all the nations of the world.

It is an astounding promise. Its ultimate fulfillment involves God healing the brokenness of His good creation. It's a promise of redemption, of setting things right. God pledges to watch over Jacob and to faithfully fulfill what He has promised.

The very ordinary place where Jacob was camping had turned into a sacred spot. Jacob had encountered God there. And he called the place "Bethel"—the house of God.

Jacob had not climbed some ladder of pious achievement. In fact, *Jacob was not very pious at all!* He had just hoodwinked his father, and ripped off his brother. And now, the deceiver was on the run.

Jacob was not engaged in some spiritual activity. He was not offering some sacrifice to God. He was sleeping on the side of a Judean hill, vulnerable and alone. Jacob was not making promises to God, but God had some promises for him.

As the swindler sleeps, God draws near, not to punish him for his sins, but to give him a stupendous promise of blessing for his descendants and for the entire world.

> *All the families of the earth shall be blessed in you and in your offspring. Know that I am with you and will keep you wherever you go, and will bring you back to this land; for I will not leave you until I have done what I have promised you* (Gn. 28:14-15).

What a remarkable picture of God's grace! The man had botched things badly, and God seeks him out and tells him of great blessings He has in store for him. Undeserved, unexpected, uncalled-for grace.

The Promise Fulfilled

In the New Testament, we discover that the promise made to Jacob has to do with the blessing of the Gospel (Gal. 3:8,16). God was committing Himself, in the presence of angels, to bring salvation to the world. Salvation basically means—He's going to rescue us from the disastrous results of the Fall. And God plans to do it through one of Jacob's descendants.

About 2,000 years go by, and one day on the banks of the Jordan River, the prophet John the Baptist sees a thirty-year old carpenter from Nazareth, and says: "That's Him! The time is fulfilled. This is the One we were waiting for."

Nathanel was among those who started to follow the Master. This is what Jesus said to him:

> *I tell you the truth, you will all see heaven open and the angels of God going up and down on the Son of Man, the one who is the stairway between heaven and earth* (Jn. 1:51 NLT).

In Genesis 28, the angels are ascending and descending on a ladder. But, in John 1:51, Jesus rearranges the vision, and now the angels are ascending and descending *upon the Son of Man*. The message is clear: *the ladder is Christ Himself.* He is the link between heaven and earth.

For centuries people have been trying in all kinds of ways to establish a connection with God. Somehow they could never quite reach Him. He was always beyond us.

Now Jesus is saying, "Remember that ladder Jacob saw in his dream that connected earth with heaven? Well, I'm that ladder. You could never make it to God—but God has come to you. There is no need to climb. I have come down. I am your connection with God."

A Ladder at Ground Level

There's an black spiritual first sung by slaves over two centuries ago:

> *We are climbing Jacob's ladder*
> *We are climbing Jacob's ladder*
> *We are climbing Jacob's ladder*
> *Soldiers of the cross.*
>
> *Every rung goes higher, higher*
> *Every rung goes higher, higher*
> *Every rung goes higher, higher*
> *Soldiers of the cross.*

It's a nice song—but it misses the point of the story. Christ is not the ladder that helps us climb up to God. Rather, in Christ, God has come down to where we are. God is not standing at the top calling out: "Climb up, you can do it!" Rather, He has descended to where we live. The ladder stands at street level. Right where we find ourselves, just like Jacob, with all the messy situations going on in our lives.

The Gospel does not say: "You must clean up your life and make yourself presentable to God." It says: "Christ has come to where you are to embrace you and to lift you up." It is not about us climbing, *it is about Jesus descending.* He is to be found, not at the level of our moral achievements, but at the level of our defeat and need.

WHAT STORY HAVE WE FALLEN INTO?

Listen to Wesley W. Nelson:

> He who cannot believe, let him come with his unbelief. He who cannot understand may come with his confusion. The rebellious man may come if he will only bring his rebellion. The indifferent and the cold person may come with his indifference and coldness. He who is troubled with bitterness and deep feeling may bring his tangled emotions. He who has no feelings may come as he is. The moral failure may come with his failures knowing that Christ will forgive and continue to forgive as often as he fails…[1]

Christ has come to meet us where we are.

> *But faith's way of getting right with God says, "Don't say in your heart, 'Who will go up to heaven?' (to bring Christ down to earth). And don't say, 'Who will go down to the place of the dead?' (to bring Christ back to life again)." In fact, it says, "The message is very close at hand; it is on your lips and in your heart." And that message is the very message about faith that we preach: If you openly declare that Jesus is Lord and believe in your heart that God raised him from the dead, you will be saved* (Rom. 10:6-9 NLT).

We do not have to go anywhere to search for Christ. He has come to us. The word we need to contact Him is in our mouth and in our heart. We don't have to scale the heights of super-spirituality. We don't have to grovel in the depths of self-loathing. There are no heights to climb or depths to plumb. Christ Himself is immediately available to all who will receive Him.

This is wonderful news, not only to the unconverted, but also to the weary Christian. Christ is the door; all may enter (Jn. 10:9). He is a door right at street level. Not at some high level for high achievers, or the super pious. He is right at the level of our failure, our weakness and our need. "No one in human history has ever been more approachable than Jesus Christ," writes Duane Ortlund. "No prerequisites. No hoops to jump through."[2]

Striving to Improve

In most bookstores, there is a large section of self-help books. The religion of self-improvement attracts a huge following. There are a thousand recipes for making ourselves better.

We are encouraged to . . . lose weight, diversify our investments, get plenty of sleep, live simply, buy organic, communicate better, declutter the garage, eat more fiber, organize our time, bring our cholesterol down, walk regularly, spend time with our children, eat more vegetables, and keep our stress levels down... just for starters.

The religion of self-improvement is preached to us daily from billboards, the internet and television. We are expected to do more, go higher, try harder. The demands of this religion are overwhelming. Many can't cope without resorting to alcohol, antidepressants and sleeping pills. They succumb to depression, anxiety and a sense of failure as they live under this religion of condemnation.

Tragically, the Christian church has often turned the Good News into Good Advice. You are told it's free, but very soon you are pressured to climb an endless ladder of good deeds. You are called upon to give more, serve more, and do more. You are exhorted to be more holy, more committed, more spiritual, more involved and more active. You can never quite do enough. And many crumble under a burden of failure and guilt.

> *Legalism says God will love us if we change. The gospel says God will change us because He loves us.*
> —Tullian Tchividjian

Rest For the Weary

Listen again to the words of Christ:

> *Come to me, all of you who are tired from carrying heavy loads, and I will give you rest. Take my yoke and put it on you, and learn from me, because I am gentle and humble in spirit; and you will find rest. For the yoke I will give you is easy, and the load I will put on you is light* (Mt. 11:28 GNT).

The Lord came to lift our burden, not to add to it. There is no condemnation, no more anxiety about God's acceptance for those who are in Christ. On the cross of Calvary, the Son of God took our guilt and our shame—and got rid of it forever. In Christ our dilemma is resolved.

The Matter of Obedience

Someone might say, "What about obedience? Isn't being a Christian all about obeying God?"

Obedience is important, and notice what Jesus had to say about it: *"Anyone who loves me will obey my teaching"* (Jn. 14:23). He didn't say: "If you want acceptance with God, obey..." He didn't say: "If you want to get blessed, obey..." He said, *"Anyone who loves me..."*

> *No person loves God except the one who has first learned that God loves him.*
> —Alexander MacLaren

Obedience is not a salvation issue, it's a *love* issue. Obedience is not something we do to score points with God. We obey Him because we love Him. And where does this love for God come from? The Bible says,

We love Him because He first loved us (1 Jn. 4:19 NKJV).

Our love goes up in response to the love that came down.

So, now we're back to the Gospel. This is where it all starts. The undeserved gift of God's love and forgiveness. We don't try to gain God's acceptance by obedience. Thanks to Christ, we *have* God's acceptance, and now we love and serve Him. To obey "from" our acceptance, not "for" our acceptance, is known as "gospel obedience."

To be fully accepted in Christ gives us wings. God's unconditional love frees us to take risks and be generous with our life. When we frolic in divine grace, submitting our life to God is not burdensome. It's liberating. It feels right. We have reason to laugh, and sing and be glad because God calls us His own.

And that's Good News if there ever was any.

PRAYER

BLESSED GOD MOST HIGH, we are grateful that when we could not come to You, You came to us. When we had lost our way, You sent your Son, who came as the Good Shepherd to find us. How we thank You for His gracious words, His deep compassion, His friendship for the fallen, His love for the wayward. Wonderful Shepherd, keep us in Your care. Do not lose sight of us when we lose sight of You. Hold us when our faith is feeble and our thoughts are confused. Lift us up when we stumble, and lead us gently home because we do not know the way, oh Blessed Shepherd of our souls. Amen.

*Paul declares his conviction that
in Christianity the final stress must
ever fall on one thing, and on one thing only,
union with Christ, life in fellowship
with Christ.*

—JAMES S. STEWART

CHAPTER TWENTY-FIVE

A DEEP CONNECTION

"Come," he replied, "and you will see."
So they went and saw where he was staying,
and they spent that day with him.
JOHN 1:38

THAT DAY by the Jordan River, Andrew and John embarked on a remarkable journey. Responding to the invitation of the Master to *"come and see,"* they followed. They were on the road to "His place"—little knowing what that meant. They were about to be drawn into a mystery. They had started on a path to the most wonderful place of all.

The journey took them to a wedding in Cana, to a well at Sychar, to a pool at Bethesda. It involved unforgettable experiences in the wilderness, on a lake called Galilee and in a cemetery near Bethany.

The journey finally took them to an upper room in Jerusalem.

This was Christ's last night with His disciples before going to the cross. John dedicates five chapters to this heart-to-heart moment. It was an occasion for final words. The Master's time in this world was about to end. There were important things to talk about.

Then, it was time to go elsewhere.

Eleven men silently follow Jesus down the stairs and into the dark streets of Jerusalem. It was quiet. Everyone was at home finishing up the Passover supper. The Lord leads them towards the Eastern Gate, and they exit the city and head towards a nearby hill—the Mount of Olives.

A New Chapter

The Master had been explaining to His disciples how His relationship with them was about to change. He would no longer be present physically but spiritually. And He would not merely be with them, *He would be in them through His Spirit.*

The new relationship would be like the one Abba's Son had always enjoyed with the Father. Jesus was going to bring them into the enjoyment of the same love and intimacy He had always known. He had often spoken of the deep spiritual connection He had with the Father—and now they would get in on it.

He would be in them and they would be in Him.

This was not easy for these disciples from Galilee to grasp.

An illustration was needed.

As they pass an old vineyard, Jesus suddenly turns aside and stops. His disciples gathered around. A grapevine on the way to Gethsemane provided the perfect example of how this new life with God works.

Peter, John, Andrew, James and the rest listen as the Son of God unfolds profound divine truth. Here are lessons every Christ-follower needs to learn.

Lessons from the Vine

Christ grasps a branch and begins to speak.

> *I am the vine; you are the branches* (Jn. 15:5).

The Lord is explaining what life with Him would be like from here on. He was about to return to heaven, and the Holy Spirit would come to take His place (Jn. 14:16-18). No longer would His disciples merely follow Him—*they would be indwelt by Him.* The Spirit would establish a spiritual connection between every believer and Christ—much the same as a branch is connected to the vine.

Pointing to the grapevine, Jesus says, in effect, "Notice how this branch is connected to the vine. There is an intimate, organic connection between the two. They live and grow and function together. And that's what goes on between my Father and me. We are connected on the inside. I receive His love, I rest in His love, and I share His love. All this time, I have been sharing it with you."

And then, Jesus explains what is about to take place: "I am going to leave you, but I'll be back, and believe it or not, it's going to be better. I'm going to be with you on the inside. We are going to be connected in the deepest way—just like this branch is connected to the vine. I am going to be with you wherever you go and whatever happens. So think of it this way: From now on . . . *I am the vine and you are the branches.*"

The Master is not sharing the secrets of the deeper Christian life. He is not pointing the way to some higher level of spirituality. He is explaining how Christ followers are to live.

His basic premise is this: *The Christian life is lived in union with Christ.*

A believer is someone who is connected to Christ on the inside.

Think for a moment of a branch on a vine. It hasn't been glued on. It hasn't been tacked or tied on. It is not simply *near* the vine. The vine and the branch are literally growing together. They share the same life. They have the same sap flowing in them. There is an organic union here.

The Master is saying: "Once you've understood that, you've understood how we are now going to do life together."

More the a Legal Matter

In the minds of many, salvation is a legal transaction. Our guilt is erased. Our name is registered in God's book. We are declared righteous. Everything is settled.

This is gloriously true.

But sin removal is only the beginning.

WHAT STORY HAVE WE FALLEN INTO?

In John's first chapter, we saw that Messiah's mission is twofold. He came to take away sin and to pour out His Spirit (Jn. 1:29,33).

To be a Christian is more than a legal arrangement—*it is relational.* It is experiential. It entails an intermingling of lives. Christ lives in me; I live in Him. Our lives have blended. It is not simply about accounting, it is about a glorious "at-one-ment" with God through the Spirit.

When I married my wife, I walked down the church aisle single, and when I walked out—I was married. My legal status had changed. Wendy and I were now a married couple. The union was duly authorized and recognized by the law of the land. This was undeniably true, but the essence of our relationship goes beyond a legal transaction. It does not consist in pulling out a marriage license and declaring, "Look, we are lawfully married." The joy of our marriage is experienced in our mutual delight in one another. It involves sharing our lives. It is a union that arises from love and for love. Marriage has a legal component, but above all, *it is experiential and relational.*

So it is in our relationship with Christ. Not only are we forgiven, we have been engrafted into the Vine by the Spirit of God. It is not simply "on the books." We have been indissolubly united to the life of Jesus Christ.

> *He who is joined to the Lord becomes one spirit with him* (1 Cor. 6:17 ESV).

Through saving faith in Christ, a connection is forged at the deepest part of our being. We are no longer two spirits, one in heaven and the other on earth. *We are one spirit.* Two have become one. We no longer know where we end and He begins. Something incredible has taken place. His life and our life have merged. Without losing our individuality, we have become inseparably connected. Included. Enfolded. Forever.

Can we even begin to perceive the magnitud of this privilege?

Oneness with Christ means (among other things) that we are joint participants in His relationship with His Father. We are equally loved, accepted and cherished. We have been included in the blessedness, wonder and glory of fellowship with the Trinity.

"Jesus so attached himself to you that if God the Father wants his Son, Jesus, he is stuck with you too," points out Robert Jenson.

Could anything be more wonderful than that?

The Central Issue

"Union with Christ is . . . what makes a Christian a Christian," declares Karl Barth. Justification, redemption, reconciliation and all other spiritual blessings are like spokes of a wheel—*but the hub is union with Christ.* Everything flows from the fact the believer has been inextricably united to the Lord Jesus Christ. *This is the core issue.*

We don't have to climb to a certain level of spirituality to reach it. We don't have to earn it. We don't have to engage in some mystical maneuvers to make it happen. It is not attained or activated by something we do. *It is a gift we receive.*

If you belong to Christ, you are one with Him.

"Union to Christ is, after all," said Charles Spurgeon, "the great point in salvation." It is not an add-on, it is an essential part of the package. It is not something we achieve—it is something that takes place at conversion. It is what *"I am the vine, you are the branches"* means. The connection has been made.

Warren W. Wiersbe writes, "Our union with Christ is a living union, so we may bear fruit; a loving union, so that we may enjoy Him; and a lasting union, so that we need not be afraid."

Union with Christ is a glorious fact that calls for a response.

Abide in me as I abide in you (Jn. 15:4 NRSV).

Here we come to the key word in this passage—*abide (meno).* It crops up ten times in John 15. The term describes a permanent place of residence as opposed to an occasional visit. First and foremost, our call is not to go somewhere, or to do something. We are called to "remain." We have been placed "in Christ"—*and now we are to live there.*

Life in Christ is encapsulated in this one fascinating term: "abide." There is much richness here worth exploring.

How Does One Abide?

At its most basic level, "abide" means: *believe it's true*. Recognize the reality of our oneness with Christ. Faith is not about activating a connection with God. It is awareness that it has already happened. It is not about trying to get into the circle of life shared by Father, Son and Spirit. It is becoming conscious of the fact that *believers are already there*.

The essence of Christian faith is discovery.

Faith sees what is there. It perceives what has taken place. It does not create, it does not construct—it merely sees with the eyes of the heart what God in Christ has done. There are no magic buttons to push, no chants to recite, no spiritual acrobatics to perform. Abiding is simply believing what is true. It is perceiving, embracing and resting in the stupendous fact we are fully and unreservedly *"accepted in the Beloved."*

Abiding is acknowledgement. It is awareness. It is ceasing to be confused about who we are in Christ. As believers, our life *"is hidden with Christ in God"* (Col. 3:3). We don't have to go anywhere to find Him. There are no heights to climb, no depths to plumb. We are in Him and He is in us (Jn. 14:20). Abiding is a hearty and continuous "amen" to the fact that in Christ we are adopted, included and embraced in this divine circle of life and blessedness.

Walking on Thick Ice

The story is told of a man who, in the dead of winter, cautiously made his way over a frozen river. About halfway across, he heard a cracking noise, and it frightened him. He quickly lay flat on his stomach to spread his weight around. That way he'd be less likely to break through the ice and fall into the freezing water.

He slowly began to pull himself forward. Little by little, he inched across the frozen river, scared the ice might give way at any moment. When he finally arrived on the other shore, he breathed a sigh of relief, and brushed himself off, glad to have made the crossing safely.

He suddenly heard a sound behind him. Turning, he saw a man on the other side, driving a team of horses harnessed to a large sled loaded with wood. They came to the frozen river and, without hesitating, began to make the crossing. The horses clopped their way across the ice, reached the other side, and continued on their journey.

Can you imagine how that man felt?

With painstaking caution, he had crawled across the ice on his stomach. And now he was watching someone else drive over nonchalantly with a team of horses!

Both men had enough faith to cross the frozen river. The first man's faith was feeble, and he inched forward, praying he wouldn't drown. The other, with absolute confidence in the strength of the ice, leisurely drove his team of horses across. Both men trusted themselves to the ice, but there was a huge difference in the *size* of their faith.

One man's faith was slim, the other's was sturdy. The magnitude of their faith, however, was not the crucial factor. What really mattered was the *object* of their faith. Their safe crossing had very little to do with the strength of their faith. *It had everything to do with the strength of the ice.*

The ice was sufficiently strong to hold them both. Sadly, the first man didn't realize that! He struggled needlessly to avoid falling through the ice. He could have danced on it, jumped on it, done cartwheels on it. The ice was good and thick. He had no need to fear. Unfortunately, he did not know that.

There are many believers like him. They hope to make it to heaven's shore, and they are inching across the ice. They seek to secure salvation by earnest activity and piety. They pray fervently. They attend church services. They read the Bible daily. They desperately hope to make it to the other side, and they are doing all they can to make sure the ice doesn't break.

WHAT STORY HAVE WE FALLEN INTO?

One is tempted to say, "Why don't you just dance across? The ice is solid. You can relax. It is important to pray and worship and study, but remember—It is not your piety that saves the day. It is not your river crossing skills that make you safe, it is the solid ice. It is not your performance that holds you up—*it is Christ.*"

Make no mistake—spiritual disciplines are vital. They need to be in our lives, but they are *not* what we are trusting in. Rather, they lead us to a more robust and untroubled reliance on the One who is mighty to save. They help us to understand how thick and strong the ice is. They guide us to greater confidence, gratitude and joy in our walk with Christ.

Our faith may be weak, it may falter. Thankfully, the greatness of our faith is not the issue, *but the greatness of our Christ.* He is the firm foundation upon which we stand. Nor do we place our faith in "faith"—we know too well how flimsy it is. Faith has value *only* if it has found a trustworthy object to lean on. We place our faith in the One who loved us and gave Himself for us. Who He is and what He has done is the strong basis of our confidence before God.

> **It is not the strength of your faith but the object of your faith that actually saves you.**
> —Timothy Keller

Faith has to do with *discovery.* It is coming to realize that in Christ we were cleansed, redeemed, reconciled, adopted and brought back to the Father. The Son of God put an end to our alienation and made us holy and blameless. Faith is discovering that in Christ we are accepted and secure in Abba's loving embrace. *We have come home.* This is what our Strong Redeemer has done, accomplished and finished. Faith is believing it, acknowledging it, embracing it, loving it and *resting in it.*

This is the astounding Good News of God's Story. Here is truth that heals hearts. It dispels demons of insecurity, shame and fear. It liberates us from religious busyness and anxiety. It teaches us to live in the staggering reality of the Father's embrace.

And it frees us to dance on the ice.

PRAYER

LORD OF LIFE AND GLORY, we are only beginning to realize that the wonder, the richness and the goodness of the Gospel is beyond our wildest dreams. Oneness with Christ, accepted in the Beloved—who could begin to fathom what that means! Who could possibly measure the blessedness and the belovedness that this entails? To be found "in Christ," to be joined by the Spirit to Him—could there be a greater privilege, a higher honor? Awaken us to the reality of this glorious fact. Overwhelm us with it. Teach us to live in the wonder of it. May we burst into song, dance with joy, fall flat on our face, and worship You in speechless wonder, oh God of goodness and grace. We pray in the name of Your Son, the Author of all this undeserved blessedness. Amen.

*Every day God is telling us
the story of how much he loves us,
but we live with spiritual dementia
and continually forget the story about us,
and we live most of our lives
in neglect of this love.*

—Jerry Root

CHAPTER TWENTY-SIX

LIVING IN HIS LOVE

*As the Father loved Me, I also have
loved you; abide in My love.*
JOHN 15:9

AT AGE TWENTY-FIVE, I found myself operating a small printing company in the city of Victoria. My interest in graphic arts had blossomed into a business, and I had been running it for about five years. My real interest, however, was missions. I longed to serve God overseas, but I had a printing business on my hands, and wondered if I would ever make it to the mission field.

Then it happened.

A middle-aged man walked into the office and asked me if I was interested in selling the business. It came out of the blue. He had recently moved to the city and was looking for a business to buy. Without thinking twice, I blurted out, "Yes, I am." I had no idea what I would do next, but I ended up selling the business, and walking out like Abraham, not knowing where I was going.

Shortly afterwards, I received an invitation to help with a mission project in Bolivia. I was "commended" by two churches in our city, and traveled to South America for two years. Two years ended up turning into 43 years (at the moment of writing this book). I have had the immense privilege and joy of living most of my life, serving in Bolivia.

Closing Shop

An infinitely more significant scenario played out in a small Galilean town. The skilled woodworker, whose Hebrew name was Yeshua, had learned the trade from His father and ran the business for many years. He was known as the carpenter of Nazareth.

Then it happened.

Word arrived in the village of a revival that had erupted near the Jordan River, in the southern province of Judea. The prophetic silence of centuries had been broken, and multitudes flocked to hear the man of God. The Lord was opening a new chapter in history.

Jesus stopped working. He laid His tools on the workbench and stood motionless, wrapt in thought. The long-awaited moment had arrived. It was time to close shop. He must now attend to a higher calling. Wood-working was about to give way to world-changing.

Not many days later, the carpenter from Nazareth waded into the Jordan River to be baptized by John. Many were being baptized by the prophet, but this time, something unusual took place. The baptism of Jesus was interrupted by a voice from heaven.

What would His Father say? Would He give advice about the work that lay ahead, or the message to be announced?

The Father had *one* word for His Son.

> *You are my Beloved Son, in whom I am well pleased*
> (Mk. 1:11 NKJV).

And with that word resounding in His ears, Jesus embarked on three years of ministry that altered the course of history. He took that heaven-sent reminder of His belovedness and wrapped his life around it. It warmed His heart. It energized His life. He dwelt in His Father's love, delighted in it and shared it with others.

This is the life of Christ in a nutshell. He lived enjoying and spreading the love of God.

Last Words

Before departing this world, our Lord left us an assignment:

> *As the Father has loved me, so have I loved you; abide in my love* (Jn. 15:9 NRSV).

"As the Father has loved me..." Is there any love greater than that? The Father's love is never-ending, unrestrained, inexhaustible, unwavering, unquenchable, unreserved, 24/7.

"So have I loved you." Did you get that? The same intensity of love has been turned towards believers. A love too great to comprehend, too vast to measure. It is passionate, it is overflowing, it is undeserved. Nothing can separate us from this love. And nothing we do can stop it. Let that sink in.

Life on the Vine

Listen again to this wonderful imperative: *"Abide in my love."*

The fact that Jesus instructs His disciples to "abide" tells us that "abiding" is not automatic. It is something we must choose to do. Jesus lived abiding in the Father's love—and this is how His disciples must live. This is where our heart must make its home. We are called to learn the sacred art of living life resting in, responding to, and sharing the love of God.

> *God is love, and those who abide in love abide in God, and God abides in them* (1 Jn. 4:16 NRSV).

What does it mean to "abide"? It involves a number of things, but here's the bottom line:

- It is accepting our acceptance
- It is relaxing in the Father's embrace
- It is basking in our belovedness
- It is resting in His love

Abiding involves awareness. It means "looking unto Jesus," recognizing His presence, believing He is in me and I am in Him, knowing I am held by a Love that will not let me go.

Sounds like a great way to live, doesn't it? It is.

But, here's the rub.

Learning to live in the strong confidence that we are loved by God is not resolved in a moment. It's something we will spend the rest of our lives discovering. Deep within us there is resistance to the idea that we are lovable. This appears to be our "default setting"—an after-effect of the Fall. The staggering fact that "in Christ" we are fully loved and accepted by God is a lesson our hearts struggle to grasp. It requires radical "renewing of our mind" and growth in faith. The Spirit and the Word are key factors in this process.

"Dare to advance in the love which has redeemed [you]... and to laugh at the preposterous idea of "worthiness," urges Thomas Merton.

Secondly, learning to live in God's love is a *battle*. The enjoyment of our belovedness will be opposed by the flesh, the world and the devil. The enemy seeks to fill our minds with doubts and fears and lies. He is eager to remind us of our failings, faults and sins. We need to remind him of the powerful truth of the Gospel. We will need to *"take the helmet of salvation and the sword of the Spirit, which is the word of God"* (Eph. 6:17). Abiding in Christ is our source of strength, but it will not go unchallenged.

Help From Above

Learning to live in the love of God requires divine assistance. We need the Spirit of God to reveal this truth to our hearts. A great prayer that is breath-taking in its scope is found in Paul's letter to the Ephesians. We would do well to memorize and pray it often for ourselves and others.

> *I pray that you, being ROOTED AND ESTABLISHED IN LOVE, may have power, together with all the Lord's holy people, TO GRASP HOW WIDE AND LONG AND HIGH*

AND DEEP IS THE LOVE OF CHRIST, and to KNOW THIS LOVE that surpasses knowledge—that you may be filled to the measure of all the fullness of God (Eph. 3:16-19).

Living in the love of God has another name in Paul's writings. He calls it—*being filled with the Spirit.* The love of God comes to us through a divine Person (Rom. 5:5; 15:30; Col. 1:8; 2 Tim. 1:7). The apostle gives us valuable pointers on how we can let this "Spirit of love" fill us. The imperative, *"Be filled with the Spirit,"* is followed by a series of supportive verbs. Pay close attention to them—they describe how we can live "filled."

> *Speaking to one another in psalms and hymns and spiritual songs, singing and making melody in your heart to the Lord, giving thanks always for all things to God the Father in the name of our Lord Jesus Christ, submitting to one another in the fear of God* (Eph. 5:19-21 NKJV).

Living in the love of God is enhanced by speaking, singing, making melody in your heart, giving thanks and serving. It involves our tongue, our hearts, and our hands. Celebrating the love of God with song, and expressing it with service intensifies our enjoyment of it. This is how we move beyond merely "knowing" to "abiding." We increase our delight in God's love by singing about it and spreading it.

Abiding and Loving

"Abiding" cannot be reduced to cultivating private ecstasies. It has an outward focus. It involves God's love flowing from the Vine through the branches to others. And the love we are called to share is the same self-giving, self-sacrificing love shown at Calvary. "Abiding" involves loving—loving others as He loved us.

> *If you keep my commandments, you will abide in my love, just as I have kept my Father's commandments and abide in his love... This is my commandment, that you love one another as I have loved you* (Jn. 15:10,12 NRSV).

We do not obey this commandment in order to be loved, but *because* we are loved. This is not about earning God's love, but about celebrating and sharing it. We are receivers of Christ's love, and as a result we become "givers." We get enough love from Christ to be empowered to love others—even if they don't love us back.

> *The purpose of redemption is to bring us to love rightly.*
> —Timothy Keller

We love because he first loved us (1 Jn. 4:19).

N. T. Wright points out,

> Love is not our duty; it is our destiny. It is the language Jesus spoke, and we are called to speak it so that we can converse with him. It is the food they eat in God's new world, and we must acquire the taste for it here and now. It is the music God has written for all his creatures to sing, and we are called to learn it and practice it now so as to be ready when the conductor brings down his baton.[1]

Mostly what God does is love you. Keep company with him and learn a life of love (Eph. 5:1 MSG).

Love is the great lesson we are in this life to learn.

Lifted by Love

For many years, my wife Wendy has visited prisons in Bolivia. These are dark places where violence, stealing, rape and murder take place regularly. Wendy and others go to show God's love in every possible way providing friendship, a birthday cake, a blanket, prayer—or whatever is needed. For many, Wendy has become the mother they never had, and numerous prisoners call her "Mama Wendy."

Another volunteer worker suggested that Wendy visit Daniel, an inmate in isolation who had attempted to take his life. Wendy and another lady were given permission to see him. Not many minutes had gone by before the young man was in her arms weeping and telling his story. As a child he had been abandoned to live on the streets. At an early age he was trained to use firearms, and to be a *sicario*—a hit-man. He killed someone for the first time at age twelve. When he was fifteen, he was sent to prison with a sentence of thirty years and another of fifteen.

Wendy listened as Daniel sobbed out his story. At that moment, God placed in her heart a special love for this young man who lived in a loveless world. She began to visit him, to pray for him and to call him regularly. At times, he did better and other times, he relapsed into a dark place. Wendy continued to reach out to him. She saw him enslaved to drugs and under the control of dark powers, and she continued to love him, and cry out to God for him.

One day, Wendy felt the urge to phone him and share a portion from Proverbs. She read verses that speak of violent men and the need to avoid them. There was silence at the other end of the line. Then Daniel said: "Mama Wendy, this is incredible. When they called me, I had a knife in my hand, and I was about to kill someone. Now I know there is a God."

Daniel was sent from one penitentiary to another. Everyone was afraid of this man. Wendy continued to keep in touch with him and to pray for him—often with tears. She persisted in loving him. And, little by little, she saw God work in his life.

Quite a few years have gone by and Daniel is now out of prison. He is walking with God and growing in his faith. His life has changed dramatically. He always talks about the Lord, and has a passion to help others come to freedom in Christ. Many of his friends cannot believe he is the same person they knew. He is a trophy of God's grace.

Before knowing the Lord, it was painful for Daniel to see fellow prisoners receive love and support from visiting family members. Daniel never had that, and it angered him that others did. He would sometimes turn on these inmates and give them a nasty thrashing. His unmet hunger for love would turn into violence. But when he came to experience the love of God, that changed completely. Daniel has become one of the most tender hearted people we know.

WHAT STORY HAVE WE FALLEN INTO?

One day he said to my wife, "Mama Wendy, years ago, if someone said to me, 'God loves you,' it made no sense to me. There was so much pain and suffering in my life that I couldn't believe God loved me. But you showed me the love of God. You didn't give up on me, and you kept loving me. I have come to believe in God and in His love, because I have seen that love in you."

"To love another person is to help him love God," writes Soren Kierkegaard. When people feel unloved and without hope, their reason for living collapses, and they easily slide into a dark place. However, when they turn to, believe in and live in the love of God, life comes back and starts to flourish. An encounter with deep affection liberates us. It thaws out the coldness of our hearts.

"Only love that cannot be changed by our behavior has the power to change our behavior," wrote Rodeen Williams.

> *Keep yourselves in God's love.*
> —JUDE 21

The Father's Delight

We are told that humans are able to remain aware of seven to nine facts per second. The most important one of all is this: *we are surrounded by God's perfect love.*

Life in Christ needs to be lived in the calm assurance of the Father's declarative word of delight: "You are my beloved son, you are my beloved daughter." If we have not heard that word spoken over us, all our "serving" will be an attempt at "earning" the love of God. We will be driven by our guilt or by our emptiness. Real joy will be absent and living for God will be burdensome. Authentic spirituality rests in the assurance of the Father's delight.

"Christians should bask daily in the awareness of God's overwhelming, incomparable love," writes J. I. Packer.

To live in the quiet assurance that "I am God's beloved" is not just for the spiritual elite; it is the blessedness of each believer. It is the home where we now reside. It is the bedrock on which we stand. It is the Story in which we now live.

It puts a song in our heart, and a spring in our step.

And what's more—it puts fruit on the Vine.

PRAYER

LOVING FATHER, we make the psalmist's cry our own: "Let me hear in the morning of your steadfast love" (Ps. 143:8). All other loves are filled with conditions and limits. Only Your love can meet the deepest needs of our hearts. Only your love can break our self-indulgent chains and set us free us for kingdom living and loving. Heavenly Father, we pray that You open our eyes to see those around us as You see them, that You give us hearts to love them as You love them. Give us the wisdom and compassion and strength to care and to love well. Help us to shoulder the burdens of family and friends. Teach me to not pull back from those who flounder in their brokenness. You lavished Your unfailing love upon us. Teach us to live in Your love and to spread it to others. Live and love in us and through us, oh Blessed Lord. We pray in the heart-transforming name of Jesus. Amen.

*Lay your life down.
Your heartbeats cannot be hoarded.
Your reservoir of breaths is draining away.
You have hands, blister them while you can.
You have bones, make them strain—they can
carry nothing in the grave. You have lungs,
let them spill with laughter.*

—N. D. Wilson

CHAPTER TWENTY-SEVEN

LEARNING TO FLY

So if the Son sets you free, you will be free indeed.
JOHN 8:36

FOR TEN YEARS, A BLACK EAGLE had been confined to a zoo in Pretoria, South Africa. It was finally decided that the bird should be given its freedom. The eagle was shipped in a large wooden crate to a suitable location for its release. The conservation officers were excited that the bird could return to its natural habitat. The cage was positioned on the edge of a cliff, and the door was opened. The captive eagle was given its freedom. However, excitement soon turned to frustration when the great bird sat with blank eyes and refused to fly. Did the eagle not realize that it was free?

It became clear that on the inside, the bird was still trapped in its confinement. It had lived in a cage for so long that it could not conceive what freedom meant. No amount of coaxing could get the eagle to take flight.

Hours later, hearing the call of another eagle, the bird looked up. Something stirred in the captive bird. The eagle within awoke. And, stretching its wings, the majestic bird soared into freedom.

Human beings experience a similar phenomenon. We live in a world imprisoned by false narratives. Someone came to set us free. When the stone was rolled away from Messiah's tomb, freedom was granted to us. The Gospel sets people free. However, the giving of freedom does not immediately translate into *living* in freedom. Freed captives must learn to fly.

Timothy Keller comments, "To get God's love and Christ's grace down into the motivational principles of our hearts, to the foundational layer of our identities, is a process, and often a slow one."[1]

Spiritual disciplines are vital for learning to live in the freedom and joy of God's story. They make space for engaging with God. They help us break free from slavery to self-interest, superficiality, doubts and fear.

Henri Nouwen writes,

> A spiritual discipline is necessary in order to move slowly from an absurd to an obedient life, from a life filled with noisy worries to a life in which there is some free inner space where we can listen to our God and follow his guidance.[2]

Liberating Truth

> *Then Jesus said to those Jews who believed Him, If you abide in My word, you are My disciples indeed. And you shall know the truth, and the truth shall make you free* (Jn. 8:31-32).

Abiding in Christ involves abiding in His life-giving Word. It nourishes our spirit, reconfigures our patterns of thought and behaviour, and helps us to align with the True Story. In Scripture we find encouragement, correction and insight—but most of all we find God.

"*You prepare a table before me*" (Psa. 23:5). The table is set for two. The Lord is our Host and we are invited to enjoy fellowship with Him. "The Christian's interest in Scripture has always been in hearing God speak, not in analyzing moral memos," points out Eugene Peterson. We enter the text not merely to find truth, but to meet the "Lover of our souls," and to turn His words into prayer, into praise, into acts of obedience and ways of love.

The goal is not to read as much as possible, but to read as meaningfully as possible. We are not simply gathering information, we are deepening a relationship. We are not merely looking for new insights; we are seeking to interact with God. This requires coming to Scripture with reverence and humility. It means reading attentively, prayerfully and thoughtfully.

Stephen Crosby said, "I do not approach the Scripture looking for principles to practice. I approach the Scriptures looking for a Person to know, a Lord to worship, and a King to yield to."

Friendship with God

On the last evening with His disciples, Jesus declared,

> *No longer do I call you servants, for a servant does not know what his master is doing; but I have called you friends, for all things that I heard from My Father I have made known to you* (Jn. 15:15).

God is usually thought of as an infinitely superior being who is to be worshipped and obeyed. Our Lord recognizes and treats His own as *friends*. A high honor, indeed! Masters are not in the custom of revealing their hearts, hopes and plans to servants, but to close friends. Such a privilege has been granted to us.

A. W. Tozer stated, "Unquestionably the highest privilege granted to man on earth is to be admitted into the circle of the friends of God."

> ***The very possibility of friendship with God transfigures life.***
> —Harry King

God did not create people because He was looking for workers. He already had millions of angels. *He was looking for friends.* It is significant that Adam was created on the sixth day of creation. The very first day for Adam was the seventh day for God—a day of rest and fellowship with his Maker. It was from that day of fellowship with God that Adam was to go out and be a co-worker with his Creator. Humans have the honor of serving God, but the foundation of our existence is friendship with the Almighty.

It is an astounding fact that the High King of Heaven desires our friendship. This is one of John's great themes.

Leaning on the Lord

Twice in the book of John, we run into the Greek word *kolpos*. It first appears in John 1:18 where the God's Son is described as living in *"the bosom (kolpos) of the Father."* This ancient metaphor denotes a close-knit relationship of love and intimacy. This beautiful togetherness has been going on forever between Father and Son.

The word crops us again near the end of the book:

> *Now there was leaning on Jesus' bosom (kolpos) one of His disciples, whom Jesus loved* (Jn. 16:23 NKJV).

Here *kolpos* is used, not to speak of the fellowship between Father and Son, but to speak of the fellowship between Christ and one of his disciples. It was at the Last Supper that John reclined his head on the Master's chest. Now the special intimacy enjoyed by the Son of God is enjoyed by one of His followers. Dwight L. Moody writes, "The Gospel of John opens with Jesus Christ in the bosom of God, and closes with the sinner in the bosom of Jesus Christ."

This illustrates beautifully the message of John's Gospel: *The One who enjoyed eternal closeness to the Father came to make us joyful participants of that fellowship.*

> *We proclaim to you what we have seen and heard, so that you also may have fellowship with us. And our fellowship is with the Father and with his Son, Jesus Christ* (1 Jn. 1:3).

We have been given an undeserved seat at God's table. We have been called into friendship with the King. This inner relatedness is the meat and drink of the spiritual life. Abiding in Christ is living in the enjoyment of this privilege.

This involves living life in His presence and turning the thoughts in our mind, the longings of our heart and the urgings of our spirit into prayer. It means making friendship with God the main business of our lives. It means weaving prayer into the fabric of our lives.

"Spiritual people are not those who engage in certain spiritual practices; they are those who draw their life from a conversational relationship with God," says Dallas Willard.[3]

In Conversation with God

Life in Christ has been described as "a secret companionship." It entails living in an interactive conversation with God—bringing to Him our questions, needs, concerns, desires, joys and failures. It means that we don't face life alone. The apostle Paul spoke of it as praying without ceasing (1 Thes. 5:17).

Willard explains: "Don't seek to develop a prayer life—seek a praying life... A 'praying life' is a life that is saturated with prayerfulness—you seek to do all that you do with the Lord."[4]

François Fénelon writes,

> Tell God the most important things that occur to you; tell Him what stands out to you as you read the Bible. Cling to your dearest Friend; live in Him with unbounded trust; speak to Him out of a heart full of love. As you learn to continually turn your spirit toward the loving presence of God within you, you will find yourself strengthened to do what is required of you.[5]

A good description of prayer is this: "Talking to God about what we are doing together."

This ongoing conversation with God is sometimes spoken, sometimes unspoken. Sometimes waking, sometimes sleeping. We don't do it because it's time for our daily devotions; we do it because it is our source of life. It is oxygen for the soul.

It is not a ritual or a burden. It is living in the joyful awareness of His presence. It is leaning on the Everlasting Arms. It is giving thanks in all circumstances and blessing the Lord at all times. It is fixing our eyes upon Jesus. It is *"casting all your cares on him, because he cares for you"* (1 Pet. 5:7). Nobody else sees it. It is an inward state. You are dwelling in the Secret Place of the Most High.

Awakening to the Wonder

Thankfulness is a vital dimension of life in God's Story. We are to "overflow" with thankfulness (Col. 2:6), and to engage in it at all times (1 Thess. 5:18). Its neglect diminishes our joy and causes spiritual wellness to falter (Rom. 1:21). To be "filled with gratitude" is a mark of being "filled with the Spirit" (Eph. 5:18-20). This holy habit needs to permeate our attitudes, reflections and prayers.

We pray for a miracle in a moment of crisis, but often fail to notice the miracles all around us. The real miracle is not physical healing or financial provision, but to be loved, forgiven, and accepted by God. The real miracle is not wealth or fame, but having toes and a tongue and fingers and knees and eyes. The real miracle is not walking on water, but walking on a planet where there are apples, sunsets, waterfalls, ice cream, romance, roses, coconuts, laughter, wine, kittens and tropical beaches.

> *Seek to cultivate a buoyant, joyous sense of the crowded kindnesses of God in your daily life.*
> —Alexander MacLaren

Life is a miracle. The entire universe is a miracle. "Life is a journey in which we heal our eyes so we can see the wonder of it all," writes Augustine.

Every enjoyment is a token of His love, a cause for gratitude: the aroma of coffee, the magic of Mozart, the taste of black-berries, the gift of hearing, sight and smell. As we walk in the light of His goodness, our lives are infused with joy.

Thomas Merton reminds us:

> To be grateful is to recognize the Love of God in everything He has given us—and He has given us everything. Every breath we draw is a gift of His love, every moment of existence is a grace, for it brings with it immense graces from Him. Gratitude therefore takes nothing for granted, is never unresponsive, is constantly awakening to new wonder and to praise of the goodness of God. For the grateful man knows that God is good, not by hearsay but by experience. And that is what makes all the difference.[6]

Truths to Remember

There are three important truths about this God-story that we should keep in mind, suggests John Eldredge.[7]

First, *things are not what they seem.*

There is more going on in this world than meets the eye. The carpenter from Nazareth, as we learn from John's prologue, is more than a carpenter—He's the Creator. His life of goodness and compassion was more than a good example—it was the revelation of God. His death on the outskirts of Jerusalem was more than a crucifixion—it was the redemption of the cosmos. There is a spiritual realm. It affects what goes on in our world. This unseen realm is real—even more than the one we can see.

Second, *we are in a battle.*

Our planet is the scenario where a great struggle takes place. Darkness is pitted against the light, falsehood against truth, evil against goodness. All war is about deception, and daily we must fight the God-denying look of things—the false narratives that cast doubt upon the Real Story. Scripture calls us to fasten truth around our waist like a belt. We are sent to tell the Story—the Truth that sets men free. This battle is for real, and casualties abound—broken hearts, broken lives, broken families. Ultimately, this is a battle for human hearts.

Third, *you have a role to play.*

No one should underestimate their role in God's Story. If Andrew had not spoken to Peter about the Messiah in the first chapter of John, this world would be a different place. If a boy had not offered his five barley loaves and two small fish, five thousand men would have gone hungry. "There's no such thing as a small act of kindness," asserted one writer. "Every act creates a ripple with no logical end." There are no trivial acts.

Spreading Goodness

The act of surrender to God's Story, as Peter discovered at the end of John's Gospel, changes us forever. Peter thought he would return to fishing, but spent the night on the lake and caught nothing. He learned, as one novel put it, *"You Can't Go Home Again."* To know Christ is to never be the same. It is to have a new identity, a new destiny, a new mission. Among the Master's last words in John's book is the call to *"feed my sheep."* There are sheep to feed, widows to visit, orphans to help, children to bless, neighbours to reach out to. We are branches on the Vine designed to bear fruit. Made to spread goodness.

> *Abide in Me, and I in you. As the branch cannot bear fruit of itself, unless it abides in the vine, neither can you, unless you abide in Me. I am the vine, you are the branches. He who abides in Me, and I in him, bears much fruit; for without Me you can do nothing* (Jn. 15:4-5 NKJV).

No Time to Lose

Frank Viola advises,

> Keep sacrificing. Keep losing. Keep laying your life down. Keep loving your enemies. Keep blessing those who despise you. Keep refusing to return fire upon those who bad-mouth you. Keep pouring your life into others, even if those same people never acknowledge it and others never notice. Keep freely sharing what God gives you.[8]

The Path to Freedom

Holy habits such as prayer, meditation, fasting, study, service, worship are not a barometer of spirituality. They are not a way to gain favor with God. They are ways of creating space for God to renew our minds and act in our lives.

They help us to focus on Christ and draw closer to His heart.
Their purpose is not bondage but freedom.
They teach us to fly.

PRAYER

GRACIOUS GOD OF OUR SALVATION, how grateful we are that You have called us and made us Your own. Stir our hearts to hunger and thirst for You, and to find our delight in You. Teach us to live in Your presence and to walk in Your ways, for we are slow to learn, prone to forget. Pour out Your grace upon us, that we may not stumble. Fulfill Your good purposes in our lives. We are in the foothills when we should be in the heights. Take us by the hand, and lead us on. Make our lives the instruments of Your goodness and grace. Break our self-indulgent chains and set us free to give and to serve. Live and love in us by the power of your Spirit, and for the glory of Your Name. Through Jesus Christ, our Lord, Amen.

*Every love story that the minds
of mortal men and women construct,
every love story that has made its appearance
in the pages of human history—whether fiction
or nonfiction—is but a reflection, a pale image,
a faint portrait, a scrambled version
of the sacred romance of the ages.*

—Frank Viola

CHAPTER TWENTY-EIGHT

THE SACRED ROMANCE

On the third day there was a wedding...
JOHN 2:1

FINDING A GOOD LIFE PARTNER can be a difficult task. However, when at the age of twenty-five I was sent as a missionary to "far flung foreign fields," the task became more complicated.

After adapting to my new land of service, I began to think about a life partner. Whom would I marry? Would it be someone from Bolivia where I was serving, or someone from my home country, Canada? I didn't expect to be spending much time in Canada, so the chance of finding a wife there seemed rather slim.

I came up with a crazy idea—I would apply Adam's method! In the Garden of Eden, the first living human obtained a wife when he went to sleep. If it worked for him, perhaps it could work for me. I wouldn't search land and sea for a life partner, I would simply do what Adam did—go to sleep on the matter. And when God wanted to bring that special person into my life, He could wake me up for the wedding. Meanwhile, I would put my hand to the task of saving the world.

And besides, in order to provide a wife for Adam, God had to *create* one. Now, with billions of women on the planet, He had it much easier.

Zealous young missionaries come up with some wacky ideas. But, as a matter of fact, this one turned out to be one of the best ones I ever had.

About four years into my missionary career, I came down with hepatitis. For a month, it was total bed rest. Many visitors came, and one topic that kept coming up was my need for a wife. Suddenly it dawned on me, "God, are you waking me up? And if so, who would the person be?" A young lady came to mind whom I had met briefly on my previous trip to Canada. Her name was Wendy. Could she be the one?

I was starting to recover, and then had a relapse. I was encouraged to return to Canada to recuperate from my illness. On the flight home, I had a strong sense I wasn't just going home to get better—I was going to get married!

And that's what happened.

Two years before, when I had spoken at the church where Wendy attended, two women heard me preach and said, "That has to be the husband for Wendy!" Unbeknown to us, they had been praying about this on a daily basis.

Was hepatitis an answer to their prayers? I don't know, but it forced me to make an unexpected trip to Canada. I arrived in September, was engaged in November, and was married in January. It happened so fast we didn't really have time to fall in love until after the wedding!

Upon returning to Bolivia with a wife, a friend said, "Hey, you went to Canada with some lame excuse about liver trouble. I think what you had was *heart* trouble!"

Adam's method worked wonderfully. Not only did God provide a life partner—but I could never have found a better one!

Are We in a Love Story?

"Romance is the deepest thing in life," argued G. K. Chesterton, "romance is deeper even than reality."

Few people would disagree.

Nothing else tugs so powerfully at human hearts.

It should come as no surprise that the Divine Drama in which we find ourselves should turn out to be a romance. The Bible starts with a wedding (Genesis 3), and ends with a wedding (Revelation 19). God's drama is essentially a Love Story—the greatest one of all.

We have been asking the question: What kind of story are we in? Clearly, it includes action, adventure, mystery and tragedy, but ultimately—*it is a Love Story.* Reality has to do with a romance.

A Prophet at the Wedding

In the first chapter of John's Gospel, John the Baptist made two momentous proclamations. The Messiah would remove sin and release the Spirit—He would be the sin-bearer and the Spirit giver. But it doesn't end there. There was a third role—a most fascinating one. Christ is also *the Heavenly Bridegroom.*

Here are the prophet's words:

> *The one who has the bride is the bridegroom. The friend of the bridegroom, who stands and hears him, rejoices greatly at the bridegroom's voice. Therefore this joy of mine is now complete* (Jn. 3:29).

John understood there was a wedding going on. A bridegroom has come from heaven to find a bride. That bridegroom is Christ. Those who believe in Him are the bride. John was the best man at the wedding, and he was delighted to see this romance take place.

Missing the Wedding

This topic arose on one occasion when a group came to question Christ. They were puzzled that Jesus and His followers did not fast as John's disciples and the Pharisees faithfully did.

The Jewish fast referred to was actually a reminder of the destruction of their temple in 586 BC by the Babylonians. According to the prophets, the fast would be turned into feasting only when the temple was correctly rebuilt and Israel's fortunes restored. This would happen when Messiah came. The Jews fasted and awaited that day.

And now, these pious Jews confront Messiah saying, "You're not doing it right. You should be fasting like the rest of us."

Listen to Jesus' response:

> *Can the wedding guests fast while the bridegroom is with them? As long as they have the bridegroom with them, they cannot fast* (Mc. 1:19).

In a few words, Jesus unloads a truckload of truth.

His bold statement could be loosely translated as: "Gentlemen, why are you still fasting? The messianic celebration you are waiting for has already started. Messiah is here; it's time to *celebrate*."

Christ abruptly moves from fasting to festivity. The celebration He is talking about is *a wedding feast!* He picks up a marriage theme familiar to the Jewish people. *"For your Maker is your husband—the Lord Almighty is his name"* (Isa. 54:5). What was not familiar to them was the idea that the Bridegroom was standing right before them!

John the Baptist had declared Jesus to be the "Bridegroom," and here the Lord Himself affirms it. He didn't come to improve religious practices or introduce new ones. He came to propose *matrimony*. His Jewish critics thought His mission had to do with making religion right—*it had to do with a heavenly romance.*

They were fasting and missing the feast.

A Marriage Made in Heaven

God purposed from eternity to create mankind to be His beloved. As a kind of a wedding present, the Lord placed Adam and Eve in a perfect paradise, and encouraged them to enjoy everything—with one exception. One tree was off limits.

Genuine love does not control or coerce. It grants freedom. The reason is clear: Love is possible only when it is freely chosen. Mankind had the freedom to accept or reject God's love.

Tragically, the Deceiver showed up to sabotage the love affair. He insinuated that the Creator was not allowing humans to enjoy life fully. He recommended they strike out on their own and run their own lives.

The unthinkable happened.

We, who are God's beloved, were lured away from our True Love. We were created for intimacy with Him, but we ran into the arms of the Enemy.

Our flight from our Heavenly Lover did not end well.

Instead of beauty, freedom and adventure, we found heartache, remorse and loneliness. Satan's lies seduced us into slavery to sin and trapped us in a false reality. We abandoned a romance "made in heaven," and ended up with a hellish nightmare.

How would God respond to this betrayal? Would he wash His hands of the whole debacle? Would he abandon the whole project?

He didn't.

He came for us.

The Heavenly Lover

One writer suggests that the most inconceivable doctrine in the Word of God is that the Creator and Sustainer of all things, who lives in inaccessible light, searches for us.

> The Bible is a love story that begins with a divorce. Everything from the third chapter of Genesis through the end of Revelation is the story of a betrayed lover wooing us back into His arms so we can enjoy the love of family forever.[1]

Philosopher Søren Kierkegaard turned our drama into a parable:

> Suppose there was a king who loved a humble maiden. The king was like no other king. Every statesman trembled before his power. No one dared breathe a word against him, for he had the strength to crush all opponents.
>
> And yet this mighty king was melted by love for a humble maiden who lived in a poor village in his kingdom. How could he declare his love for her? In an odd sort of way, his kingliness tied his hands. If he brought her to the palace and

crowned her head with jewels and clothed her body in royal robes, she would surely not resist—no one dared resist him. But would she love him?

She would say she loved him, of course, but would she truly? Or would she live with him in fear, nursing a private grief for the life she had left behind? Would she be happy at his side? How could he know for sure? If he rode to her forest cottage in his royal carriage, with an armed escort waving bright banners, that too would overwhelm her. He did not want a cringing subject. He wanted a lover...[2]

So the king disguised himself as a beggar and approached her cottage incognito to win her heart.

It is a parable of God coming to our world in the person of Jesus of Nazareth. The King of creation set aside His royal splendor, robed Himself with our humanity, and came to win our hearts. This is the astonishing Love Story in which we find ourselves.

Abba's Son put the beauty of God on display. His splendor was not the glitter of external elegance, but the majestic shining forth of true goodness within. His miracles did not exhibit the love of power, but the undeniable power of His love. And there was tenderness, patience, gentleness, humility, compassion, courage, fearlessness and wisdom. All these are the fuller unfolding of love, the arresting attractiveness of God. This is the Divine Lover captivating our hearts, drawing us to Himself.

Pursued by Love

Helen of Troy must have been a stunningly beautiful woman. Two kingdoms went to war over her; thousands of men laid down their lives so one man could get her back. It is said that her's was "the face that launched a thousand ships."

Helen was the wife of Menelaus, King of Sparta in the ninth Century, B.C. This royal couple lived in a peaceful kingdom in Southern Greece until the arrival of Paris, Prince of Troy. Paris stole the heart of Helen, and fled with the beautiful queen, taking her back to Troy. That triggered the Trojan War. Menelaus mobilized his mighty army and laid siege on Troy to get Helen back.

Few people have been so pursued.

Far greater, however, was the pursuit launched by the kingdom of heaven. The Heavenly Lover set in motion the greatest campaign in the history of the world. The unfolding drama of God's pursuit of lost humanity began. In staggering grace, God "launched his ships" and set out to find us in our darkness and win us back.

Gordon D. Fee writes,

> The genius of the biblical story is what it tells us about . . . a God who would not let us go, but who would pursue us—all of us, even the worst of us—so that he might restore us into joyful fellowship with himself.[3]

A cosmic romance is what Scripture is all about.

An Astounding Story

Like Helen of Troy, our King has come for us—in spite of our unfaithfulness. We were sought for, fought over, pursued, desired and loved. *We were even bled for.* The Divine Prince moved heaven and earth to rescue us.

It seems too good to be true—*but this is our story.*

We are caught up in the most remarkable romance of all—*pursued by a Heavenly Lover.* The false god of this world would keep us in the dark about it, but this is the astonishing narrative "we have fallen into." The great difference between this story and all other fairy tales is *this one is really taking place.*

> *Be persuaded, timid soul, that He has loved you too much to cease loving you.*
> —François Fénelon

When the light of our King's love shone in the darkness of this world, the darkness could not "extinguish" it (Jn. 1:5). The verb used by John is in past tense; it refers to a single event. It is likely a reference to what took place at the Cross.

WHAT STORY HAVE WE FALLEN INTO?

Darkness had so penetrated human hearts that we did the unthinkable: *we put the Divine Lover to death on a cross*. We tried to extinguish the light by crucifixion.

It only caused the light to shine more brightly.

- His love surpasses knowledge (Eph. 3:19)
- His power defies imagination (Eph. 3:20)
- His riches transcend calculation (Eph. 3:8)
- His plans exceed our wildest dreams (1 Cor. 2:9)

> *If the suffering Jesus endured did not make him give up on us, nothing will.*
> —Tim Keller

Holy Scripture is the record of the Heavenly Lover's relentless ambition to recapture our hearts. It tells us of a staggering out-pouring of grace. Of the in-breaking of a hope beyond all dreams. It is the ultimate Love Story.

The prophet Isaiah uses a stunning metaphor to open a window into the inner feelings God for His people. Give this verse some thought:

> *As a bridegroom rejoices over his bride, so will your God rejoice over you* (Isa. 62:5).

Here God is portrayed as a newly married groom deliriously in love. Could this be true? Could the Lord possibly delight in us to that extent?

Puritan writer, Thomas Goodwin, comments,

> It is as if Jesus had said: "The truth is, I cannot live without you. I shall never be quiet till I have you where I am, that we may never part again. Heaven shall not hold me, nor my Father's company, if you are not with me – my heart is so set upon you. And if I have any glory, you shall be part of it too."[6]

Is this miracle enough for anyone?

PRAYER

HIGH LORD OF HEAVEN, we cannot begin to fathom that we are loved by the King of glory. We are prone to think that it cannot be true, that surely there must be a mistake. Break through our blindness and dullness, and awaken our hearts to this glorious truth. You see our unworthiness, yet You have called us to be a part your broken-yet-beloved bride. You know everything about us, yet You love us with a love beyond all measure, a love that will not let us go. May this staggering fact become evermore precious and real to us. Rouse us from our sluggishness. Capture our hearts. Intensify our astonishment. Teach us to live in the joy of our belovedness as we wait for day when faith gives way to sight, and we are with You forever, oh Blessed Lord and Mighty Redeemer. Amen.

*The renewal of creation
has been promised by
the same Word who made it
in the beginning.*

—Athanasius of Alexandria

CHAPTER TWENTY-NINE

THE ULTIMATE MAKE-OVER

It is finished.
JOHN 19:30

ON NUMEROUS OCCASIONS, I have crossed the footbridge that straddles the Parapetí River near the town of Camiri in southeastern Bolivia. The hanging bridge provides access to a farm and a Bible school. I have enjoyed going there many times to teach students in the one-year program.

The school is located on the bend of a river that flows steady and strong. At times, the water level rises precipitously and rages dangerously close to the bridge. By all appearances, the Parapetí River is in a hurry to get somewhere. You would expect it to join other rivers downstream and end up at some point in the Atlantic Ocean—but it doesn't. *It doesn't go anywhere.* It finally peters out and disappears into a marshland. A rather inglorious finish.

Not all rivers finish well.

And not all people finish well.

Every person embarks on the river of life with the hope of finding his way into something larger, fuller and better. Sadly, the stories we come up with turn out to be too shallow, too empty, too inadequate for people who carry "eternity" in their hearts. Many get trapped in false narratives that ultimately land them in a swamp.

WHAT STORY HAVE WE FALLEN INTO?

We are all confronted by the question: *What story are we going to live in?*

We all choose a story.

There's only one story that's big enough for our hearts. There's only one with a truly fabulous ending—and it's the one God is telling. No other story can carry the quantity and calibre of glory we are hungry for. No other narrative can make good sense of the complexity, the beauty and the mystery of our world.

The Story According to John

John's Gospel has allowed us to look through a crack in time and peer into eternity. We have stood like Moses looking through a gap in the rock to catch sight of the glory of God. We have seen the heart and purpose of the Father before the foundation of the world. We have seen His passionate desire that we would be with Him as His beloved.

We heard in John's opening line an echo of the first words of the Bible. It sounds as if he were writing a New Genesis, a new creation story. And, as a matter of fact—he is.

In the beginning...

The apostle gathers up the thread of the story that began at creation. The Word who spoke the universe into existence speaks again. The Light-giver of Genesis comes to dispel the darkness that invaded His creation. The seven "signs" or miracles of Christ recorded in the Fourth Gospel are likely an intentional recasting of the seven days of creation.

1. Water is turned into wine - chapter 2
2. A sick child gets healed - chapter 4
3. A paralytic gets restored - chapter 5
4. A hungry multitude is fed - chapter 6
5. Blind eyes are opened - chapter 9
6. A dead man comes back to life - chapter 11
7. Christ dies and is resurrected - chapter 19-20

These miraculous signs are not an interference with the laws of nature—rather they are the *restoration* of the natural order of things. When Christ drives out disease, deformity and death, He is expelling intruders that do not belong in God's good creation. These miracles are evidence of His power to untangle the brokenness of our world and a foretaste of the glorious restoration He will finally bring about.

Jesus declared that He had been sent by Father, not to condemn, but "to save the world" (Jn. 3:17). This leads us to understand that God's purpose is to deal with and ultimately eradicate the presence of evil in God's world.

Love on a Cross

It was on the sixth day of the week that Messiah died on a cross. Before bowing his head in death, He cried out, *"It is finished!"* (Jn. 19:30). It is one word in Greek, *tetelestai*. It reminds us of the word used in the Genesis account to describe the completion on the sixth day of the work of creation. *"God had FINISHED the work he had been doing"* (Gn. 2:2). Further echoes of the Genesis story.

Tetelestai carries the weight of the whole biblical narrative that ultimately culminates in a new heaven and new earth. "Never before and never after was ever spoken one word which contains and means so much," declared one scholar. It reaches far beyond the salvation of souls to the renewal of the entire creation. Listen to the words of Paul:

> *By a Carpenter mankind was made, and only by that Carpenter can mankind be remade.*
> —Desiderio Erasmo

For God was pleased . . . to reconcile to himself all things, whether things on earth or things in heaven, by making peace through his blood, shed on the cross (Col. 1:19-20).

He made known to us the mystery of his will . . . to bring unity to all things in heaven and on earth under Christ (Eph. 1:9-10).

This is the final goal of redemption—*"the restoration of all things"* (Acts 3:21). Christ referred to this in Matthew 19:28 with the word *"palingenesia"*—a word that literally means a new Genesis, a rebirth, the renewal of creation.

Chaos in the Cosmos

At the beginning of history, when God's creation mutinied against its Maker, a rift took place between heaven and earth. C. S. Lewis referred to this disconnection as *The Great Divorce*. The phrase is well chosen, because earth was designed to relate to heaven in a relationship akin to marriage. The world was made to be wedded to the source of all goodness—but the sacred bond was broken. A breakdown took place.

When all the constituent parts of a system work together in harmony, wholeness, wellness and flourishing happens. When the different components turn against each other and begin to clash and collide, chaos results. The breakdown of fellowship with God unleashed a destructive process of disintegration the Bible calls *sin*.

Sin is the great "separator." It tears things apart. It debilitates the process of integration that is essential to the well-being and health of individuals, families, and societies.

We now find ourselves in a world where things that were meant to work together tend to fall apart. Like an autoimmune disease which causes one's immune system to attack his own body, the disintegrating force of sin wreaks havoc everywhere. People adopt self-destructive behaviours, they harm the lives of others, they inflict damage on the environment.

Societies fragment as tension grows between different groups —men and women, blacks and whites, rich and power, left and right. The list goes on.

This disuniting force affects every area of life. Sex gets separated from love, art gets separated from beauty, science gets separated from truth, education gets separated from virtue. When man ceases to be integrated with his Master, *everything disintegrates*.

The Restoration of All Things

But, here is the good news. The apostle John has a message of hope for our sin-fractured world: *"The Word became flesh."*

Why is this good news?

This resolves the central issue.

This reconnects divinity and humanity.

God and man, so long at odds, are brought together through the God-man Jesus Christ. The mystery of the Incarnation in the life, death and resurrection of Jesus deals with the human dilemma at its very heart.

This Incarnate Christ entered a ruined world to carry out a massive rescue operation. The goal was not just to redeem people, *but to restore the entire cosmos.* All fear, shame, sorrow, pain and brokenness will be banished. All things that were split, divided, detached, separated, fragmented, disconnected, disintegrated—however you want to describe it—are brought together and made whole in Christ. God's world will be released into its full glory and beauty. Heaven and earth will be one. Everything will be made new. *Tetelestai.*

A New Day Begins

On the seventh day, Jesus rests in a tomb. As the Creator rested on the seventh day from His work of creation, now He rests from His work of *redemption.* God rests, not because He is weary, but because His work is done. The One who cried, *"It is finished,"* now lies in a borrowed tomb.

Then comes the eighth day, the resurrection day. *"Early on the FIRST day of the week..."* (Jn. 20:1) John says it again in verse 19, *"On the evening of that FIRST day of the week..."* The repetition is intentional. John wants us to notice *when* the resurrection took place. This is the beginning of a new week—the first day of a new creation. Christ has risen from the dead—a new era has begun.

Early in the morning, Mary Magdalene goes to the tomb and finds it empty. She stands weeping. As the new day dawns, she is

the first person to encounter the risen Christ. It is no accident that, like the creation story in Genesis, this takes place in a garden.
Mary thinks He is the gardener.
Was she wrong?
Not really.
Adam, the first gardener, failed, and took creation down with him. Jesus, the second gardener triumphed, and creation rose up with Him. Instead of extending Eden to the far corners of the earth, Adam extended sin, sorrow, thorns and thistles. Christ, the gardener par excellence, will "Edenize" the world and, when He is done, *"the earth will be filled with the knowledge of the glory of the Lord, as the waters cover the sea"* (Hab. 2:14).

Genesis Revisited

Because of Adam, paradise was lost. Because of Christ, it is recovered. *"For as in Adam all die, so in Christ all will be made alive"* (1 Cor. 15:22). Access is regained to the Tree of Life—*which turns out at last to be a cross.* Through His death and resurrection, Christ cancels death, reverses the curse and turns everything around.

> *The resurrection of Jesus Christ is the Big Bang of the New Creation.*
> —Brian Zahnd

"The gospel of Jesus Christ announces that what God did for Jesus at Easter He will do not only for all those who are "in Christ" but also for the entire cosmos."[1] A glorious hope has risen from the grave.

Later that day, Jesus appears to His disciples, breathes on them, and says, *"Receive the Holy Spirit"* (Jn. 21:22).

Remember when God breathed life into Adam? Now the risen Christ breathes on and imparts spiritual life to His followers. Genesis is being reenacted. A new creation is emerging.

> *Therefore, if anyone is in Christ, the new creation has come: The old has gone, the new is here!* (2 Cor. 5:17).

Making All Things New

The incarnation and bodily resurrection of Christ sends a clear message—our Maker is *not* finished with His material creation. *He has joined Himself to it.* The "enfleshment" of God is no passing fad. He has involved Himself in the human drama in a deep and permanent way. Our story will not be tossed in some cosmic trash bin. He will bring it to a glorious conclusion—the renewal and restoration of all things.

> *All the broken and dislocated pieces of the universe—people and things, animals and atoms—get properly fixed and fit together in vibrant harmonies, all because of his death, his blood that poured down from the cross* (Col. 1:20 MSG).

Randy Alcorn writes,

> God has never given up on His original creation. Yet somehow we've managed to overlook an entire biblical vocabulary that makes this point clear. *Reconcile. Redeem. Restore. Recover. Return. Renew. Regenerate. Resurrect.* Each of these biblical words begins with the re-prefix, suggesting a return to an original condition that was ruined or lost.[2]

The biblical narrative doesn't end with souls dwelling in an otherworldly heaven. It ends with the Heavenly Jerusalem descending to earth. It does not finish with destruction, but with God saying, *"I am making everything new!"* (Rev. 21:5).

We will not exist as disembodied souls. We will have eyes to see, ears to hear, knees to bow and tongues to confess. We will obviously need a face if God is going to wipe away our tears and if His name is to be on our foreheads (Rev. 22:4).

We will live in a material world that has been transformed and made more beautiful than ever. One writer describes it like this:

The whole world looks different. High-rises have become orchards. Children are no longer hiding indoors for fear of neighbors or potential predators, but are chasing and laughing and playing in the streets. The desert is in bloom. The mountains and the hills have broken forth into singing. The trees of the fields are clapping their hands. Death is no more, and neither is there any mourning, or crying, or pain, for the former things have passed away.[3]

A Good Ending

In his book *Guide to the Gospels,* Graham Scroggie points out that:

- Matthew ends with the resurrection
- Mark ends with the ascension
- Luke ends with the promise of the Holy Spirit
- John ends with the promise of the second coming

We are immersed in a narrative that moves towards a glorious finale. History does not go around in cycles. It flows in a particular direction. There is a beginning, and there is an end. There is a plan and a purpose. This story is going somewhere.

C. S. Lewis describes the final chapter as follows:

> God will invade... When that happens, it is the end of the world. When the author walks on to the stage the play is over... It will be God without disguise; something so overwhelming that it will strike either irresistible love or irresistible horror into every creature. It will be too late then to choose your side. There is no use saying you choose to lie down when it has become impossible to stand up. That will not be the time for choosing; it will be the time when we discover which side we really have chosen, whether we realized it before or not. Now, today, this moment, is our chance to choose the right side. God is holding back to give us that chance. It will not last forever. We must take it or leave it.[4]

The seven signs recorded in John's Gospel send a message and elicit a response:

> *Jesus performed many other signs in the presence of his disciples, which are not recorded in this book. But these are written that you may believe that Jesus is the Messiah, the Son of God, and that by believing you may have life in his name* (Jn. 20:30-31).

John's Gospel unveils the mystery of the Author and Finisher of our story. He is seen as the Revealer of God, the Grace Bringer, the Lamb of God, the Heavenly Bridegroom, the Fountain of Living Water, the Bread of Life, the Tender Healer, the Kind Forgiver, the Light of the World, the Good Shepherd and the Way to the Father. John's book was designed to point us to Him.

Light, Life and Love

One writer outlines God's Story beautifully:

> In the beginning there was light, life and love. A Father loving His Son in the joy of the Holy Spirit. And everything has come from life and light and love.
> But we look today at the world and we see it's not like that. We see a world full of darkness, and death and disconnection.
> Where has that come from?
> Well, we've turned from the light. And when you turn from the light, where else do you go but darkness? And when you turn from the love, where else do you go but disconnection? And when you turn from the life, where else do you go but death?
> But then, what does love do when love sees the beloved in trouble? Love says, your pit will be my pit, your debts will be my debts, your darkness will be my darkness. Your death will be my death.
> So who is Jesus?

WHAT STORY HAVE WE FALLEN INTO?

> He's the Son of the Father who came as our Brother to be with us in the darkness. To take on Himself that darkness, that death, that disconnection that we all deserve for turning from God. He took it on Himself on the cross. He plunged it down into the hell that it deserves. And then He rose up again to light and life and love.
>
> And He says, "You in the darkness, do you want my light? You in the death, do you want my life? You in the disconnection, do you want my love?"
>
> And anyone who turns and says yes to Jesus—we now belong to Him. We get His Father as our Father. We get His Spirit as our Spirit. We get His future as our future.
>
> It's for free and it's forever—so do you want Jesus?[5]

This is the crucial question.

To trust Jesus Christ, the Eternal Word, is to choose light and life and love. It is to abandon our nonstory and surrender to the Real Story. Without Him we flounder in our lostness forever. Peter Kreeft states,

> If all of life's roads lead to the same place, it makes no ultimate difference which road we choose. But if they lead to opposite places, to infinite bliss or infinite misery, unimaginable glory or unimaginable tragedy . . . then life is a life-or-death affair, a razor's edge, and our choice of roads is infinitely important.[6]

The invitation of Christ stands:

> *Most assuredly, I say to you, he who believes in Me has everlasting life* (Jn. 6:47 NKJV).

This Gospel is like a river. It is the river of God's love that flows on toward a glorious future of endless day. It crosses the border into a land of infinite joy where there is no loneliness, anger, hatred or heartache. We are invited to step into the river, and let it take us where it's going.

PRAYER

LORD GOD ON HIGH, I am grateful that You created me to be a part of Your Story of light and life and love. I confess that I have lived believing false narratives and acting in false ways that dishonor You. Thank You, Lord Jesus, that on the cross You gave your life to free me from darkness and death and lovelessness. Shine Your light upon my life, cleanse me from all that is hurtful and wrong, and fill me with your life and love and goodness. I surrender to your Story. I surrender to your redeeming grace. I gladly bow to You, Lord Jesus Christ, as king and lord of my life. Fulfill your good purposes in me. May I live giving honor and glory to the One who loved me and gave Himself for me. In Jesus' Name, amen.

*At present we are on the outside
of the world, the wrong side of the door.
We discern the freshness and purity of morning...
We cannot mingle with the splendours we see.
But all the leaves of the New Testament are rustling
with the rumour that it will not always be so.
Some day, God willing, we shall get in.*

—C. S. Lewis

CHAPTER THIRTY

A FABULOUS FINALE

You will see greater things than these.
JOHN 1:50

ALBERT EINSTEIN WAS ONCE traveling on a train when the conductor came through the cabin, perforating the ticket of each passenger. When he came to Einstein, the great scientist reached into his vest pocket, but couldn't find his ticket. He checked his trouser pockets. It wasn't there. He searched his briefcase. He looked on the seat, but couldn't find it.

The conductor said, "Dr. Einstein, I know who you are. I'm sure you bought a ticket. Don't worry about it."

Einstein nodded appreciatively. The conductor continued down the aisle punching tickets. Before moving on to the next car, he turned and saw the famous physicist down on his hands and knees looking under his seat for his ticket.

The conductor rushed back to say, "Dr. Einstein, please don't worry, I know who you are. It's not a problem. I don't need to see your ticket. I'm sure you bought one."

Einstein looked at him and said, "Young man, I also know who I am. What I don't know is *where* I'm going."

Many people ask the same question.

WHAT STORY HAVE WE FALLEN INTO?

They wonder where the story of our world is going. They want to see the big picture. They want to know how we fit into the grand scheme of things.

The Bible offers a true map of reality. The truth about who God is, who we are, the truth about life and death and the world we live in. The Christian story is the story of the universe; it provides a set of lenses that allow us to see our place in the divine drama. It furnishes us with a magnificent story.

What Story Have We Fallen Into?

We have tumbled into a tale far more beautiful, dramatic and dangerous than we imagined. The Gospel is not merely about resolving the problem of sin; though marvelous indeed, this is a *part* of a larger richer narrative. To shrink the biblical message to a "gospel of sin management" is to miss the mystery and wonder of the Story.

> The gospel says that we, who are God's beloved, created a cosmic crisis. It says we, too, were stolen from our True Love and that he launched the greatest campaign in the history of the world to get us back. God created us for intimacy with him. When we turned our back on him he promised to come for us.[1]

This story involves being pursued by a Heavenly Lover. It involves being ransomed and rescued from the kingdom of darkness, indwelt by the Spirit of Christ and enveloped in the love of the Father. It involves a mission, a battle and a romance beyond our wildest dreams. It promises an incomparable *"eternal weight of glory."* It is a cosmic drama of unimaginable proportions.

The biblical record reveals a God who lays down His life for His enemies, who would rather die than be without us, and who comes into our story to make us a part of His.

> We deserve nothing but get everything; that we deserve hell but get heaven; that we deserve to be wiped out, obliterated, but we get his tender embrace; that we deserve rejection and judgment but get to become his children, to bear his like-

ness, to call him Father. This is the story of the Bible, God's story, which at the same time is also our own. Indeed, he even let his human creatures have a part in writing it![2]

We have been written into an epic that is greater and better than we ever thought. A Triune God of unsurpassable love and goodness went to the unthinkable lengths to rescue a rebellious race, adopt them into his family and share His glory with them. We have been caught up in an astonishing story. It is, in the words of Lewis, the greatest myth ever told, though unlike all other myths—*this one is true.*

"We wake, if ever at all, to mystery," declares Annie Dillard.

Love is Why We Are Here

When John gets to the final section of his book, the point he emphasizes is not that Jesus had taught his disciples, or had shown them His power—but that He had *loved* them (13:1,34; 14:21; 15:9,12).

> *Jesus knew that the hour had come for him to leave this world and go to the Father. Having loved his own who were in the world, he loved them to the end* (Jn. 13:1).

Notice the calibre of love that Christ has for His own:

- Loved from the beginning - *"having loved his own"*
- Loved in the present - *"who were in the world"*
- Loved forever - *"He loved them to the end"*

Here is a love without cracks or glitches. It will not fail, falter or diminish. We are loved in our brokenness, our weakness and our incompleteness. God is fully aware of the wrong turns we have made, the moments of selfishness, degraded love and dishonesty, yet His love for us is absolute, unwavering and endless. "God is not moody or capricious; God knows no seasons of change. God has a single relentless stance toward us: God loves us," stated Brennan Manning.

WHAT STORY HAVE WE FALLEN INTO?

John Eldredge writes,

> The life, death, and resurrection of Jesus of Nazareth answer once and for all the question, "What is God's heart toward me?" At the point of our deepest betrayal, when we had run our farthest from him and gotten so lost we could never find our way home, God came and died to rescue us. You have never been loved like this. He has come to save you in every way a person can be saved. This is God's heart toward you.[3]

We are living in a love story. As in most dramas, there are segments that look like tragedy or comedy. Misfortune, pain and sorrow are very much present in our world—as in all great stories. However, when we step back and view the big picture of biblical revelation, we catch sight of a love story like none other. "The heart of reality is a suffering romance," states Leonard Sweet, "a bloody Calvary beauty."

> *The whole of the Bible does nothing but tell of God's love.*
> —Augustine of Hippo

The fact that God is love means, of course, that love is ultimately what His story is all about. *Love is why we are here.* It is no accident our hearts yearn for intimacy, beauty and adventure. These longings were placed there by the One who made us. We were created for a cosmic romance—one that towers above every other love story ever heard of. We were made to be God's beloved.

An Exquisite Moment

While waiting in an airport for the arrival of a friend, a young theologian gained a profound insight. As he sat reading a newspaper, he noticed a young man anxiously checking the arrivals monitor and looking out at the runway.

Before long, an airplane arrived and taxied to the terminal. Apparently this was the flight the man was waiting for. He positioned himself in front of the doors through which the arriving passengers emerged. He watched as people of every description streamed into the airport.

Then it happened.

A little blond-headed boy came through the doors and stopped, his eyes scanning the crowd for a familiar face. He suddenly heard his dad's voice and their eyes met. The little fellow broke into a run. As he dashed through the airport, many eyes turned to watch.

They were witnessing an exquisite moment.

The boy raced towards his father, and leaped into his awaiting arms. The two embraced in a moment of undiluted joy and delight. Many onlooking eyes were filled with tears.

As the theologian gazed upon this emotive encounter between father and son, a profound realization came over him: "There is the gospel being played out before my eyes. I am looking at a picture of the resurrected Christ returning to His Father. The Son of God does not go home alone—*He takes us with Him*. When He is embraced, we are embraced. When the Father rejoices over Him, He also rejoices over us. We are included, accepted and loved. This is who we are. This is what it means to be 'in Christ.'"

> *All this is God's doing, for he has reconciled us to himself through Jesus Christ* (2 Cor. 5:18 PHLP).

This is the heart-stopping good news of the gospel.

Accepted in the Beloved

Ponder again these words of Christ:

> *Father . . . you loved me before the creation of the world* (Jn. 17:24).

How much does the Father love His Son?

Where could we possibly find words to describe the unsurpassed richness of this relationship? Here is a Son who is prized, treasured, cherished—the object of sheer delight. His Father contemplates Him with unrestrained affection and boundless pleasure.

Here there is no fear, no apprehension, no reservation. Jesus is the apple of the Father's eye—and He knows it. The blissfulness of such belovedness fills His soul with a symphony of assurance and joy. It generates a togetherness of deep unhindered openness and trust. It gives rise to flourishing and thriving of the highest order.

There's a Beautiful Dance going on here. We have only heard rumors of such a relationship. But here is the staggering part:

> *Then the world will know that you . . . have loved them even as you have loved me* (Jn. 17:23).

Abba's Beloved Son came to share His Father's love with us.

The One who lives in the steadfast embrace of His Father came to say—*"Come, this is for you too!"*

Could anything be more amazing?

Stop and take this in.

The Sacred Romance

The biblical narrative begins and ends with a marriage. The story commences with the union of Adam and Eve and culminates in the climax of the ages, the wedding of Christ and His church—the Marriage Supper of the Lamb.

Both Adam and Christ obtained their brides in a similar manner. Eve was created when the first man was put into a deep sleep. Similarly, our Lord went into the sleep of death. It was there He destroyed the sin that would destroy his bride and separate her from Him eternally. It was through His death that she would be made holy, spotless and without blame.

John is the only Gospel writer who mentions that *"one of the soldiers pierced Jesus' side with a spear, bringing a sudden flow of blood and water"* (Jn. 19:34). It reminds us of Adam, whose side was opened and a rib was extracted from which the Lord God created the first woman. Our Savior's side also was opened and His blood flowed out. As a result of His death, Christ obtained a bride, purchased by His precious blood. His scared side assures us that there is a place at His side for those whom He has redeemed.

History ends with the ultimate wedding banquet—the feast to end all feasts. This is the "joy" Christ looked forward to when He went to the cross (Heb. 12:2). It will be the moment when those whom Jesus loved, His bride, will finally be united with Him. The most rapturous love of a wedded couple on earth is but a faint hint of that glorious future reality.

We will be overwhelmed by the generosity and beauty of the Love that is Father, Son and Holy Spirit. The unhindered vision of the glory of Christ will inspire awe, gratitude and worship beyond anything we have ever known. If we did not have glorified bodies, it would blow all our circuits!

When Sad Things Become Untrue

Peter Kreeft states, "All of history is a kind of broken marriage. And God puts it back together again." Not only does the biblical narrative culminate with the union of Christ and His bride, but also with the reconnection of heaven and earth. This was the original plan. Heaven and earth were always intended for one another, and finally that's what's going to happen.

And then begins the most glorious chapter of all.

> *Then I saw a new heaven and a new earth, for the first heaven and the first earth had passed away, and there was no longer any sea. I saw the Holy City, the new Jerusalem, coming down out of heaven from God, prepared as a bride beautifully dressed for her husband. And I heard a loud voice from the throne saying, "Look! God's dwelling place is now among the people, and he will dwell with them. They will be his people, and God himself will be with them and be their God. 'He will wipe every tear from their eyes. There will be no more death' or mourning or crying or pain, for the old order of things has passed away* (Rev. 21:2-4).

Sir Thomas Moore said it beautifully: "Earth has no sorrow that Heaven cannot heal."

The biblical story comes to a glorious end. We will not be living forever in a far off heaven. Something far more interesting will take place. Heaven is going to come down and renew this world. Every tear will be wiped away. Death will be swallowed up in victory. God's creation will be drenched in a glory greater than that which it had at the beginning.

Sam Storms describes the endless avalanche of future joy:

> Heaven is not simply about the reality or experience of joy, but its eternal increase... Our relishing and rejoicing in God will sharpen and spread and extend and progress and mature and flower and blossom and widen and stretch and swell and snowball and inflate and lengthen and augment and advance and proliferate and accumulate and accelerate and multiply and heighten and reach a crescendo that will even then be only the beginning of an eternity of new and fresh insights into the majesty of who God is![4]

A Happy Ending

Human beings seem to be hardwired for happy endings. When our hero fights against impossible odds, endures betrayal and pain and loss, defeats the villain, and wins the day, we breathe a sigh of relief. It's what we were hoping for. "And they lived happily ever after." We close the book, satisfied that things ended well.

God's story has the happiest ending of all.

In fact, as C. S. Lewis points out in one of his novels, this life is merely the introduction to the Real Story. Our earthly existence is only "the cover and the title page." Beyond this life, as Lewis puts it, we come to "the beginning of Chapter One of the great Story, which no one on earth has read; which goes on forever: in which every chapter is better than the one before."[5]

We will discover that the happy ending we long for is *not* a fairy tale.

The greatest love story we could ever imagine is actually true.

PRAYER

SOVEREIGN LORD, we are grateful that Your Story is full of goodness and unshakeable hope. We thank You that history will end, not with the triumph, but with the overthrow of evil. The kingdoms of this world will become the kingdoms of our Lord and of His Christ. We are thankful that we can run the race with this strong confidence. We can engage in working and serving and giving knowing that our labors in the Lord are not in vain.

> *Teach us, good Lord, to serve Thee as Thou deservest:*
> *To give and not to count the cost;*
> *To fight and not to heed the wounds;*
> *To toil and not to seek for rest;*
> *To labor and not ask for any reward,*
> *Save that of knowing that we do Thy will.*[6]

We ask this in the name of the One whose name is above every other name, Jesus Christ our Lord. Amen.

NOTES

Introduction

1. John Polkinghorne, *Quarks, Chaos, and Christianity* (New York: Crossroad, 1997), 13.
2. C. S. Lewis, *The Voyage of the Dawn Treader.*
3. N.T. Wright, *The New Testament and the People of God* (Minneapolis: Fortress, 1992), 41-42.
4. Dorothy L. Sayers, *The Greatest Drama Ever Staged.* https://gutenberg.ca/ebooks/sayers-greatest/sayers-greatest-00-h.html. Accessed 29 Jan 2021.
5. Alexander Whyte, *Bible Characters,* Part Two (Grand Rapids, MI: Zondervan, 1975), 45.

Chapter 1: The Over-Arching Story

1. N. D. Wilson, *Death by Living: Life Is Meant to Be Spent* (Nashville, TN: Thomas Nelson, 2013), 11.
2. Madeleine L'Engle, *Dragons in the Waters* (New York: Crosswicks, 1976).
3. Madeleine L'Engle, *The Summer of the Great-Grandmother* (New York: Open Road Media, 2020).
4. Nancy Pearcey, *Finding Truth: 5 Principles for Unmasking Atheism, Secularism, and Other God Substitutes* (Colorado Springs: David C Cook, 2015), 139.
5. Sarah Ban Breathnach, *Simple Abundance* (New York: Grand Central Publishing, 1995), 51.
6. C. S. Lewis, *Miracles* (New York: Macmillan, 1947), 212.
7. Michael Horton, *The Gospel-Driven Life* (Grand Rapids, MI: Baker Book House, 1986), 12.

WHAT STORY HAVE WE FALLEN INTO?

Chapter 2: The Story Begins

1. G. K. Chesterton, *Heretics*, www.gutenberg.net, Originally published in 1905. Public domain.
2. Paul Dukes, cited in: https://directionjournal.org/17/2/literary-features-in-gospel-of-john.html. Accessed 10 Sept 2019.
3. Mark Buchanan, *The Holy Wild* (Sisters, OR: Multnomah, 2003), 79-80.
4. William Barclay provides this information: "Clement of Alexandria says that John wrote 'urged by his companions'" (Eusebius, *The Ecclesiastical History* 6:14.5). Jerome in his prologue to the Fourth Gospel says that John wrote urged by all the bishops of Asia Minor and by the delegates of the Churches... Almost the first account of the New Testament books is called the Muratorian Canon (c. A.D. 170). It says that John in his old age was asked to set down the story. They decided to fast and pray to see what they should do. The divine revelation came..." William Barclay, *The Men, The Meaning, The Message of the Books* (Toronto: G.R. Welch, 1976), 24.
5. G. K. Chesterton, *The Everlasting Man*, Originally Published 1925. Public domain.
6. I am indebted to Peter Hiett for the idea of using this illustration.
7. William Temple, *Readings in John's Gospel* (London: Macmillan, 1947), 3.
8. S. D. Gordon, *Quiet Talks On John's Gospel*, 1915. Public domain, 51.
9. J. Gresham Machen, *What Is Faith?* rev. ed. (Edinburgh: Banner of Truth, 1991), 153.
10. Evelyn Underhill, *The Spiritual Life* (London: Hodder & Stoughton, 1955), 14-15.

Chapter 3: The Original Word

1. G. K. Chesterton, *The Man Who Was Thursday*, 1908. Public domain.
2. G. Kingsley Barrett, *The Gospel According to St. John*, 2nd ed. (London: SPC, 1978), 156.
3. C. S. Lewis, *Miracles* (New York: HarperCollins, 1996), ch. 14.
4. E. Stanley Jones, *The Word Became Flesh* (Nashville, Abingdon Press, 1963), 196.
5. Michael Horton@MichaelHorton_. Twitter post. 26 Sept 2018. https://twitter.com/MichaelHorton_/status/1044983769806065665

6. Leonard Sweet, *Out of the Question ... Into the Mystery* (Colorado Springs, CO: Waterbrook Press, 2004), 146.

Chapter 4: The Matrix of the Story

1. The great search in philosophy has been: How do we explain the unity in diversity in our world? The word "university" (to find unity in diversity) addresses this idea. Where did the unity in diversity originate? The Tri-unity of God provides philosophical answers found nowhere else.

    There are religions that are monotheistic and others that are polytheistic. Only the Christian faith views God as both One and Plural. The triune God of the Bible is both one God and three persons; both unity and multiplicity are present in the being of God.

    In his book, *He is There and He Is Not Silent,* philosopher and theologian Francis A. Schaeffer argues: "Nobody else, no philosophy, has ever given us an answer for unity and diversity [in the universe]... Every philosophy has this problem and no philosophy has an answer. Christianity does have an answer in the existence of the Trinity. The only answer to what exists is that he, the triune God, is there."

    Christians need not be defensive about the idea of a Trinity. We should celebrate it. We should proclaim it. Only God in three persons can make sense of the world around us. As one man said, Trinity is not a problem to solve, it's the answer.

2. C. S. Lewis, *Mere Christianity* (New York: HarperCollins, 2001), 175.

3. Karl Barth, *Church Dogmatics, II/1,* trans. T. H. L. Parker et al., ed. Bromiley, G. W. and Torrance, T. F. (London: T&T Clark, 1957), 659-61.

4. Michael Reeves, *Delighting In The Trinity* (Downers Grove, IL: InterVarsity, 2012), 9.

5. Philip Yancey, *Vanishing Grace* (Grand Rapids, MI: Zondervan, 2014), 32.

6. Darrell Johnson, *Experiencing the Trinity* (Vancouver, B.C.: Regent College Publishing, 2002), 38.

7. Timothy Keller, *The Reason for God* (New York: Dutton, 2008), 215.

WHAT STORY HAVE WE FALLEN INTO?

Chapter 5: Love Was Here First

1. Glen Scrivener. Trinity Sermon. *Christ the Truth,* https://christthetruth.net/2014/06/10/trinity-sermon-2/. Accessed 16 Dec 2019.
2. Michael Reeves, *Delighting In The Trinity,* 9.
3. C. H. Dodd, *The Johannine Epistles* (London: Hodder & Stoughton, 1946), 112.
4. D. Martyn Lloyd-Jones, *Life in Christ: Studies in 1 John. Vol. 4: The Love of God* (Wheaton, IL: Crossway Books, 1994).
5. N. T. Wright, *Simply Good News: Why the Gospel Is News and What Makes It Good* (New York: Harper Collins, 2015), 114.
6. Timothy Keller, *The Reason for God,* 215.
7. Cornelius Plantinga, *Engaging God's World: A Christian Vision of Faith, Learning, and Living* (Grand Rapids: Eerdmans, 2002), 20.
8. https://stevebell.com/symphony-and-trinity/. Accessed 19 Sept 2019.
9. C. Baxter Kruger, *The Secret* (www.perichoresis.org: Perichoresis Press), 10.
10. Michael Reeves, *Delighting In The Trinity* (Downers Grove, IL: InterVarsity, 2012), 62.
11. Peter Kreeft, *Three Philosophies of Life: Ecclesiastes, Job, and Song of Songs* (San Francisco: Ignatius Press, 1989), 132.

Chapter 6: Expansive Goodness

1. Michael Reeves, *Delighting in the Trinity* (Downers Grove, IL: InterVarsity, 2012), 127.
2. C. S. Lewis, *The Four Loves* (New York: Hardcourt Brace Jovanovich, 1960), 175-76.
3. Irenæus, (2nd century) *Against Heresies* 4.14.1.
4. https://www.islamreligion.com/articles/336/why-did-god-create-mankind-part-1/. Accessed 31 Dec 2020.
5. Richard Sibbes, "The Successful Seeker," in *Works of Richard Sibbes* (Edinburgh: James Nichol, 1862-64), 6:113.
6. Jean Vanier, *Drawn into the Mystery of Jesus* (Ottawa, ON: Novalis, 2004), 21.

7. Numerous Scriptures attest to the fact that believers are called to share in the glory of God: Jn. 17:22; Rom. 5:2; 8:18; 9:23; 1 Cor. 2:7; 2 Cor. 4:17; 1 Thes. 2:12; 2 Thes. 2:14; 2 Tim. 2:10; Heb. 2:10; 1 Pet. 5:1,4,10.
8. C. Baxter Kruger, *The Great Dance* (Jackson, MS: Perichoresis Press, 2000), 76.
9. Jeremy Berg, *The Father's Song,* 2017, p. 9, https://jeremyberg.files.wordpress.com/2017/05/pocket-book-fathers-song.pdf. Accessed 2 Sept 2018.
10. Michael Reeves, *Delighting In The Trinity,* 56.
11. Thomas F. Torrance, *Trinitarian Faith: The Evangelical Theology of the Ancient Catholic Faith* (London: T & T Clark, 1993), 94-95.
12. C. S. Lewis, *The Problem of Pain,* (New York: HarperCollins, 1996), 40-41.
13. Michele Perry, *Love has a Face* (Bloomington, MN: Chosen Books, 2009), 189.

Chapter 7: Amusing Grace

1. G. K. Chesterton, Selections from G. K.Chesterton, Humor and Gravity, http://www.gkc.org.uk/gkc/books/Man_Orthodox.html. Accessed 30 Jan 2021.
2. Cited by Leslie B. Flynn, Serve Him With Mirth, The Place of Humor in the Christian Life (Grand Rapids: Zondervan, 1960).
3. C. S. Lewis, *Collected Letters: Books, Broadcasts, and War,* 1931–1949, ed. Walter Hooper (New York: HarperCollins, 2004), 930.
4. G. K. Chesterton, *Orthodoxy* (London: Hodder & Stoughton, 1996), 240.

Chapter 8: God's Self-Portrait

1. Howard Peskett & Vinoth Ramachandra, *The Message of Mission* (Downer Grove, IL: InterVarsity: 2003), 38.
2. Chris Wright, *The Uniqueness of Jesus* (London: Monarch Books, 2001), 109-110.
3. N. D. Wilson, *Death by Living,* 6.
4. Charles Everett Koop, Francis August Schaeffer, *Whatever Happened to the Human Race?* (Wheaton, IL: Crossway Books, 1983), 10.

5. Richard Dawkins, *River Out of Eden: A Darwinian View of Life* (New York: Basic Books, 1995), 133.
6. Helmut Thielicke, *Nihilism*, trans. John W. Doberstein (London: Routledge and Kegan Paul, 1962), 110.
7. James Bryan Smith, *The Magnificent Story* (Downers Grove, IL: InterVarsity, 2017), 31.

Chapter 9: The Giver of Life

1. C. S. Lewis, *Mere Christianity*, 50.
2. Baxter Kruger, *Across All Worlds* (Vancouver, BC: Regent College Publishing, 2007), 8.
3. C. S. Lewis, *The Weight of Glory, and Other Addresses* (Grand Rapids, MI: Eerdmans: 1977).
4. Andreas Köstenberger, Scott Swain, *Father, Son and Spirit: The Trinity and John's Gospel* (Downers Grove, IL: InterVarsity, 2008), 187.

Chapter 10: Dispelling the Darkness

1. Christine Caine, Light Looking for Darkness. *FaithGateway*, https://www.faithgateway.com/light-looking-darkness/. Accessed 26 June 2021.
2. John Owen, *Communion with God*, abridged by J.J.K. Law (Carlisle, PA: Banner of Truth, 1991), 32.
3. E. Stanley Jones, *The Christ of Every Road* (Toronto: McClelland & Stewart, 1930), 62-63.
4. N. T. Wright, *The Challenge of Jesus* (Downers Grove: InterVarsity Press, 2015), 69.
5. Brennan Manning, *Lion and Lamb* (Grand Rapids, MI: Baker Book House, 1986), 121.
6. Andrew Purves, *Reconstructing Pastoral Theology* (Louisville, KY: Westminster John Knox Press, 2004), 47.
7. S. D. Gordon, *Quiet Talks On John's Gospel*, 51.

Chapter 11: The Twist in the Story

1. Denis Covington, *Salvation on Sand Mountain* (New York: Addison-Wesley, 1995), 203-4.

2. Frederick Buechner, *The Magnificent Defeat* (New York: HarperCollins, 1966), 86.

Chapter 12: The Big Blunder

1. I am indebted for this insight to: Leonard Sweet, Frank Viola, *Jesus Manifesto* (Nashville, TN: Thomas Nelson, 2010), 6.
2. E. Stanley Jones, *Christ at the Round Table* (Toronto: McClelland & Steward, 1928), 262-263.
3. George MacDonald, *Unspoken Sermons,* Third Series, "*The Truth,*" https://ccel.org/ccel/macdonald/unspoken3.v.html. Accessed 5 May 2020.
4. This story is attributed to Harald Bredeson.
5. E. Stanley Jones, *Christ at the Round Table,* 263.
6. Frederick Buechner, *The Magnificent Defeat* (New York: HarperCollins, 1985), 71.

Chapter 13: The God Who Stoops

1. Daniel Barker, "We Were Just Thrust Into a New Age in Astronomy." *Futurism,* https://futurism.com/we-were-just-thrust-into-a-new-age-in-astronomy. Accessed 21 Feb 2021.
2. E. Stanley Jones, *The Christ of Every Road* (Toronto: McClelland & Stewart, 1930), 65.
3. Os Guinness, *Fool's Talk: Recovering the Art of Christian Persuasion* (Downers Grove, IL: IVPress, 2015), 174.
4. Diane Langberg, PhD @DianeLangberg. Twitter post. 11 March 2021. https://twitter.com/dianelangberg/status/1370057054296145929

Chapter 14: The God Who Is Abba

1. J. I. Packer, *Knowing God* (Downers Grove, IL: IVPress, 1973), 188.
2. Michael P. V. Barrett, *Complete in Him* (Greenville, SC: Emerald House, 2000), 170.
3. Geerhardus Vos, *Redemptive History and Biblical Interpretation: The Shorter Writings of Geerhardus Vos* (Phillipsburg, NJ: P &R Publishing Company, 2001), 298.
4. C. S. Lewis, *Mere Christianity,* 159.
5. John Owen, *Communion with God,* 29-30.

6. Brennan Manning, *Abba's Child* (Colorado Springs, NavPress: 1994), 50.

Chapter 15: The Human Face of God

1. Albert Einstein, Leopold Infeld (1938). *The Evolution of Physics: The Growth of Ideas from Early Concepts to Relativity and Quanta.* Cambridge University Press. Quoted in https://en.wikipedia.org/wiki/Wave%E2%80%93particle_duality (accessed June 25, 2020)
2. J. I. Packer, *Knowing God* (Downers Grove, IL: IVPress, 1973), 53.
3. William Barclay, *The Daily Study Bible, The Gospel of John, Vol. I* (Toronto, ON: G. R. Welch, 1975), 66.
4. David Bentley Hart, *The Beauty of the Infinite* (Grand Rapids: Wm. B. Eerdmans Publishing, 2004), viii.
5. Michael Reeves, *The Good God: Enjoying Father, Son and Spirit* (Carlisle, UK: Send The Light, 2012).
6. Baxter Kruger. https://www.goodreads.com/author/quotes/769673.C_Baxter_Kruger. Accessed 2 Feb 2021.

Chapter 16: The Story of His Glory

1. For further reading on the self-giving nature of the Trinity: J. Scott Horrell, *The Self-Giving Triune God, The Imago Dei And The Nature Of The Local Church: An Ontology Of Mission,* found at: https://bible.org/article/self-giving-triune-god-iimago-deii-and-nature-local-church-ontology-mission
2. N. T. Wright, *Following Jesus* (Grand Rapids: Eerdmans, 1994), 34.
3. John Calvin, quoted by John Stott, *The Cross of Christ,* 206.
4. Alexander MacLaren, *Expositions of Holy Scripture, First Timothy,* 312-313. Originally published in 1902. Public domain.
5. Glen Scrivener, *What is Glory? and Why does it Matter?* p. 2, https://static1.squarespace.com/static/563a2ea1e4b0fe22768d81dd/t/59f20aa9ccc5c55e186a3e76/1509034667637/What+is+Glory.pdf. Accessed 21 Feb 2021.

Chapter 17: Grace and Truth

1. W. Griffith Thomas, *Christianity is Christ* (New Canaan, CN: Keats Publishing, 1981), 7.
2. E. Stanley Jones, *The Christ of Every Road* (Toronto: McClelland & Stewart, 1930), 63-64.

NOTES

3. E. Stanley Jones, *The Christ of Every Road*, 63-65.
4. Brennan Manning, *The Ragamuffin Gospel* (Colorado Springs, CO: Multnomah, 2005), 40.
5. Brian Zahnd, *Beauty Will Save The Word, Rediscovering the Allure and Mystery of Christianity* (Lake Mary, FL: Charisma House, 2012), 69-71.

Chapter 18: Outrageous Grace

1. Doug Wilson, Bones and Silicon. *Blog and Mablog,* https://dougwils.com/books/bones-and-silicon.html. Accessed 22 July 2020.
2. Glen Scrivener, *What is Glory? and Why does it Matter?* p. 21, https://static1.squarespace.com/static/563a2ea1e4b0fe22768d81dd/t/59f20aa9ccc5c55e186a3e76/1509034667637/What+is+Glory.pdf. Accessed 2 Feb 2021.
3. Glen Scrivener, *Ibid.*
4. For a good discussion of this topic, see Paul Copan, *"Divine Narcissism? A Further Defense of God's Humility",* http://www.paulcopan.com/articles/pdf/divine-narcissism.pdf
5. C.J. Mahaney with Kevin Meath, *The Cross-Centered Life* (Colorado Springs, CO: Multnomah, 2001), 42.
6. Edward Judson ,*"Life under pressure: a Lenten sermon,"* in The Outlook, v. XCVII, Lyman Abbott, ed., Outlook Co., 1911, 749.
7. Robert Farrar Capon, *Kingdom, Grace, Judgment* (Grand Rapids, MI: Eerdmans, 2002), 25.
8. Philip Yancey, *What's So Amazing About Grace* (Grand Rapids: Zondervan, 1997), 71.
9. Lewis B. Smedes, *Shame and Grace* (New York: HarperCollins, 1994)
10. Mitch Chase@mitchellchase. Twitter post. 21 Jan 2021. https://twitter.com/i/web/status/1352242545892458496

Chapter 20: The Unveiling of God

1. William Hoste, Christ: *The Interpreter of the Father* (Kilmarnock, Scotland: John Ritchie, 1927), 12.
2. From a sermon by Charles Spurgeon, The Pleading of the Last Messenger, preached March 6, 1887.

3. Thomas F. Torrance, "The Christ Who Loves Us," in *A Passion for Christ: The Vision That Ignites Ministry* (Eugene, OR: Wipf & Stock, 2010), 17.
4. Jason Micheli@JasonMicheli. Twitter post. 5 March 2021. https://twitter.com/jasonmicheli/status/1367902055134822410
5. S. D. Gordon, *Quiet Talks On John's Gospel*, 51.

Chapter 21: The Way to the Father

1. George MacDonald, *Unspoken Sermons* (series 1 to 3), 155, https://www.gutenberg.org/ebooks/9057. Accessed 3 Feb 2021.

Chapter 22: The Giver of the Spirit

1. Theolgian Ray Ortlund comments: "God's holiness extends to all that he is. His grace is holy—unlike our grace. His wrath is holy—unlike our wrath. Etc., etc. Hosea 11:8-9 powerfully affirms God's holiness as *the very reason* he loves so deeply. Again, in contrast with our touchy, demanding hearts. To frame our thoughts of God in such a way that we perceive his holiness as diminishing his loving heart—this is the very error the Bible intends to correct. His all-encompassing holiness *heightens* everything about him as truly, fully divine, including his love. To contend for God's holiness *as if we need to worry about too clear a declaration of his loving heart*—that's arguing for and against God simultaneously. It is not biblical thinking. I used to make this mistake a lot. I meant well. But I was foolish. Don't be like me." Ray Ortlund@rayortlund. Twitter post. 18 Mar 2021. https://twitter.com/rayortlund/status/1372591678436032512
2. Henri Nouwen, *Making All Things New: An Invitation to the Spiritual Life* (San Francisco: Harper and Row, 1981), 54.

Chapter 23: A New Place to Live

1. George MacDonald, *Unspoken Sermons,* Series II, *"The Truth in Jesus."*
2. T. Austin-Sparks, The Belovedness of Christ. *oChristian.com,* http://articles.ochristian.com/article1476.shtml. Accessed 4 Feb 2021.

Chapter 24: A Ladder to Heaven

1. Wesley W. Nelson, *Captivated by Christ* (Fort Washington, PA: Christian Literature Crusade, 1974), 23.

2. Dane Ortlund, *Gentle and Lowly, The Heart of Christ for Sinners and Sufferers* (Wheaton, IL: Crossway, 2020), 20.

Chapter 26: Living in His Love

1. N. T. Wright, *Surprised by Hope: Rethinking Heaven, the Resurrection, and the Mission of the Church* (New York: Harper Collins, 2009), 288.

Chapter 27: Living in His Love

1. Timothy Keller, *The Prodigal Prophet, Jonah and the Mystery of God's Mercy,* (New York: Penguin Random House, 2018), 239.
2. Henri Nouwen, *Making all Things New,* (San Francisco: Harper & Row, 1981), 67-68.
3. Dallas Willard, *Hearing God: Developing a Conversational Relationship with God,* (Downers Grove, IL: InterVarsity Press, 2012), 228.
4. Dallas Willard, Dallas Willard's Definitions. *SoulShepherding,* https://www.soulshepherding.org/dallas-willards-definitions/. Accessed 5 Nov 2020.
5. Cited in Gene Edwards, *100 Days In The Secret Place,* (Shippenburg, PA: Destiny Image Publishers, 2015).
6. Thomas Merton, *Thoughts in Solitude,* (New York: Farrar, Straus, Giroux, 1998), 33.
7. John Eldredge, *Epic, The Story God is Telling,* (Nashville, TN: Thomas Nelson, 1997), 102.
8. Frank Viola, An Audience of One. *Frank Viola Author,* https://violafrank.wordpress.com/2015/02/26/an-audience-of-one/. Accessed 14 April 2021.

Chapter 28: The Sacred Romance

1. Larry Crabb, *66 Love Letters: A Conversation with God That Invites You into His Story* (Nashville: Thomas Nelson, 2011), xviii.
2. Søren Kierkegaard, *Philosophical Fragments* (1844), ch. 2.
3. Gordon D. Fee and Douglas Stuart, *How to Read the Bible Book by Book: A Guided Tour* (Grand Rapids, MI: Zondervan, 2009), 55.
4. Thomas Goodwin, *The Heart of Christ in Heaven, Towards Sinners on Earth,* Originally published in 1645. Public domain.

Chapter 29: The Ultimate Makeover

1. N. T. Wright, *Surprised by Hope: Rethinking Heaven, the Resurrection, and the Mission of the Church* (New York: Harper Collins, 2009), 99.
2. Randy Alcorn, *Heaven* (Carol Stream, IL: Tyndale, 2004), 88.
3. Andrew Wilson, Alastair Roberts, *Echoes of Exodus: Tracing Themes of Redemption Through Scripture* (Wheaton, IL: Crossway Books, 1983), 202.
4. C. S. Lewis, *Mere Christianity,* 65.
5. Glen Scrivener, *Good News in 90 Seconds,* https://speaklife.org.uk/videos/. Accessed 5 Feb 2021. Used with permission from author.
6. Peter J. Kreeft, *Everything You Ever Wanted to Know About Heaven* (San Francisco: Ignatius Press, 1990), 17.

Chapter 30: A Fabulous Finale

1. Brent Curtis & John Eldridge, *The Sacred Romance: Drawing Closer To The Heart of God* (Nashville, TN: Thomas Nelson, 1997), 169.
2. Gordon D. Fee and Douglas Stuart, How to Read the Bible Book by Book: A Guided Tour (Grand Rapids, MI: Zondervan, 2009), 55-56.
3. John Eldredge, *Epic, The Story God is Telling* (Nashville, TN: Thomas Nelson, 1997), 72.
4. Andrew Wilson, Alastair Roberts, *Echoes of Exodus,* 201.
5. Sam Storms, *When The Perfect Comes: The Ever-Increasing Joy of Heaven* (1 Corinthians 13:8-13), https://www.samstorms.org/all-articles/post/when-the-perfect-comes:-the-ever-increasing-joy-of-heaven--1-corinthians-13:8-13-. Accessed 20 Feb. 2021.
6. C. S. Lewis, adapted from *The Last Battle.*
7. St. Ignatius of Loyola, included in *A Treasury of Sermon Illustrations,* Charles Langworthy Wallis, ed., (Nashville, TN: Abingdon-Cokesbury Press, 1950, [1548]), 61.
8. Alastair Roberts, Andrew Wilson, *Echoes of Exodus,* 201.

Scripture quotations marked ESV taken from *English Standard Version*. Copyright © 2001 by Crossway Bibles, a division of Good News Publishers. All rights reserved.

Scripture quotations marked CEV taken from the *Contemporary English Version*. Copyright © 1995 by American Bible Society. Used by permission. All rights reserved.

Scripture quotations marked ISV taken from the *International Standard Version*. Copyright © 1995–2014 by ISV Foundation. All rights reserved.

Scripture quotations marked MOF are taken are from the *James Moffatt, A New Translation of the Bible,* Containing the Old and New Testaments. New York: Doran, 1926. Revised edition, New York and London: Harper and Brothers, 1935. Reprinted, Grand Rapids: Kregel, 1995.

Scripture quotations marked MSG are taken from *The Message*, copyright © 1993, 2002, 2018 by Eugene H. Peterson. Used by permission of NavPress, represented by Tyndale House Publishers. All rights reserved.

Scripture quotations marked NASB are taken from the *New American Standard Bible*, Copyright© 1960, 1962, 1963, 1968, 1971, 1972, 1973, 1975, 1977, 1995 by The Lockman Foundation. Used by permission.

Scripture quotations marked NET are taken from the *New English Translation* (NET) NET Bible® copyright ©1996-2017 by Biblical Studies Press, L.L.C. http://netbible.com All rights reserved

Scripture quotations marked NJB are from *The New Jerusalem Bible,* copyright © 1985 by Darton, Longman & Todd, Ltd. and Doubleday, a division of Random House, Inc. Reprinted by Permission.

Scripture quotations marked NKJV taken from the *New King James Version*. Copyright © 1982 by Thomas Nelson, Inc. Used by permission. All rights reserved.

Scripture quotations marked NLT taken from *The New Living Translation Holy Bible.* Copyright © 1996 by Tyndale Charitable Trust. Used by permission of Tyndale House Publishers. All rights reserved.

Scripture quotations marked NLV are taken from the Holy Bible, *New Life Version,* Copyright 1969, 1976, 1978, 1983, 1986 by Christian Literature International, PO Box 777, Canby, OR 97013. Used by permission.

Scripture quotations marked NRSV taken from the *New Revised Standard Version.* Copyright © 1989 by the Division of Christian Education of the National Council of Churches of Christ in the USA. Used by permission. All rights reserved.

Scripture quotations marked OEB taken from the *Open English Bible,* Public domain.

Scripture quotations marked PHLP are taken from the *Phillips Modern English Bible,* by J. B. Phillips, "The New Testament in Modern English", Copyright© 1962 edition, published by HarperCollins.

Scripture quotations marked RGT taken from the *Revised Geneva Translation* (RGT) © 2019 by Five Talents Audio. All rights reserved.

Scripture quotations marked TLB taken from *The Living Bible* (TLB) The Living Bible copyright © 1971 by Tyndale House Foundation. Used by permission of Tyndale House Publishers Inc., Carol Stream, Illinois 60188. All rights reserved.

Scripture quotations marked TLP taken from *The Passion Translation,* Copyright © 2017, 2018, 2020 by Passion & Fire Ministries, Inc. Used by permission. All rights reserved. thePassionTranslation.com

Scripture quotations marked TLV taken from the *Tree of Life Version* (TLV) Tree of Life (TLV) Translation of the Bible. Copyright © 2015 by The Messianic Jewish Family Bible Society.

Scripture quotations marked WE are taken *The Worldwide English* (New Testament) (WE) © 1969, 1971, 1996, 1998 by SOON Educational Publications. All rights reserved.

Ingram Content Group UK Ltd.
Milton Keynes UK
UKHW021254300323
419413UK00018B/199